KASHMIR
A VALLEY OF TERROR

KASHMIR
A VALLEY OF TERROR

Sunil Sardana

MD PUBLICATIONS PVT LTD
NEW DELHI
www.mdppl.com

Published by :

MD Publications Pvt Ltd
"MD House", 11, Darya Ganj,
New Delhi - 110 002
Phone : +91-11-45355555
E-mail : contact@mdppl.com
Website: www.mdppl.com

ISBN: 978-81-7533-331-4

Published and Printed by Mr. Pranav Gupta on behalf of MD Publications Pvt Ltd at Mohit Enterprises, Delhi.

PREFACE

The Kashmir conflict refers to the territorial dispute over Kashmir, the north western most region of South Asia. The parties to the dispute are India, Pakistan, China, and the people of Kashmir. India claims the entire former princely state of Jammu and Kashmir and presently administers approximately 43% of the region including most of Jammu, Kashmir Valley, Ladakh and the Siachen Glacier. India's claim is contested by Pakistan which controls approximately 37% of Kashmir, mainly Azad Kashmir and the northern areas of Gilgit and Baltistan. In addition, China controls 20% of Kashmir including Aksai Chin which it occupied following the brief Sino-Indian War of 1962 and the Trans-Karakoram Tract, also known as the Shaksam Valley that was ceded to it by Pakistan in 1963.

India's official position is that Kashmir is an integral part of India. Pakistan's official position is that Kashmir is a disputed territory whose final status must be determined by the people of Kashmir. China's official position is that Aksai Chin is a part of Tibet, which is a part of China. Certain Kashmiri independence groups believe that Kashmir should be independent of both India and Pakistan.

Since 1987, disputed State elections have resulted in some of the state's legislative assembly forming militant wings, creating the catalyst for the insurgency, the Indian-administered Jammu and Kashmir has been the site of conflict between the Indian Armed Forces, militants and separatists. Furthermore, India alleges these militants are supported by Pakistan. The turmoil in Jammu and Kashmir has resulted in thousands of deaths, but has become less deadly in recent years. On the other hand, there have been protest movements in Indian Administered Kashmir since 1989. The movements were created to voice Kashmir's disputes and grievances with the Indian government, specifically the Indian Military. Elections held in 2008 were generally regarded as fair by the United Nations High Commissioner for Refugees, had a high voter turnout in spite of calls by militants for a boycott, and led to the pro India Jammu & Kashmir National Conference forming the government in the state. According to Voice of America, many analysts have interpreted the high voter turnout in this election as a sign that the people of Kashmir have endorsed Indian rule in the state.

Pakistan's claims to the disputed region are based on the rejection of Indian claims to Kashmir, namely the Instrument of Accession. Pakistan insists that the Maharaja was not a popular leader, and was regarded as a tyrant by most Kashmiris; Pakistan also maintains that the Maharaja used brute force to suppress the population. Pakistan also accuses India of hypocrisy, as it refused to recognize the accession of Junagadh to Pakistan and Hyderabad's independence, on the grounds that those two states had Hindu majorities. Furthermore, as he had fled Kashmir due to Pakistani invasion, Pakistan asserts that the Maharaja held no authority in determining Kashmir's future. Additionally, Pakistan argues that even if the Maharaja had any authority in determining the plight of Kashmir, he signed the Instrument of Accession under duress, thus invalidating the legitimacy of his actions.

Pakistan also claims that Indian forces were in Kashmir before the Instrument of Accession was signed with India, and that therefore Indian troops were in Kashmir in violation of the Standstill Agreement, which was designed to maintain the status quo in Kashmir. A comprehensive volume containing almost everything that a reader might want to know about Kashmir: its terror, terrorism, insurgency and problem of LOC.

I am very grateful to Mr. Pranav Gupta, Director of MD Publications Pvt Ltd, New Delhi, for his kind cooperation and support for this book.

Sunil Sardana

CONTENTS

1

Terrorism in Jammu & Kashmir

Introduction

The low-intensity conflict in Jammu and Kashmir (J&K) has been the most important issue in India's internal security scenario. Possession of the State has been an issue of dispute between India and Pakistan since 1947. After two unsuccessful attempts to seize the territory by force, Pakistan has largely refrained from making any direct attempt at challenging control in the area of J&K still in India's possession. Rather, the focus of Pakistan's efforts, channelled through the Inter Services Intelligence (ISI), is on aiding Pakistan-based militant groups who are waging a proxy war against Indian security forces in the State. With the two countries going overtly nuclear in 1999, the issue is also percieved globally as a nuclear flash point.

The proxy war has claimed 26226 lives between 1988 and 2000 in an estimated 43956 incidents of terrorist violence. Of these casualties 10310 (40 per cent) were civilians, 3520 (13 per cent) were security forces personnel, and 12396 (47 per cent) terrorists.

The emergence of the protracted insurgency in J&K, which began with two explosions in 1988 (in Srinagar, the State capital), coincides with the withdrawal of Soviet forces from Afghanistan. The insurgency was preceded by a long phase of political turmoil in the State, which began after the death of Sheikh Abdullah, the then Chief Minister, in 1982. Political squabbles between the National Conference (NC, the dominant political outfit in the State) and the Congress government at the Centre, saw the dismissal of two State governments. While Farooq Abdullah's (Sheikh Abdullah's son) government was dismissed in 1984, the successor Ghulam Mohammad Shah government was dismissed in 1986.

In the same year, the then Prime Minister, Rajiv Gandhi, concluded an Accord with Farooq Abullah under which the Congress and the NC formed an alliance to contest the State Assembly elections held in 1987. The alliance won and Farooq Abdullah was once again sworn in as Chief Minister of the State. The Congress-NC alliance was opposed, in the 1987 elections, by a coalition of Islamic parties, the United Muslim Front. Allegations of rigging in these elections gained wide credibility and generated domestic unrest in the State.

Pakistan set out to channelise this civilian discontent into an armed insurgency against India. Pakistan had successfully aided and abetted the *Jihad* against the Soviet presence in Afghanistan by arming and training the Afghan *mujahiddeen*. Several training camps were now set up on the same model for disaffected elements who were willing to take up arms against India's control in J&K. The ISI initially used the Jammu and Kashmir Liberation Front (JKLF) in this effort. The JKLF, formed in 1965, was was originally a Pakistan-based militant outfit committed to challenge India's control over the State. This organisation was used to bring militant youth of the State, train them and send them back to forment insurgency.

JKLF was the first militant group to advocate secession of J&K from India. From the time of its inception till 1988, the JKLF focussed on propagating its secessionist cause, and building its militant base through indoctrination and arms training. A co-founder of the JKLF, Maqbool Butt, was arrested and sentenced to death for the murder of an Indian intelligence operative. In an attempt to secure his release, JKLF activists, in early 1984, kidnapped an Indian diplomat posted in London, Ravindra Mahtre. Mahtre was executed him when the release demand was not met. Maqbool Butt was hanged in February 1984.

While several minor incidents occurred in the second half of the Eighties, insurgency began with two bomb blasts triggered by the JKLF in Srinagar during the evening of July 31, 1988. In late 1989, Dr Rubaiya Sayeed, daughter of the then Union Home Minister Mufti Mohammad Sayeed, was kidnapped and the release of some militants was demanded. The government succumbed to pressure, and the militants were released. This incident gave a new confidence to the militants and an enormous impetus to the their movement. The Union government in 1989, re-appointed Jagmohan (a retired bureaucrat and former governor of the State in the first half of the eighties) as governor of the State. Several public protests during this period led to police firing which claimed several lives. These incidents increased the anti-state fervour within sections of the population and encouraged insurgency.

JKLF was initially used by the ISI, as it was the only established militant group in Kashmir. The State in Pakistan had serious differences with JKLF as the outfit was committed to J&K's independence rather than accession to Pakistan. Pakistan recognised that the element of *Kashmiriyat*, the spirit of independence among sections of the state and JKLF, had to be countered with Islamic nationalism which could be subsequently subsumed into Pakistani nationalism.

Between August 1988 and end 1989, JKLF was the only organisation involved in the insurgency. Later, the ISI facilitated the formation and promotion of various other militant groups. Prominent groups included the *Hizb-ul Mujahideen* (militant wing of the Islamic organisation *Jamat-e-Islami*), *Harkat-ul-Ansar* and *Lashkar-e-Toiba*. Unlike the JKLF which favoured independence for the state, these organisations were more adaptable to the pan-Islamic Pakistani nationalism being promoted by Pakistan.

With Pakistani material aid and indoctrinated cadre drawn largely from the madarssas of Pakistan and Afghanistan, pro-Pakistan militant groups grew very effective during the early nineties as the statistics on civilian casualties indicates. Since 1994 there has been increasing evidence of foreign militants participating and dominating the insurgency in J&K. Meanwhile, devoid of Pakistani support, the JKLF stagnated into an ineffective militant organisation focussing on other means to propagate its aims. The influx of foreign mercenaries prompted several local mercenaries to break ranks, in the mid-1990s, and aid Indian security forces against the militants.

Insurgency was first predominant in the Srinagar Valley, particularly when militants were largely Kashmiri youth. Indian Intelligence reports indicate that two major developments motivated a change in strategy, whereby the ISI-controlled militancy gradually shifted from the Valley to the Jammu region. First, the resumption of a democratic government led by Farooq Abdullah took office in 1996. The restoration of democratic governance in the State helped in reducing dissatisfaction within the people of the State and consequently popular support for the insurgency in the Valley. Second, increasing availability of foreign militants, indoctrinated in Islamic orthodoxy, facilitated a strategy of targeting minority groups for massacres. The minority groups in the State are largely concentrated in Jammu. These indoctrinated militants, fighting their version of *Jihad,* had no qualms about indulging in massacres of civilians of minority groups, particularly Hindus. The broad aim was ethnic cleansing of the State. Several such massacres have been perpetrated with Sikhs being a new target as witnessed in Chattisinghpora, Anantnag district where 35 Sikhs were massacred on March 20 2000 and later at Mehjoor Nagar in Srinagar where six Sikhs were on February 3, 2001.

Massacres by J&K Militants

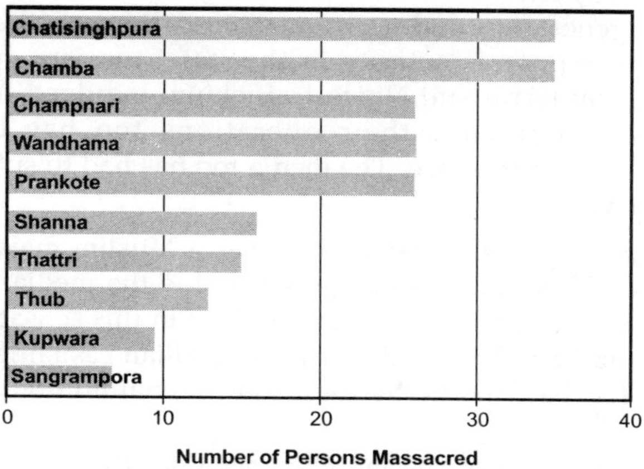

The first few years of insurgency saw a relative domination of the terrorist groups when the casualties were mainly civilian. Since than Indian security forces have been gaining an upper hand in eliminating terrorists though civilian casualties continued to mount. The constant supply of terrorists generated from religious institutions in Pakistan and Afghanistan has helped keep up terrorist violence despite the fact that each year Indian security forces have succeeded in eliminating a substantial number of terrorists.

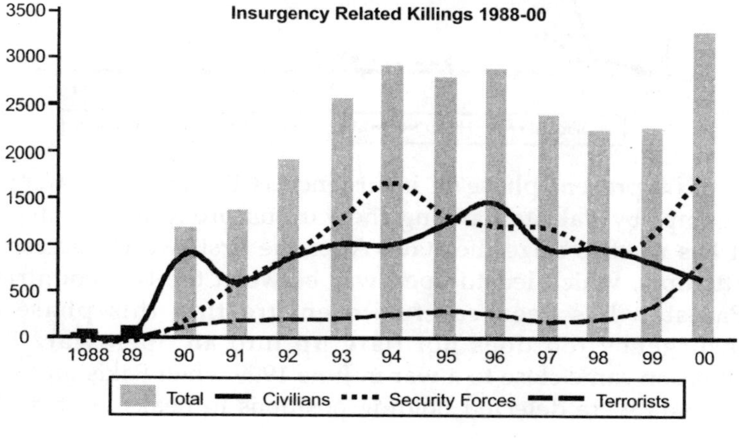

The impact of insurgency in J&K has been felt most by the civilian population. Human casualty is one consequence, refugee generation and economic stagnation are the others. The main economic activity in the state, tourism, has been badly hit by terrorism. Narco trafficking, indulged in by the terrorists to finance their operations too has been an unwelcome consequence. The media too has had to suffer from terrorist violence.

Insurgency in the State, which has a Muslim majority, has been given a communal image partly due the media focus on massacres perpetrated by militants. Lost in this sensationalism is the brutal reality that the brunt of civilian casualties in this conflict has been borne by the majority community.

Religious Identity of Civilian Casualties in J&K

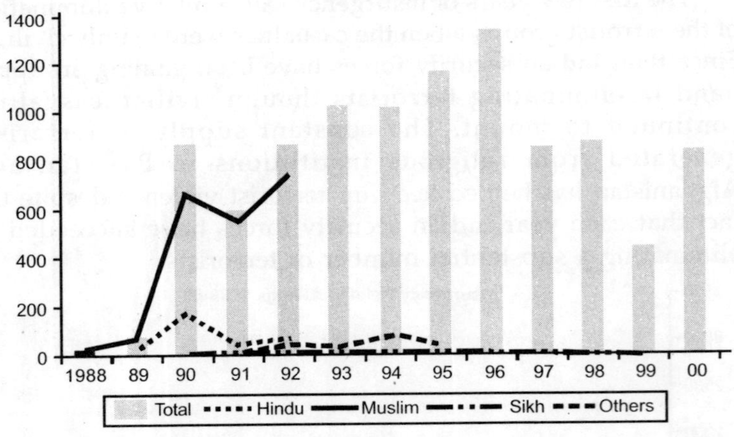

The present phase of insurgency is the most threatening attempt by Pakistan among the various proxy war strategies it has used to seize the state. After the first two unsuccessful attempts, which led to open war between the two countries, Pakistan has been careful to ensure that this phase of insurgency too does not flare up into an open war. The situation came close to a war in June 1999 when Pakistan army regulars were detected holding positions in peaks west of the

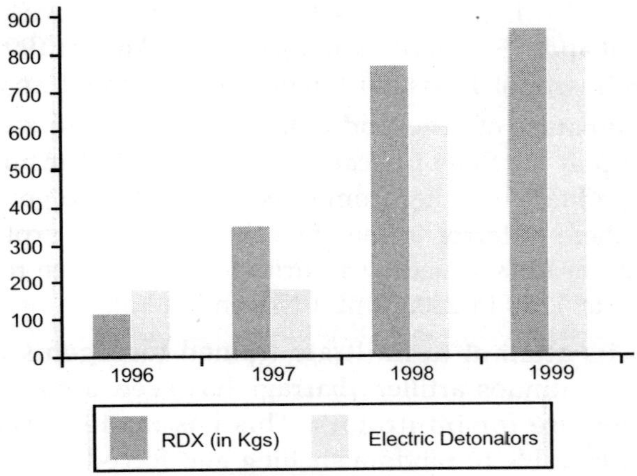

Explosives Seizures

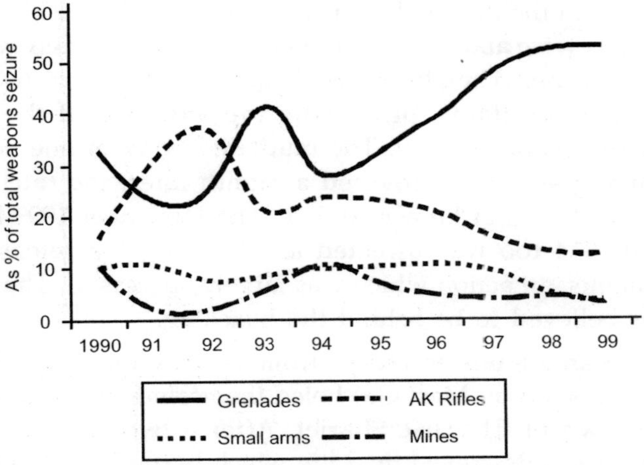

Weapon Seizures

Line of Control (LoC) in the Kargil region and warding off attempts by Indian forces to reclaim these peaks. India's restraint and US intervention during July-August 1999, ensured a withdrawal of Pakistani forces and prevented an open war.

The nature of arms and ammunition being seized from the militants in the State indicates that the focus of insurgency has been gradually shifting from selective killings to generating an atmosphere of terror in the State through bomb explosions.The quantity of RDX seized by security forces has risen from 104 kg in 1996 to 1280 in 2000 (untill November 15).

In its attempt to infiltrate trained insurgents across the LoC, a continuos artillery barrage has been used by Pakistan as cover fire for infiltrators. This has made areas near the LoC vulnerable to random shelling and forced people to move from these areas. Substantial segments of the Kashmiri Pundit community (which has been targeted by some of the terrorist groups for attacks and massacres) too have migrated from the Valley and are refugees in other parts of the State and in other States.

There have been several dramatic actions taken by militant groups in the decade long insurgency. In July 1995, six foreign tourists were abducted by a relatively unknown militant group, the *Al-Faran*. The abductors demanded release of twenty-one detained militants, principally top members of the militant group, *Harkat-al-Ansar*. The mutilated body of one hostage, a Norwegian, was recovered a month later; the fate of other hostages are not known to date. The December 1999 hijacking of IC 814 too was directed at obtaining the release of top militants, an action which was largely successful. The *Al-Faran* was believed to be behind the hijacking.

In an attempt to escape from security forces in May 1995, militants led by Mast Gul holed themselves in a Sufi shrine in the town of Charar-e Sharief. After a two month siege, the shrine was destroyed by a fire which burned most of the town too and led to cancellation of the government's plan to hold elections.

Counter-insurgency operations have led to several instance where innocent civilians have fallen victim to the bullets of the security forces. In the initial stages of the conflict, security forces have had to resort to firing when several mass protest demonstrations turned violent leading to high casualties in police firing. Prominent among these are the cases of firings Bij Behara (October 1993, 60 killed), Sopore (January 1993, 40 killed) and Srinagar (January 20, 1990, 35 killed). On April 5, 2000, protestors in Brakpora, Anantnag too were fired upon by security forces leaving seven dead. In a recent incident on February 16 at Haigam, Sopore, five civilians were killed when a passing army convoy, which was blocked by a protesting mob, and opened fire. The quick response of State authorities in these cases, has reflected a new responsive attitude of the State administration. The State government had released the inquiry reports into the Pathribal firing promptly and promised action against security personnel found guilty. An inquiry by a sitting High Court judge into the Maisuma firing too has been ordered.

The February 1999 visit of the Indian Prime Minister to Lahore and the subsequent Lahore declaration had generated expectations that there would be some let down in the terrorist pressure. In contrast, the Kargil episode has only intensified terrorist violence, particularly increasing incidences of suicide attacks on bases of security forces. This has translated into a rising proportion of casualties among the security forces in the total casualties of the conflict.

Several initiatives have been taken by the government to settle the problem. While the early nineties was marked by an excessive reliance on security forces, several political steps were taken in the later years. In a move to initiate the political process in 1994, the then Prime Minister Narasimha Rao ordered the release of some militant leaders like Yasin Malik and Shabir Shah. The democratic process was revived first in April 1996 when elections where held to the six parliament seats from the state. In September 1996 elections where held to the state assembly where the National Conference won a majority and formed the government under the chief ministership of Dr. Farooq Abdullah. The elections have been marked by terrorist violence in a bid to disrupt the democratic process.

Several economic initiatives too have been taken by the government. These are aimed at addressing the lack of socio-economic development in the State. The Central government declared J&K as a backward state under the new industrial policy in 1995 to encourage new industries and generate employment opportunities. This was followed by the announcement of a Rs. 7200 crore (US $ 1714.28 million) economic package the State in February 1997. Following complaints of human rights violations by security forces, the State government set up a State Human Rights Commission in January 1997.

Prime Minister Atal Bihari Vajpayee took a major peace initiative on November 14 when he announced that security forces would observe a unilateral cease-fire during the holy Islamic month of Ramadan begining November 27. This was subsequently extended twice for one month each and a third extension for three months was announced on February 22. The unilateral cessation of hostility being observed by security forces in the State would be in force until May 27.

This peace initiative did elicit some favourable responses but failed to evoke any positive reaction from the main source of the problem, indigenous and foreign terrorists who have converted the insurgency into a profitable enterprise. Even as the secessionist All Party Hurriyat Conference welcomed the government's cease-fire and expressed the hope that it would be converted into a comprehensive cease-fire, terrorist outfits under the umbrella of the Pakistan based Muttahida Jehad Council (MJC) rejected the cease-fire in words and action.

Several major incidents of violence such as massacres (two instances in Doda district on November 21 and 23, 2000 in which 10 civilians were killed; on February 3 in Srinagar where six Sikhs were killed and on February 10 in Rajouri district where fifteen civilians were killed), attacks on security forces (nine personnel killed in two landmine explosions in Rajouri on January 18, 2001) including suicide attacks (at Srinagar airport on January 7 and 16, 2001 and the Army Headquarters in Srinagar on December 25, 2000) and storming bases (in Rajouri on December 16 and the Red Fort in New Delhi on December 22, 2000) marked the terrorist response.

In contrast, the response from overground secessionist forces has been encouraging though a huge gap still exists between their demands and what the government is prepared to concede. The most positive impact has been the explicit distancing of most Hurriyat leaders from the terrorist outfits, especially those dominated by foreign merceanaries, that operate in the State. This was most evident fromt the observations made by leaders such as Abdul Lone and the Hurriyat Chairman Abdul Ghani Bhat against foreign mercenaries. The Hurriyat has also given up its insistence on trilateral negotiations between the governments of India, Pakistan and the Hurriyat and has instead proposed bilateral dialogue between the Hurriyat and the two respective governments. There is also a proposal for a Pakistan visit by a Hurriyat delegation to hold talks with terrorist outfits based in that country.

As is evident from the present situation in the State, insurgency is far from beign brought under control. The mere installation of a democratically elected regime in the State or a cease-fire by security forces has not helped the restoration process and the annual casualty rates are considerably high. Efforts to isolate Pakistan in the international community, for its sponsorship of terrorism in the State, have yet to yield significant results. The proxy war in the State gained prominence in the international agenda after the 1998 nuclear tests, the 1999 Kargil flare-up, and the IC 814 hijacking in 1999. Kashmir figured prominently in the US President's agenda during his South Asian visit in March 2000 where he reiterated the futility of force and interventions across the LoC as a solution to the crisis. As expected, Pakistan has refused to commit itself to the principles of peaceful resolution. Terrorist outfits active in J&K and based in Pakistan continue to raise finance and operate training camps within that country. The recent explicit outburst by these outfits against Interior Minister Moinuddin Hyder's directive to prohibit fund raising by *jehadi* groups, demonstrates their power vis-a-vis the State. Military ruler Gen. Pervez Musharraf continues to publicly back these terrorist outfits. Hence the scenario of conflict is likely to continue.

2

Kashmir Conflict
Developing Negotiation Strategies

Introduction

The Kashmir conflict refers to the territorial dispute over Kashmir, the northwesternmost region of South Asia. The parties to the dispute are India, Pakistan, China, and the people of Kashmir.

India claims the entire former princely state of Jammu and Kashmir and presently administers approximately 43% of the region including most of Jammu, Kashmir Valley, Ladakh and the Siachen Glacier. India's claim is contested by Pakistan which controls approximately 37% of Kashmir, mainly Azad Kashmir and the northern areas of Gilgit and Baltistan. In addition, China controls 20% of Kashmir including Aksai Chin which it occupied following the brief Sino-Indian War of 1962 and the Trans-Karakoram Tract, also known as the Shaksam Valley, that was ceded to it by Pakistan in 1963.

India's official position is that Kashmir is an integral part of India. Pakistan's official position is that Kashmir is a disputed territory whose final status must be determined by the people of Kashmir. China's official position is that Aksai Chin is a part of Tibet, which is a part of China. Certain Kashmiri independence groups believe that Kashmir should be independent of both India and Pakistan.

India and Pakistan have fought three wars over Kashmir: in 1947, 1965, and 1999. India and Pakistan have also been involved in several skirmishes over the Siachen Glacier.

Since 1987, disputed State elections have resulted in some of the state's legislative assembly forming militant wings, creating the catalyst for the insurgency; the Indian-administered Jammu and Kashmir has been the site of conflict between the Indian Armed Forces, militants and separatists. Furthermore, India alleges these militants are supported by Pakistan. The turmoil in Jammu and Kashmir has resulted in thousands of deaths, but has become less deadly in recent years. On the other hand, there have been protest movements in Indian Administered Kashmir since 1989. The movements were created to voice Kashmir's disputes and grievances with the Indian government, specifically the Indian Military. Elections held in 2008 were generally regarded as fair by the United Nations High Commissioner for Refugees, had a high voter turnout in spite of calls by militants for a boycott, and led to the pro India Jammu & Kashmir National Conference forming the government in the state. According to Voice of America, many analysts have interpreted the high voter turnout in this election as a sign that the people of Kashmir have endorsed Indian rule in the state.

A 2001 report 'Pakistan's Role in the Kashmir Insurgency' of US think tank RAND Corporation noted that 'More intrinsically, the nature of the Kashmir conflict has been transformed from what was originally a secular, locally based struggle (conducted via the Jammu Kashmir Liberation Front - JKLF) to one that is now largely carried out by foreign militants and rationalized in pan-Islamic religious terms.' Most of the militant organizations are composed of foreign mercenaries mostly from the Pakistani Punjab In 2010 with the support of its intelligence agencies Pakistan has been once again 'boosting' Kashmir militants and recruitment of 'martyrs' in Pakistani state of Punjab has increased.

In the 18th century Kashmir was ruled by the Muslim Pashtun Durrani Empire. In 1819 Kashmir was conquered by the Sikh ruler Ranjit Singh. Following the First Anglo-Sikh War in 1845 and 1846, Kashmir was first ceded by the Treaty of Lahore to the East India Company, and shortly after sold by the Treaty of Amritsar to Gulab Singh, Raja of Jammu, who thereafter was given the title Maharaja of Jammu and Kashmir. From then until the Partition of India, Kashmir was ruled by the Hindu Maharajas of the princely state of Kashmir and Jammu, although the majority of the population were Muslim, except in the Jammu region.

Partition and Dispute

In 1947, British rule in India ended with the creation of two new nations: the Union of India and the Dominion of Pakistan while British suzerainty over the 562 Indian princely states ended. According to the Indian Independence Act 1947, "the suzerainty of His Majesty over the Indian States lapses, and with it, all treaties and agreements in force at the date of the passing of this Act between His Majesty and the rulers of Indian States", so the states were left to choose whether to join India or Pakistan or to remain independent. Jammu and Kashmir, the largest of the princely states, had a predominantly Muslim population while having a Hindu ruler (Maharaja Hari Singh.) On partition Pakistan expected Kashmir to be annexed to it.

In October 1947, Muslim revolutionaries in western Kashmir and Pakistani tribals from Dir entered Kashmir intending to liberate it from Dogra rule. Unable to withstand the invasion, the Maharaja signed the Instrument of Accession that was accepted by the government of India on 27 October 1947.

Indo-Pakistani War of 1947

The Indo-Pakistani War of 1947, sometimes known as the First Kashmir War, was fought between India and Pakistan over the region of Kashmir from 1947 to 1948. It was the first of four wars fought between the two newly independent nations. The result of the war still affects the geopolitics of both the countries.

The war was fought within the borders of the former princely state of Kashmir and Jammu by Indian Army, paramilitary and the erstwhile princely state forces opposed by Pakistan Army, paramilitary and local militias from the NWFP. The princely state forces were unprepared for the initial assault of the Pakistani forces, having been deployed thinly on the borders of the princely state for purposes of maintaining border security and deterring militant activity. The state defenses quickly collapsed in the face of the assault, some individuals and units joining the tribal forces. The Pakistani forces referred to themselves as the Azad Kashmir forces (AZK forces), *Azad* in Urdu meaning liberated or free.

The initial successes by AZK forces were not vigorously pressed, giving an opportunity for India to airlift its forces into Kashmir after the state had acceded to India. With Indian reinforcements opposing AZK forces, the offensive ran out of steam towards the end of 1947, except in the High Himalayas sector where AZK forces made substantial progress until they were turned back at the outskirts of Leh in late 1948. Throughout 1948 many small-scale battles were fought, but none gave a strategic advantage to either side. The Indian Army gradually captured a large area in Rajouri and Poonch and ejected Pakistanis from the Indus valley till Kargil, securing the Dras valley and the Zojila pass. The fronts gradually solidified along what would became known as the Line of Control. A formal cease-fire was declared at 2359 hrs on night of 1/2 January 1949.

Background

Prior to 1815 the area now known as "Jammu and Kashmir" comprised 22 small independent states (16 Hindu and 6 Muhammadan) carved out of territories controlled by the Afghanistan Amir (King) combined with those of local small rulers. These were collectively referred to as the "Panjab Hill States". These small states, ruled by Rajput kings, were vassals of the Mughal Empire since 1757. Following the decline of the Mughals, the hill States fell one by one under the dominance of the Sikhs under Ranjit Singh, who merged them into into a single state to be called the State of Jammu.

The First Anglo-Sikh War (1845–46) was fought between the Sikh Empire, which asserted sovereignty over Kashmir, and the East India Company. In the Treaty of Lahore in 1846, the Sikhs were made to surrender the valuable region (the Jullundur Doab) between the Beas River and Sutlej River and required to pay an indemnity of 1.2 million rupees. Because they could not readily raise this sum, the East India Company allowed the Dogra ruler Gulab Singh to acquire Kashmir from the Sikh kingdom in exchange for making a payment of 750,000 rupees to the East India Company. Gulab Singh became the first Maharaja of the newly formed princely state of Jammu and Kashmir, founding a dynasty, that was to rule the state, the second-largest principality during the British Raj, until India gained its independence in 1947.

Partition of India

Before and after the withdrawal of the British from India in 1947, the princely state of Kashmir and Jammu came under pressure from both India and Pakistan to agree to become part of one of the newly independent countries. According to the instruments of accession relating to the Partition of India, the rulers of princely states were to be given the choice of either acceding to India or Pakistan, or remaining independent. The Maharaja of Kashmir, Hari Singh chose the latter and tried to avoid accession to either country. When British forces ceded responsibility for security to the two dominions, Muslim troops rebelled in the some state force units and alongwith Pashtun tribals from the North West Frontier Province (NWFP), invaded the state, thereby triggering the war.

Fearing that his forces would be unable to withstand the assault, the Maharaja asked for Indian military assistance. India set a condition that Kashmir must accede to India for it to receive assistance. Whereupon the Government of India recognized the accession of the erstwhile princely state to India, and was considered the new Indian state of Jammu and Kashmir, Indian troops were sent to the state to defend it against the Pakistani forces. The legitimacy of this accession is still disputed.

Pakistan was of the view that the Maharaja of Kashmir had no right to call in the Indian Army, because it held that the Maharaja of Kashmir was not a heredity ruler, that he was merely a British appointee. There had been no such position as the "Maharaja of Kashmir" prior to British rule. Hence Pakistan decided to take action, but the Army Chief of Pakistan General Douglas Gracey did not send troops to the Kashmir front and refused to obey the order to do so given by Muhammad Ali Jinnah, Governor-General of Pakistan. Gracey's justified his insubordination by arguing that Indian forces occupying Kashmir represented the British Crown and hence he could not engage in a military encounter with Indian forces. Pakistan finally did manage to send troops to Kashmir but by then the Indian forces had taken control of approximately two thirds of the former principalty. The Gilgit and Baltistan territories were secured for Pakistan by the Gilgit Scouts and the forces of the state of Chitral, another princely state that had acceded to Pakistan.

Operation Gulmarg

The objective of the tribal invasion was to capture control of the Kashmir valley including its principal city, Srinagar, the summer capital of the state (Jammu being the winter capital). The entire was codenamed Operation Gulmarg. Maj Gen Akbar Khan of the Pakistan Army, codename "Jebel Tariq", was made the commander.

Deputy Commissioners and Political Agents invited each tribe in the North West Frontier Province to form "lashkars" of upto a thousand men each for invading Jammu and Kashmir for plunder, thereby reversing decades of British policy of restricting tribals to the east of the Durand Line. The lashkars were formed at Bannu, Wana, Thal, Kohat and Peshawar and Nowshera where they were armed by the local brigade commanders from army stocks. Two regular army officers, and some soldiers disguised as tribals, were provided to each lashkar as also deserters from State forces as guides. The lashkars were to concentrate at a segregated area near Abbottabad where they would be briefed and dispersed for the various missions.

The overall plan for the capture of Jammu and Kashmir was as follows:-

- Ten lashkars would advance along the axis Domel - Baramulla - Srinagar, capture the seat of govt and announce Pakistani rule or accession of the state to Pakistan by a puppet govt. The forces would capture the Srinagar airfield and push southward to secure the Banihal Pass to cut of possible ingress from India.
- Two lashkars would support the main offensive by advancing through the Haji Pir Pass and outflanking the defences from the south while another two laskars did the same from the North through the Nastachhun pass.
- Another force of ten lashkars would infiltrate into Jammu district from Kotli, Mirpur and Sialkot to capture Poonch, Rajauri and expand eastward towards Jammu.
- In consonance with Operation Gulmarg, Pakistani forces comprising regular troops from Gilgit Scouts, tribal lashkars and deserters of State Forces would capture the Northern territories and Ladakh including Gilgit, Skardu, Kargil, Leh and the Shyok/Nubra valleys.

Stages of the War

Initial invasion: The state forces stationed in the border regions around Muzaffarabad and Domel were quickly defeated by AZK forces (some state forces mutinied and joined the AZK) and the way to the capital was open. Rather than advancing toward Srinagar before state forces could regroup or be reinforced, the invading forces remained in the captured cities in the border region engaging in looting and other crimes against their inhabitants. In the Poonch valley, the state forces retreated into towns where they were besieged.

Indian operation in the Kashmir Valley

After the accession, India airlifted troops and equipment to Srinagar, where they reinforced the princely state forces, established a defense perimeter and defeated the AZK forces on the outskirts of the city. The successful defence included an outflanking manoeuvre by Indian armoured cars. The defeated AZK forces were pursued as far as Baramulla and Uri and these towns were recaptured.

In the Poonch valley, AZK forces continued to besiege state forces. In Gilgit, the state paramilitary forces (the Gilgit Scouts) joined the invading AZK forces, who thereby obtained control of this northern region of the state. The AZK forces were also joined by troops from Chitral, whose ruler, the Mehtar of Chitral, had acceded to Pakistan.

Attempted Link-up at Poonch and Fall of Mirpur

Indian forces ceased pursuit of AZK forces after recapturing Uri and Baramula, and sent a relief column southwards, in an attempt to relieve Poonch. Although the relief column eventually reached Poonch, the siege could not be lifted. A second relief column reached Kotli, and evacuated the garrisons of that town and others but were forced to abandon it being too weak to defend it. Meanwhile, Mirpur was captured by AZK forces on the 25th of November 1947. Then there was a massacre of Hindus and Sikhs and loot, and more later in Alibeg camp. Around 20 thousand people were reported killed, with atrocities on women reported.

Fall of Jhanger and Attacks on Naoshera and Uri

The Pakistani/AZK forces attacked and captured Jhanger. They then attacked Naoshera unsuccessfully. Other Pakistani/

AZK forces made a series of unsuccessful attacks on Uri. In the south a minor Indian attack secured Chamb. By this stage of the war the front line began to stabilise as more Indian troops became available.

Operation Vijay: Counterattack to Jhanger

The Indian forces launched a counterattack in the south recapturing Jhanger and Rajauri. In the Kashmir Valley the Pakistani/AZK forces continued attacking the Uri garrison. In the north Skardu was brought under siege by Pakistani/AZK forces.

Indian Spring Offensive

The Indians held onto Jhanger against numerous counterattacks from the AZK, who were increasingly supported by regular Pakistani Forces. In the Kashmir Valley the Indians attacked, recapturing Tithwail. The AZK made good progress in the High Himalayas sector, infiltrating troops to bring Leh under siege, capturing Kargil and defeating a relief column heading for Skardu.

Operations Gulab and Eraze

The Indians continued to attack in the Kashmir Valley sector driving north to capture Keran and Gurais (Operation Eraze). They also repelled a counterattack aimed at Tithwal. In the Jammu region, the forces besieged in Poonch broke out and temporarily linked up with the outside world again. The Kashmir State army was able to defend Skardu from the Gilgit Scouts impeding their advance down the Indus valley towards Leh. In August the Chitral Forces under Mata-ul-Mulk besieged Skardu and with the help of artillery were able to take Skardu. This freed the Gilgit Scouts to push further into Ladakh.

Operation Bison

During this time the front began to settle down. The siege of Poonch continued. An unsuccessful attack was launched by

77 Parachute Brigade (Brig Atal) to capture Zoji La pass. Operation Duck, the earlier epithet for this assault, was renamed as Operation Bison by Cariappa. M5 Stuart light tanks of 7 Cavalry were moved in dismantled conditions through Srinagar and winched across bridges while two field companies of the Madras Sappers converted the mule track across Zoji La into a jeep track. The surprise attack on 1 November by the brigade with armour supported by two regiments of 25 pounders and a regiment of 3.7 inch guns, forced the pass and pushed the enemy back to Matayan and later Dras. The brigade linked up on 24 November at Kargil with Indian troops advancing from Leh while the enemy eventually withdrew northwards toward Skardu.

Operation Easy: Poonch Link-up

The Indians now started to get the upper hand in all sectors. Poonch was finally relieved after a siege of over a year. The Gilgit forces in the High Himalayas, who had previously made good progress, were finally defeated. The Indians pursued as far as Kargil before being forced to halt due to supply problems. The Zoji La pass was forced by using tanks (which had not been thought possible at that altitude) and Dras was recaptured.

Moves up to Cease-fire

At this stage Indian Prime Minister Jawahar Lal Nehru decided to ask UN to intervene. A UN cease-fire was arranged for the 31 December 1948. A few days before the cease-fire the Pakistanis launched a counter attack, which cut the road between Uri and Poonch. After protracted negotiations a cease-fire was agreed to by both countries, which came into effect. The terms of the cease-fire as laid out in the UNCIP resolution. This required Pakistan to withdraw its forces, both regular and irregular, while allowing India to maintain minimum strength of its forces in the state to preserve law and order. On compliance of these conditions a plebiscite was to be held to determine the future of the territory. In all, 1,500 soldiers died on each side during the war and Pakistan was able to acquire roughly two-fifths of Kashmir, including five of the fourteen eight thousanders plus peaks of the world, while India maintained the remaining three fifths of Kashmir, including the most populous and fertile regions.

Indo-Pakistani War of 1965

The Indo-Pakistani War of 1965 was a culmination of skirmishes that took place between April 1965 and September 1965 between India and Pakistan. This conflict became known as the Second Kashmir War fought by India and Pakistan over the disputed region of Kashmir, the first having been fought in 1947. The war began following Pakistan's Operation Gibraltar, which was designed to infiltrate forces into Jammu and Kashmir to precipitate an insurgency against rule by India. The five-week war caused thousands of casualties on both sides. It ended in a United Nations (UN) mandated ceasefire and the subsequent issuance of the Tashkent Declaration.

Much of the war was fought by the countries' land forces in Kashmir and along the International Border between India and Pakistan. This war saw the largest amassing of troops in Kashmir since the Partition of British India in 1947, a number that was overshadowed only during the 2001–2002 military standoff between India and Pakistan. Most of the battles were fought by opposing infantry and armored units, with substantial backing from air forces, and naval operations. Many details of this war, like those of other Indo-Pakistani Wars, remain unclear.

Pre-war Escalation

Since Partition of British India in 1947, Pakistan and India remained in contention over several issues. Although the Kashmir conflict was the predominant issue dividing the nations, other border disputes existed, most notably over the

Rann of Kutch, a barren region in the Indian state of Gujarat.On March 20, 1965, and later in April 1965, fighting broke out between India and Pakistan in the Rann of Kutch due to intentional provocation by the latter. Initially involving border police from both nations, the disputed area soon witnessed intermittent skirmishes between the countries' armed forces. In June 1965, British Prime Minister Harold Wilson successfully persuaded both countries to end hostilities and set up a tribunal to resolve the dispute. The verdict, which came later in 1968, saw Pakistan awarded 350 square miles (900 km^2) of the Rann of Kutch, as against its original claim of 3500 square miles.

After its success in the Rann of Kutch, Pakistan, under the leadership of General Ayub Khan, believed the Indian Army would be unable to defend itself against a quick military campaign in the disputed territory of Kashmir as the Indian military had suffered a loss to China in 1962. Pakistan believed that the population of Kashmir was generally discontented with Indian rule and that a resistance movement could be ignited by a few infiltrating saboteurs. Pakistan attempted to ignite the resistance movement by means of a covert infiltration, codenamed Operation Gibraltar. The Pakistani infiltrators were soon discovered, however, their presence reported by local Kashmiris, and the operation ended in a complete failure.

The War

On August 5, 1965 between 26,000 and 33,000 Pakistani soldiers crossed the Line of Control dressed as Kashmiri locals headed for various areas within Kashmir. Indian forces, tipped off by the local populace, crossed the cease fire line on August 15.

Initially, the Indian Army met with considerable success, capturing three important mountain positions after a prolonged artillery barrage. By the end of August, however, both sides had relative progress; Pakistan had made progress in areas such as Tithwal, Uri and Punch and India had captured the Haji Pir Pass, eight kilometers into Pakistan-occupied Kashmir.

On September 1, 1965, Pakistan launched a counterattack, called Operation Grand Slam, with the objective to capture the vital town of Akhnoor in Jammu, which would sever communications and cut off supply routes to Indian troops. Attacking with an overwhelming ratio of troops and technically superior tanks, Pakistan made gains against Indian forces, who were caught unprepared and suffered heavy losses. India responded by calling in its air force to blunt the Pakistani attack. The next day, Pakistan retaliated, its air force attacked Indian forces and air bases in both Kashmir and Punjab. India's decision to open up the theater of attack into Pakistani Punjab forced the Pakistani army to relocate troops engaged in the operation to defend Punjab. Operation Grand Slam therefore failed, as the Pakistan Army was unable to capture Akhnoor; it became one of the turning points in the war when India decided to relieve pressure on its troops in Kashmir by attacking Pakistan further south.

India crossed the International Border on the Western front on September 6, marking an official beginning of the war. On September 6, the 15th Infantry Division of the Indian Army, under World War II veteran Major General Prasad, battled a massive counterattack by Pakistan near the west bank of the Ichogil Canal (BRB Canal), which was a *de facto* border of India and Pakistan. The General's entourage itself was ambushed and he was forced to flee his vehicle. A second, this time successful, attempt to cross the Ichhogil Canal was made over the bridge in the village of Barki, just east of Lahore. These developments brought the Indian Army within the range of Lahore International Airport. As a result, the United States requested a temporary ceasefire to allow it to evacuate its citizens in Lahore. However, the Pakistani counter attack took Khem Karan from Indian forces which tried to divert the attention of Pakistanis from Khem Karan by an attack on Bedian and the adjacent villages.

The thrust against Lahore consisted of the 1st Infantry Division supported by the three tank regiments of the 2nd Independent Armoured Brigade; they quickly advanced across the border, reaching the Ichhogil (BRB) Canal by 6 September. The Pakistani Army held the bridges over the canal or blew up those it could not hold, effectively stalling any further advance by the Indians on Lahore. One unit of the Indian Jat Regiment, 3 Jat, had also crossed the Ichogil canal and captured the town of Batapore (Jallo Mur to Pakistan) on the west side of the canal. The same day, a counter offensive consisting of an armored division and infantry division supported by Pakistan Air Force Sabres forced the Indian 15th Division to withdraw to its starting point. Although 3 Jat suffered minimal casualties, the bulk of the damage being taken by ammunition and stores vehicles, the higher commanders had no information of 3 Jat's capture of Batapore and misleading information led to the command to withdraw from Batapore and Dograi to Ghosal-Dial. This move brought extreme disappointment to Lt-Col Desmond Hayde, CO of 3 Jat. Dograi was eventually recaptured by 3 Jat on 21 September, for the second time but after a much harder battle due to Pakistani reinforcements.

On September 8, 1965, a company of 5 Maratha Light Infantry was sent to reinforce a Rajasthan Armed Constabulary (RAC) post at Munabao a strategic hamlet about 250 kilometres from Jodhpur. Their brief was simple. To hold the post and to keep Pakistan's infantry battalions from overrunning the post at bay. But at Maratha Hill (in Munabao) - as the post has now been christened the Indian company could barely manage to thwart the intense attack for 24 hours. A company of 3 Guards with 954 heavy mortar battery ordered to reinforce the RAC post at Munabao could never reach. The Pakistani Air Force had strafed the entire area, and also hit a railway train coming from Barmer with reinforcements near Gadra road railway station. On September 10, Munabao fell into Pakistani hands, and efforts to capture the strategic point did not succeed.

On the days following September 9, both nations' premiere formations were routed in unequal battles. India's 1st

Armoured Division, labeled the "pride of the Indian Army", launched an offensive towards Sialkot. The Division divided itself into two prongs, was forced back by the Pakistani 6th Armoured Division at Chawinda and was forced to withdraw after suffering heavy losses of nearly 100 tanks. The Pakistanis followed up their success by launching Operation Windup, which forced the Indians back farther. Similarly, Pakistan's pride, the 1st Armoured Division, pushed an offensive towards Khem Karan, with the intent to capture Amritsar (a major city in Punjab, India) and the bridge on River Beas to Jalandhar.

The Pakistani 1st Armored Division never made it past Khem Karan, however, and by the end of September 10 lay disintegrated by the defences of the Indian 4th Mountain Division at what is now known as the Battle of *Asal Uttar* (lit. meaning "Real Answer", or more appropriate English equivalent – "Fitting Response"). The area became known as 'Patton Nagar' (Patton Town), because of the large number of US-made Pakistani Patton tanks. Approximately 97 Pakistani tanks were destroyed or abandoned, with only 32 Indian tanks destroyed or damaged. The Pakistani 1st Armoured Division less 5th Armoured Brigade was next sent to Sialkot sector behind Pakistani 6th Armoured Division where it didn't see action as 6th Armoured Division was already in process of routing Indian 1st Armoured Division which was superior to it in strength.

The war was heading for a stalemate, with both nations holding territory of the other. The Indian army suffered 3,000 battlefield deaths, while Pakistan suffered 3,800. The Indian army was in possession of 710 mile^2 (1,840 km^2) of Pakistani territory and the Pakistan army held 210 mile^2 (545 km^2) of Indian territory. The territory occupied by India was mainly in the fertile Sialkot, Lahore and Kashmir sectors, while Pakistani land gains were primarily south in deserts opposite to Sindh and in Chumb sector near Kashmir in north.

Aerial Warfare

The war saw aircraft of the Indian Air Force (IAF) and the Pakistan Air Force (PAF) engaging in combat for the first time since independence. Though the two forces had previously faced off in the First Kashmir War during the late 1940s, that engagement was very limited in scale compared to the 1965 conflict.

The IAF was flying large numbers of Hawker Hunter, Indian-manufactured Folland Gnats, de Havilland Vampires, EE Canberra bombers and a squadron of MiG-21s. The PAF's fighter force comprised 102 F-86F Sabres and 12 F-104 Starfighters, along with 24 B-57 Canberra bombers. During the conflict the PAF was out-numbered by around 5:1.

The PAF's aircraft were largely of American origin, whereas the IAF flew an assortment of Soviet and European aeroplanes. It has been widely reported that the PAF's American aircraft were superior to those of the InAF, but according to some experts this is untrue because the InAF's MiG-21, Hawker Hunter and Folland Gnat fighters actually had higher performance than their PAF counter-part, the F-86 Sabre. Although the InAF's de Havilland Vampire fighter-bombers were outdated in comparison to the F-86 Sabre, the Hawker Hunter fighters were superior in both power and speed to the F-86 according to Air Cdre (retired) Sajjad Haider, who lead the PAF's No.19 Squadron in combat during the war.

According to the Indians, the F-86 was vulnerable to the diminutive Folland Gnat, nicknamed "Sabre Slayer." The PAF's F-104 Starfighter of the PAF was the fastest fighter operating in the subcontinent at that time and was often referred to as "the pride of the PAF". However, according to Air Cdre (retired) Sajjad Haider who flew with the PAF's No.19 Squadron, the F-104 did not deserve this reputation. Being "a high level interceptor designed to neutralise Soviet strategic bombers in altitudes above 40,000 feet," rather than engage in dogfights with agile fighters at low altitudes, it was "unsuited to the tactical environment of the region." It can be argued that, although the IAF is believed to have feared the Starfighter, in combat it was not as effective as the IAF's far more agile, albeit much slower, Folland Gnat fighter.

The two countries have made contradictory claims of combat losses during the war and few neutral sources have verified the claims of either country. The PAF claimed it shot down 104 IAF planes and lost 19 of its own, while the IAF claimed it shot down 73 PAF planes and lost 35. According to one independent source, the PAF flew 86 F-86 Sabres, 10 F-104 Starfighters and 20 B-57 Canberras in a parade soon after the war was over. Thus disproving the IAF's claim of downing 73 PAF fighters, which at the time constituted nearly the entire Pakistani front-line fighter force.

Indian sources have pointed out that, despite PAF claims of losing only a squadron of combat craft, Pakistan sought to acquire additional aircraft from Indonesia, Iraq, Iran, Turkey and China within 10 days of the beginning war. But this could be explained by the 5:1 disparity in numbers faced by the PAF.

Tank Battles

The 1965 war witnessed some of the largest tank battles since World War II. At the beginning of the war, the Pakistani Army had both a numerical advantage in tanks, as well as better equipment overall. Pakistani armour was largely American-made; it consisted mainly of Patton M-47 and M-48 tanks, but also included many M4 Sherman tanks, some M24 Chaffee light tanks and M36 Jackson tank destroyers, equipped with 90 mm guns. The bulk of India's tank fleet were older M4 Sherman tanks; some were up-gunned with the French high velocity CN 75 50 guns and could hold their own, whilst some older models were still equipped with the inferior 75 mm M3 L/40 gun. Besides the M4 tanks, India fielded the British-made Centurion Tank Mk 7, with the 105 mm Royal Ordnance L7 gun, and the AMX-13, PT-76, and M3 Stuart light tanks. Pakistan fielded a greater number and more modern artillery; its guns out-ranged those of the Indian artillery, according to Pakistan's Major General T.H. Malik.

At the outbreak of war in 1965, Pakistan had about 15 armoured cavalry regiments, each with about 45 tanks in three squadrons. Besides the Pattons, there were about 200 M4 Shermans re-armed with 76 mm guns, 150 M24 Chaffee light tank and a few independent squadrons of M36B1 tank destroyers. Most of these regiments served in Pakistan's two armoured divisions, the 1st and 6th Armoured divisions the latter being in the process of formation.

The Indian Army of the time possessed 17 cavalry regiments, and in the 1950s had begun modernizing them by the acquisition of 164 AMX-13 light tanks and 188 Centurions. The remainder of the cavalry units were equipped with M4 Shermans and a small number of M3A3 Stuart light tanks. India had only a single armoured division, the 1st 'Black Elephant' Armoured Division, also called 'Fakhr-i-Hind' ('Pride of India'), which consisted of the 17th Cavalry (The Poona Horse), the 4th Hodson's Horse, the 16th 'Black Elephant' Cavalry, the 7th Light Cavalry, the 2nd Lancers, the 18th Cavalry and the 62nd Cavalry, the two first named being equipped with Centurions. There was also the 2nd Independent Armoured Brigade, one of whose three regiments, the 3rd Cavalry, was also equipped with Centurions.

Despite the qualitative and numerical superiority of Pakistani armour, Pakistan was outfought on the battlefield by India, which made progress into the Lahore-Sialkot sector, whilst halting Pakistan's counteroffensive on Amritsar; they were sometimes employed in a faulty manner, such as charging prepared defenses during the defeat of Pakistan's 1st Armoured Division at Assal Uttar.

Although India's tank formations experienced same results, India's attack at the Battle of Chawinda, led by its 1st Armored Division and supporting units, was brought to a grinding halt by the newly raised 6th Armoured Division (ex-100th independent brigade group) in the Chawinda sector. The Indians lost 120 tanks at Chawinda. One true winner to emerge was India's Centurion battle tank, with its 105 mm gun and heavy armour, which proved superior to the overly complex Pattons and their exaggerated reputations.However, in the Sialkot sector outnumbered Pattons performed exceedingly well in the hands of the 25th Cavalry and other regiments of the 6th

Armoured Division, which exacted a disproportionately heavy toll of Centurions from the Poona Horse and Hodson's Horse. The Indian Army has made much of the fact that some of its Centurions survived repeated hits; yet have failed to point out that the majority of tanks in the Sialkot sector were Shermans whose guns were inadequate even in 1944. Neither the Indian nor Pakistani Army showed any great facility in the use of armoured formations in offensive operations, whether the Pakistani 1st Armoured Division at Asal Uttar or the Indian 1st Armoured Division at Chawinda. In contrast, both proved adept with smaller forces in a defensive role such a the 2nd Armoured Brigade at Asal Uttar and the 25th Cavalry at Chawinda, where they defeated their better equipped but clumsier foes.

Naval Hostilities

The navies of India and Pakistan did not play a prominent role in the war of 1965, although Pakistani accounts dispute this. On September 7, a flotilla of the Pakistani Navy carried out a small scale bombardment of the Indian coastal town and radar station of Dwarka, which was 200 miles (300 km) south of the Pakistani port of Karachi. Codenamed Operation Dwarka, it did not fulfill its primary objective of disabling the radar station and there was no immediate retaliatory response from India. Later, some of the Indian fleet sailed from Bombay to Dwarka to patrol the area and deter further bombardment. Foreign authors have noted that the "insignificant bombardment" of the town was a "limited engagement, with no strategic value."

According to some Pakistani sources, one submarine, PNS Ghazi, kept the Indian Navy's aircraft carrier INS Vikrant besieged in Bombay throughout the war. Indian sources claim that it was not their intention to get into a naval conflict with Pakistan, and wished to restrict the war to a land-based conflict. Moreover, they note that the Vikrant was in dry dock in the process of refitting. Some Pakistani defence writers have also discounted claims that the Indian Navy was bottled up in Bombay by a single submarine, instead stating that 75% of the Indian Navy was under maintenance in harbour.

Covert Operations

The Pakistan Army launched a number of covert operations to infiltrate and sabotage Indian airbases. On September 7, 1965, the Special Services Group (SSG) commandos were parachuted into enemy territory. According to Chief of Army Staff General Musa Khan, about 135 commandos were airdropped at three Indian airfields(Halwara, Pathankot and Adampur). The daring attempt proved to be an "unmitigated disaster". Only 22 commandos returned to Pakistan as planned, 93 were taken prisoner (including one of the Commanders of the operations, Major Khalid Butt), and 20 were killed in encounters with the army, police or civilians. The reason for the failure of the commando mission is attributed to the failure to provide maps, proper briefings and adequate planning or preparation.

Despite failing to sabotage the airfields, Pakistan sources claim that the commando mission affected some planned Indian operations. As the Indian 14th Infantry Division was diverted to hunt for paratroopers, the Pakistan Air Force found the road filled with transport, and destroyed many vehicles.

India responded to the covert activity by announcing rewards for captured Pakistani spies or paratroopers. Meanwhile, in Pakistan, rumors spread that India had retaliated with its own covert operations, sending commandos deep into Pakistan territory, but these rumors were later determined to be unfounded.

Assessment of Losses

India and Pakistan make widely divergent claims about the damage they inflicted on each other and the amount of damage suffered by them. The following summarizes each nation's claims.

	Indian Claims	Pakistani Claims	Independent Sources
Casualties	-	-	3,000 Indian soldiers, 3,800 Pakistani soldiers
Combat flying effort	4,073+ combat sorties	2,279 combat sorties	
Aircraft lost	35 IAF (official), 73 PAF.Other sources based on the Official Indian Armed Forces History put actual IAF losses at 30 including 19 accidents (non combat sortie rate is not known) and PAF's combat losses alone at 43.	19 PAF, 104 IAF	20 PAF, Pakistan claims India rejected neutral arbitration.
Aerial victories	17 + 3 (post war)	30	-
Tanks destroyed	128 Indian tanks, 152 Pakistani tanks captured, 150 Pakistani tanks destroyed. Officially 471 Pakistani tanks destroyed and 38 captured	165 Pakistan tanks	
Land area won	1,500 mi^2 (3,885 km^2) of Pakistani territory	250 mi^2 (648 km^2) of Indian territory	India held 710 mi^2(1,1840 km^2) of Pakistani territory and Pakistan held 210 mi^2(545 km^2) of Indian territory

Neutral Assessments

There have been several neutral assessments of the losses incurred by both India and Pakistan during the war. Most of these assessments agree that India had a upper hand over Pakistan when ceasefire was declared. Some of the neutral assessments are mentioned below –

- According to the United States Library of Congress Country Studies:

  The war was militarily inconclusive; each side held prisoners and some territory belonging to the other. Losses were relatively heavy on the Pakistani side, twenty aircraft, 200 tanks, and 3,800 troops. Pakistan`s army had been able to withstand Indian pressure, but a continuation of the fighting would only have led to further losses and ultimate defeat for Pakistan. Most Pakistanis, schooled in the belief of their own martial prowess, refused to accept the possibility of their country`s military defeat by "Hindu India" and were, instead, quick to blame their failure to attain their military aims on what they considered to be the ineptitude of Ayub Khan and his government.

- TIME magazine reported that India held 690 mi^2 of Pakistan territory while Pakistan held 250 mi^2 of Indian territory in Kashmir and Rajasthan. Additionally, Pakistan had lost almost half its armour temporarily. The same article stated that -

  Severely mauled by the larger Indian armed forces, Pakistan could continue the fight only by teaming up with Red China and turning its back on the U.N.

- Devin T. Hagerty wrote in his book *"South Asia in world politics"* –

  The invading Indian forces outfought their Pakistani counterparts and halted their attack on the outskirts of Lahore, Pakistan`s second-largest city. By the time United Nations intervened on September 22, Pakistan had suffered a clear defeat.

- In his book *"National identity and geopolitical visions"*, Gertjan Dijkink writes –

The superior Indian forces, however, won a decisive victory and the army could have even marched on into Pakistani territory had external pressure not forced both combatants to cease their war efforts.

- An excerpt from Stanley Wolpert's *India,* summarizing the Indo-Pakistani War of 1965, is as follows:

  In three weeks the second Indo-Pak War ended in what appeared to be a draw when the embargo placed by Washington on U.S. ammunition and replacements for both armies forced cessation of conflict before either side won a clear victory. India, however, was in a position to inflict grave damage to, if not capture, Pakistan 's capital of the Punjab when the cease-fire was called, and controlled Kashmir 's strategic Uri-Poonch bulge, much to Ayub 's chagrin.

- In his book titled *The greater game: India's race with destiny and China,* David Van Praagh wrote –

  India won the war. It gained 1,840 square kilometers of Pakistani territory: 640 square kilometers in Azad Kashmir, Pakistan 's portion of the state; 460 square kilometers of the Sailkot sector; 380 square kilometers far to the south of Sindh; and most critical, 360 square kilometers on the Lahore front. Pakistan took 540 square kilometers of Indian territory: 490 square kilometers in the Chhamb sector and 50 square kilometers around Khem Karan.

- Dennis Kux's *"India and the United States estranged democracies"* also provides a summary of the war.

  Although both sides lost heavily in men and materiel, and neither gained a decisive military advantage, India had the better of the war. New Delhi achieved its basic goal of thwarting Pakistan 's attempt to seize Kashmir by force. Pakistan gained nothing from a conflict which it had instigated.

- *"A region in turmoil: South Asian conflicts since 1947"* by Robert Johnson mentions –

  India 's strategic aims were modest it aimed to deny Pakistani Army victory, although it ended up in possession of 720 square miles of Pakistani territory for the loss of just 220 of its own.

- An excerpt from William M. Carpenter and David G. Wiencek's *"Asian security handbook: terrorism and the new security environment"* –

  A brief but furious 1965 war with India began with a covert Pakistani thrust across the Kashmiri cease-fire line and ended up with the city of Lahore threatened with encirclement by Indian Army. Another UN-sponsored cease-fire left borders unchanged, but Pakistan`s vulnerability had again been exposed.

- English historian John Keay's *"India: A History"* provides a summary of the 1965 war –

  The 1965 Indo-Pak war lasted barely a month. Pakistan made gains in the Rajasthan desert but its main push against India`s Jammu-Srinagar road link was repulsed and Indian tanks advanced to within a sight of Lahore. Both sides claimed victory but India had most to celebrate.

- Uk Heo and Shale Asher Horowitz write in their book *"Conflict in Asia: Korea, China-Taiwan, and India-Pakistan"* –

  Again India appeared, logistically at least, to be in a superior position but neither side was able to mobilize enough strength to gain a decisive victory.

- Newsweek magazine, however, praised the Pakistani military's ability to hold of the much larger Indian Army.

  "By just the end of the week, in fact, it was clear that the Pakistanis were more than holding their own."

Ceasefire

The United States and the Soviet Union used significant diplomatic tools to prevent any further escalation in the conflict between the two South Asian nations. The Soviet Union, led by Premier Alexei Kosygin, hosted ceasefire negotiations in Tashkent (now in Uzbekistan), where Indian Prime Minister Lal Bahadur Shastri and Pakistani President Ayub Khan signed the Tashkent Agreement, agreeing to withdraw to pre-August lines no later than February 25, 1966.

With declining stockpiles of ammunition, Pakistani leaders feared the war tilting in India's favor. Therefore, they quickly accepted the ceasefire in Tashkent. Despite strong opposition from Indian military leaders, India budged to growing international diplomatic pressure and accepted the ceasefire. On September 22, the United Nations Security Council unanimously passed a resolution that called for an unconditional ceasefire from both nations. The war ended the following day.

India's Prime Minister, Shastri, suffered a fatal heart attack soon after the declaration of the ceasefire. As a consequence, the public outcry in India against the ceasefire declaration transformed into a wave of sympathy for the ruling Indian National Congress. The ceasefire was criticized by many Pakistanis who, relying on fabricated official reports and the controlled Pakistani press, believed that the leadership had surrendered military gains. The protests led to student riots. Pakistan State's reports had suggested that their military was performing admirably in the war which they incorrectly blamed as being initiated by India and thus the Tashkent Declaration was seen as having forfeited the gains. Some recent books written by Pakistani authors, including one by ex-ISI chief titled "The Myth of 1965 Victory", allegedly exposed Pakistani fabrications about the war, but all copies of the book were bought by Pakistan Army to prevent publication because the topic was "too sensitive".

India and Pakistan accused each other of ceasefire violations; India charged Pakistan with 585 violations in 34 days, while Pakistan countered with accusations of 450 incidents by India. In addition to the expected exchange of small arms and artillery fire, India reported that Pakistan utilized the ceasefire to capture the Indian village of Chananwalla in the Fazilka sector. This village was recaptured by Indian troops on 25 December. On October 10, a B-57 Canberra on loan to the PAF was damaged by 3 SA-2 missiles fired from the IAF base at Ambala. A Pakistani Army Auster was shot down on 16 December, killing one Pakistani army captain and on 2 February 1967, an AOP was shot down by

IAF Hunters. The ceasefire remained in effect until the start of the Indo-Pakistani War of 1971.

Intelligence Failures

Strategic miscalculations by both India and Pakistan ensured that the war ended in a stalemate –

Indian miscalculations

Indian military intelligence gave no warning of the impending Pakistan invasion. The Indian Army failed to recognize the presence of heavy Pakistani artillery and armaments in Chumb and suffered significant losses as a result.

The "Official History of the 1965 War", drafted by the Ministry of Defence of India in 1992, was a long suppressed document that revealed other miscalculations. According to the document, on September 22 when the Security Council was pressing for a ceasefire, the Indian Prime Minister asked commanding Gen. Chaudhuri if India could possibly win the war, were he to delay accepting the ceasefire. The general replied that most of India's frontline ammunition had been used up and the Indian Army had suffered considerable tank losses. It was determined later that only 14% of India's frontline ammunition had been fired and India held twice the number of tanks as Pakistan. By this time, the Pakistani Army had used close to 80% of its ammunition.

Air Chief Marshal (retd) P.C. Lal, who was the Vice Chief of Air Staff during the conflict, points to the lack of coordination between the IAF and the Indian army. Neither side revealed its battle plans to the other. The battle plans drafted by the Ministry of Defence and General Chaudhari, did not specify a role for the Indian Air Force in the order of battle. This attitude of Gen. Chaudhari was referred to by ACM Lal as the "Supremo Syndrome", a patronizing attitude sometimes held by the Indian army towards the other branches of the Indian Military.

Pakistani miscalculations

The Pakistani Army's failures started with the supposition that a generally discontented Kashmiri people, given the opportunity provided by the Pakistani advance, would revolt against their Indian rulers, bringing about a swift and decisive surrender of Kashmir. The Kashmiri people, however, did not revolt. Instead, the Indian Army was provided with enough information to learn of Operation Gibraltar and the fact that the Army was battling not insurgents, as they had initially supposed, but Pakistani Army regulars.

The Pakistani Army also failed to recognize that the Indian policy makers would order an attack on the southern sector in order to open a second theater of conflict. Pakistan was forced to dedicate troops to the southern sector to protect Sialkot and Lahore instead using them to support penetrating into Kashmir.

"Operation Grand Slam", which was launched by Pakistan to capture Akhnoor, a town north-east of Jammu and a key region for communications between Kashmir and the rest of India, was also a failure. Many Pakistani commentators criticized the Ayub Khan administration for being indecisive during Operation Grand Slam. These critics claim that the operation failed because Ayub Khan knew the importance of Akhnur to India (having called it India's "jugular vein") and did not want to capture it and drive the two nations into an all-out war. Despite progress being made in Akhnur, General Ayub Khan relieved the commanding Major General Akhtar Hussain Malik and replaced him with Gen. Yahya Khan. A 24-hour lull ensued the replacement, which allowed the Indian army to regroup in Akhnur and successfully oppose a lackluster attack headed by General Yahya Khan. "The enemy came to our rescue", asserted the Indian Chief of Staff of the Western Command. Later, Akhtar Hussain Malik criticized Ayub Khan for planning Operation Gibraltar, which was doomed to fail, and for relieving him of his command at a crucial moment in the war. Malik threatened to expose the truth about the war and the army's failure, but later dropped the idea for fear of being banned.

Some authors have noted that Pakistan might have been emboldened by a war game - conducted in March 1965, at the Institute of Defence Analysis, USA. The exercise concluded that, in the event of a war with India, Pakistan would win. Other authors like Stephen Philip Cohen, have consistently commented that the Pakistan Army had "acquired an exaggerated view of the weakness of both India and the Indian military the 1965 war was a shock".

Pakistani Air Marshal and Commander-in-Chief of PAF during the war, Nur Khan, later said that the Pakistan Army, and not India, should be blamed for starting the war. However propaganda in Pakistan about the war continued; the war was not rationally analyzed in Pakistan, with most of the blame being heaped on the leadership and little importance given to intelligence failures that persisted until the debacle of the 1971 war, when then East Pakistan was invaded by India and seceded from West Pakistan, leading to the creation of Bangladesh.

Involvement of Other Nations

The United States of America, which had previously supplied military equipment to India and Pakistan, imposed an embargo against further supplies to both countries once the war had started. The US was apprehensive that military equipment that it had provided to be used in a battle against communism, would instead be used by the countries to fight one another. The American embargo especially affected Pakistan since the majority of its equipment was provided by America. This would cause Pakistan to believe that it could not continue the war beyond September.

Following imposition of the American embargo, other NATO allies (including the UK) discontinued providing military equipment to the nations.

Both before and during the war, China had been a major military associate of Pakistan and had invariably admonished India, with whom it had fought a war in 1962. There were also reports of Chinese troop movements on the Indian border to support Pakistan. As such, India agreed to the UN mandate in order to avoid a war on both borders.

India's participation in the Non-Aligned Movement yielded little support from its members. Pakistan, however, gained assistance from countries of Asia with large Islamic populations, including Turkey, Iran and Indonesia. The USSR was more neutral than most other nations during the war and even invited both nations to talks that it would host in Tashkent.

Aftermath

India

Despite the declaration of a ceasefire, India was perceived as the victor due to its success in halting the Pakistan-backed insurgency in Kashmir. In its October 1965 issue, the TIME magazine quoted a Western official assessing the consequences of the war –

> *Now it `s apparent to everybody that India is going to emerge as an Asian power in its own right.*
>
> *In light of the failures of the Sino-Indian War, the outcome of the 1965 war was viewed as a "politico-strategic" victory in India. The Indian premier, Lal Bahadur Shastri, was hailed as a national hero in India.*

While the overall performance of the Indian military was praised, military leaders were criticized for their failure to effectively deploy India's superior armed forces so as to achieve a decisive victory over Pakistan. In his book *"War in the modern world since 1815"*, noted war historian Jeremy Black said that though Pakistan "lost heavily" during the 1965 war, India's hasty decision to call for negotiations prevented further considerable damage to the Pakistan Armed Forces. He elaborates –

> *India `s chief of army staff urged negotiations on the ground that they were running out ammunition and their number of tanks had*

become seriously depleted. In fact, the army had used less than 15% of its ammunition compared to Pakistan, which had consumed closer to 80 percent and India had double the number of serviceable tanks.

As a consequence, India focussed on enhancing communication and coordination within and among the triservices of the Indian Armed Forces. Partly as a result of the inefficient information gathering preceding the war, India established the Research and Analysis Wing for external espionage and intelligence. Major improvements were also made in command and control to address various shortcomings and the positive impact of these changes was clearly visible during the Indo-Pakistani War of 1971 when India achieved a decisive victory over Pakistan within two weeks.

China's repeated threats to intervene in the conflict in support of Pakistan increased pressure on the government to take an immediate decision to develop nuclear weapons. Despite repeated assurances, the United States did little to prevent extensive use of American arms by Pakistani forces during the conflict which irked India. At the same time, the United States and United Kingdom refused to supply India with sophisticated weaponry which further strained the relations between the West and India. These developments led to a significant change in India's foreign policy India, which had previously championed the cause of non-alignment, distanced itself further from Western powers and developed close relations with the Soviet Union. By the end of 1960s, the Soviet Union emerged as the biggest supplier of military hardware to India. From 1967 to 1977, 81% of India's arms imports were from the Soviet Union. After the 1965 war, the arms race between India and Pakistan became even more asymmetric and India was outdistancing Pakistan by far.

Pakistan

At the conclusion of the war, many Pakistanis considered the performance of their military to be positive. September 6 is celebrated as 'Defence Day' in Pakistan, in commemoration of the successful defence of Lahore against the Indian army. The performance of the Pakistani Air Force, in particular, was praised.

However, the Pakistani government was accused by foreign analysts of spreading disinformation among its citizens regarding the actual consequences of the war. In his book "*Mainsprings of Indian and Pakistani foreign policies*", S.M. Burke writes –

> *After the Indo-Pakistani war of 1965 the balance of military power had decisively shifted in favor of India. Pakistan had found it difficult to replace the heavy equipment lost during that conflict while her adversary, despite her economic and political problems, had been determinedly building up her strength.*

Most observers agree that the myth of a mobile, hard hitting Pakistan Army was badly dented in the war, as critical breakthroughs were not made. Several Pakistani writers criticized the military's ill-founded belief that their "martial race" of soldiers could defeat "Hindu India" in the war. Rasul Bux Rais, a Pakistani political analyst wrote -

> *The 1965 war with India proved that Pakistan could neither break the formidable Indian defenses in a blitzkrieg fashion nor could she sustain an all-out conflict for long.*

Moreover, Pakistan had lost more ground than it had gained during the war and, more importantly, failed to achieve its goal of occupying Kashmir; this result has been viewed by many impartial observers as a defeat for Pakistan.

Many high ranking Pakistani officials and military experts later criticized the faulty planning of Operation Gibraltar that ultimately led to the war. The Tashkent declaration was also criticized in Pakistan, though few citizens realised the gravity of the situation that existed at the end of the war. Political leaders were also criticized. Following the advice of Zulfikar Ali Bhutto, Pakistan's foreign minister, Ayub Khan had raised very high expectations among the people of Pakistan about the superiority if not invincibility - of its armed forces, but

Pakistan's inability to attain its military aims during the war, created a political liability for Ayub. The defeat of its Kashmiri ambitions in the war led to the army's invincibility being challenged by an increasingly vocal opposition.

One of the most far reaching consequences of the war was the wide-scale economic slowdown in Pakistan. The cost of the 1965 war put an end to the impressive period economic growth Pakistan had experienced during early 1960s. Between 1964 and 1966, Pakistan's defence spending rose from 4.82% to 9.86% of GDP, putting tremendous strain on Pakistan's economy. By 1970–71, defence spending comprised a whopping 55.66% of government expenditure.

Pakistan was surprised by the lack of support by the United States, an ally with whom the country had signed an Agreement of Cooperation. USA declared its neutrality in the war by cutting off military supplies to both sides, leading Islamabad to believe that they were "betrayed" by the United States. After the war, Pakistan would increasingly look towards China as a major source of military hardware and political support.

Another negative consequence of the war was the growing resentment against the Pakistani government in East Pakistan (present day Bangladesh), particularly for West Pakistan's obsession with Kashmir. Bengali leaders accused the central government of not providing adequate security for East Pakistan during the conflict, even though large sums of money were taken from the east to finance the war for Kashmir. In fact, despite some Pakistan Air Force attacks being launched from bases in East Pakistan during the war, India did not retaliate in that sector, although East Pakistan was defended only by an understrenghted infantry division (14 Division), sixteen planes and no tanks. Sheikh Mujibur Rahman was critical of the disparity in military resources deployed in East and West Pakistan, calling for greater autonomy for East Pakistan, which ultimately led to the Bangladesh Liberation war and another war between India and Pakistan in 1971.

Indo-Pakistani War of 1971

The Indo-Pakistani War of 1971 was a military conflict between India and Pakistan. Indian, Bangladeshi and international sources consider the beginning of the war to be Operation Chengiz Khan, Pakistan's December 3, 1971 pre-emptive strike on 11 Indian airbases. Lasting just 13 days it is considered one of the shortest wars in history. However, Pakistan considers it to be a part of the overall Bangladesh Liberation War, in which India had been providing direct financial and military support for the Mukti Bahini Bengali operatives.

During the course of the war, Indian and Pakistani forces clashed on the eastern and western fronts. The war effectively came to an end after the Eastern Command of the Pakistan Military signed the Instrument of Surrender on December 16, 1971 following which East Pakistan seceded as the independent state of Bangladesh. Around 97,368 West Pakistanis who were in East Pakistan at the time of its independence, including some 79,700 Pakistan Army soldiers and paramilitary personnel and 12,500 civilians, were taken as prisoners of war by India.

Background

The Indo-Pakistani conflict was sparked by the Bangladesh Liberation war, a conflict between the traditionally dominant West Pakistanis and the majority East Pakistanis. The Bangladesh Liberation war ignited after the 1970 Pakistani election, in which the East Pakistani Awami League won 167 of 169 seats in East Pakistan and secured a simple majority in the 313-seat lower house of the Majlis-e-Shoora (Parliament of Pakistan). Awami League leader Sheikh Mujibur Rahman presented the Six Points to the President of Pakistan and claimed the right to form the government. After the leader of the Pakistan Peoples Party, Zulfikar Ali Bhutto, refused to yield the premiership of Pakistan to Mujibur, President Yahya Khan called the military, dominated by West Pakistanis to suppress dissent.

Mass arrests of dissidents began, and attempts were made to disarm East Pakistani soldiers and police. After several days of strikes and non-cooperation movements, the Pakistani military cracked down on Dhaka on the night of 25 March 1971. The Awami League was banished, and many members fled into exile in India. Mujib was arrested on the night of 25–26 March 1971 at about 1:30 a.m. (as per Radio Pakistan's news on 29 March 1971) and taken to West Pakistan.

On 27 March 1971, Ziaur Rahman, a rebellious major in the Pakistani army, declared the independence of Bangladesh on behalf of Mujibur. In April, exiled Awami League leaders formed a government-in-exile in Baidyanathtala of Meherpur. The East Pakistan Rifles, a paramilitary force, defected to the rebellion. A guerrilla troop of civilians, the Mukti Bahini, was formed to help the Bangladesh Army.

India's Involvement in Bangladesh Liberation War

The Pakistan army conducted a widespread genocide against the Bengali population of East Pakistan, aimed in particular at the minority Hindu population, leading to approximately 10 million people fleeing East Pakistan and taking refuge in the neighboring Indian states. The East Pakistan-India border was opened to allow refugees safe shelter in India. The governments of West Bengal, Bihar, Assam, Meghalaya and Tripura established refugee camps along the border. The resulting flood of impoverished East Pakistani refugees placed an intolerable strain on India's already overburdened economy.

General Tikka Khan earned the nickname 'Butcher of Bengal' due to the widespread atrocities he committed. General Niazi commenting on his actions noted 'On the night between 25/26 March 1971 General Tikka struck. Peaceful night was turned into a time of wailing, crying and burning. General Tikka let loose everything at his disposal as if raiding an enemy, not dealing with his own misguided and misled people. The military action was a display of stark cruelty more merciless than the massacres at Bukhara and Baghdad by Chengiz Khan and Halaku Khan General Tikka resorted to the killing of civilians and a scorched earth policy. His orders to his troops were: 'I want the land not the people...' Major General Farman had written in his table diary, "Green land of East Pakistan will be painted red". It was painted red by Bengali blood.'

The national Indian government repeatedly appealed to the international community, but failing to elicit any response, Prime Minister Indira Gandhi on 27 March 1971 expressed full support of her government for the independence struggle of the people of East Pakistan. The Indian leadership under Prime Minister Gandhi quickly decided that it was more effective to end the genocide by taking armed action against Pakistan than to simply give refuge to those who made it across to refugee camps. Exiled East Pakistan army officers and members of the Indian Intelligence immediately started using these camps for recruitment and training of Mukti Bahini guerrillas.

India's Official Engagement with Pakistan

Objective

By November, war seemed inevitable; a massive buildup of Indian forces on the border with East Pakistan had begun. The Indian military waited for winter, when the drier ground would make for easier operations and Himalayan passes would be closed by snow, preventing any Chinese intervention. On 23 November, Yahya Khan declared a state of emergency in all of Pakistan and told his people to prepare for war.

On the evening of 3 December Sunday, at about 5:40 p.m., the Pakistani Air Force (PAF) launched a pre-emptive strike on eleven airfields in north-western India, including Agra which was 300 miles (480 km) from the border. During this attack the Taj Mahal was camouflaged with a forest of twigs and leaves and draped with burlap because its marble glowed like a white beacon in the moonlight.

This preemptive strike known as Operation Chengiz Khan, was inspired by the success of Israeli Operation Focus in the

Arab-Israeli Six Day War. But, unlike the Israeli attack on Arab airbases in 1967 which involved a large number of Israeli planes, Pakistan flew no more than 50 planes to India and failed to inflict the intended damage. As a result, Indian runways were cratered and rendered non-functional for several hours after the attack.

In an address to the nation on radio that same evening, Prime Minister Gandhi held the air strikes as a declaration of war against India and the Indian Air Force responded with initial air strikes that very night that were expanded to massive retaliatory air strikes the next morning.

This marked the official start of the Indo-Pakistani War of 1971. Prime Minister Gandhi ordered the immediate mobilization of troops and launched the full-scale invasion. This involved Indian forces in a massive coordinated air, sea, and land assault. Indian Air Force started flying sorties against Pakistan from midnight and quickly achieved air superiority. The main Indian objective on the western front was to prevent Pakistan from entering Indian soil. There was no Indian intention of conducting any major offensive into West Pakistan.

Naval hostilities

In the western theatre of the war, the Indian Navy, under the command of Vice Admiral Kohli, achieved success by attacking Karachi's port in the code-named Operation Trident on the night of 4–5 December, which resulted in the sinking of the Pakistani destroyer PNS Khyber and a minesweeper PNS Muhafiz; PNS Shajehan was badly damaged. This resulted in tactical Indian success: 720 Pakistani sailors were killed or wounded, and Pakistan lost reserve fuel and many commercial ships, thus crippling the Pakistan Navy's further involvement in the conflict. Operation Python followed Operation Trident which was on the night of 8–9 December, in which Indian rocket-armed motor torpedo boats attacked the Karachi Roads that resulted in further destruction of reserve fuel tanks, and in the sinking of three Pakistani commercial ships in Karachi Harbour.

In the eastern theatre of the war, the Indian Eastern Naval Command, under Vice Admiral Krishnan, completely isolated East Pakistan by establishing a naval blockade in the Bay of Bengal, trapping the Eastern Pakistani Navy and eight foreign merchant ships in their ports. From 4 December onwards, the aircraft carrier INS Vikrant was deployed in which its Sea Hawk fighter-bombers attacked many coastal towns in East Pakistan including Chittagong and Cox's Bazaar. Pakistan responded by sending the submarine PNS Ghazi to negate the threat. Indian Eastern Naval Command laid a trap to sink the submarine and Indian Navy destroyer INS Rajput sank Pakistani submarine PNS Ghazi through depth charges off Vishakapatnam's coast reducing Pakistan's control of Bangladeshi coastline. But on 9 December, the Indian Navy suffered its biggest wartime loss when the Pakistani submarine PNS Hangor sank the frigate INS Khukri in the Arabian Sea resulting in a loss of 18 officers and 176 sailors.

The damage inflicted on the Pakistani Navy stood at 7 gunboats, 1 minesweeper, 1 submarine, 2 destroyers, 3 patrol crafts belonging to the coast guard, 18 cargo, supply and communication vessels, and large scale damage inflicted on the naval base and docks in the coastal town of Karachi. Three merchant navy ships - Anwar Baksh, Pasni and Madhumathi and ten smaller vessels were captured. Around 1900 personnel were lost, while 1413 servicemen were captured by Indian forces in Dhaka. According to one Pakistan scholar, Tariq Ali, the Pakistan Navy lost a third of its force in the war.

East Pakistan Air Operations, 1971

East Pakistan Air Operations incorporate the interdiction, air defence, ground support, and logistics missions flown by the Indian Air Force and the Bangladesh Air Force in support of the advancing Mitro Bahini in the then eastern theatre during the Indo-Pakistani conflict of 1971. Although the first of the engagements between the opposing airpowers occurred before the formal declaration of hostilities, the events described below include only those conducted after the declaration of war. Indian Air force also helped the Mukti Bahini form a formation of light aircraft called *Kilo flight*, which was manned and serviced by Bengali pilots and technicians of who had defected from the Pakistan Air Force, and this unit had launched attacks on targets in Bangladesh on December 3, 1971, prior to the start of formal combat between India and Pakistan.

Background

The Indo-Pakistani War of 1971 will be noted in history as one of the defining conflicts which led to the birth of the new nation of Bangladesh. The engagements between the Mitro Bahini against the Pakistani Army lasted a short but intense 14 days, between 3 December and 16 December 1971. The speedy conclusion was only possible because the objectives set by the Mitro Bahini in the east were achieved in that time. This was only possible due to excellent co-ordination between the Indian Army, Air Force, and the Navy and the Mukti Bahini.

Although the western theatre saw engagements that have defined the rules of 20th century warfare, including the Battle of Longewala, Operation Trident, as well as Battle of the bases between the two rival Air Forces, the eastern theatre would be marked by a near total domination by the Indian Forces and the Mitro Bahini. Two major reasons stand out, the first and major was the fact that the Bengali population and the Awami League led resistance had already greatly weakened the Pakistani Forces. The second, and possibly equally important, is the total air supremacy that the IAF came to achieve within the opening days of the war.

The Eastern Theater: Historical Background

East Pakistan saw no air combat when Pakistan and India came to blows over Kashmir in 1947, although both countries possessed functional air forces. All Pakistani air assets were deployed in West Pakistan at the time, and India also concentrated on the Western front as well. India began upgrading its air capabilities on its eastern border after the war– in 1958 the Eastern operational group was formed in Kolkata, which was upgraded into a command the following year. Following the Sino-Indian War of 1962, the Eastern Air command HQ shifted to Shillong and extensive efforts to increase its operational capabilities (in terms of number of squadrons and modernization of its warplanes and operational infrastructure) began, as added emphasis was given to countering any possible Chinese threat. In contrast, Pakistan High Command posted only 1 squadron of 12 F-86 Canadair Sabres in East Pakistan. The Sabres were deployed at Dhaka on October 1964, while PAF infrastructure development in the province was largely ignored.

1965 Indo-Pakistan War: Eastern Theater

Air forces of both countries actively launched attacks against each other during the Indo-Pakistan War of 1965 in the eastern theater. The IAF bombed airfields and airstrips located in East Pakistan and the PAF managed to launch two celebrated raids on the Indian Air Force base at Kalaikudda, West Bengal. The PAF raids, which took place on September 7, destroyed several Canberra bombers and Vampire aircraft on the ground while the IAF claimed 2 aerial kills (Pakistani sources record 1 F-86 lost). The first PAF Kalaikudda raid by 5 Sabres had achieved total surprise but the second wave was opposed by Indian interceptors, leading to the loss. The PAF also launched attacks on Bagdogra on September 10 and Barrackpur on September 14, with varying results. The IAF did hit back with airstrikes on Dacca, Jessore and Lalmunirhat, but failed to destroy any aircraft. Mid-air interceptions and dogfights rarely happened, and barring some skirmishing between the EPR and BSF along the border, the air forces of both countries provided most of the combat activities in the eastern theater during the 1965 War. The final tally was 12 Indian aircraft destroyed on the ground (PAF claim is 21 aircraft destroyed) and 2 Pakistani Sabres shot down (PAF records one aircraft lost) and 1 PAF Sabre lost due to accident. Following the war, the IAF continued its steady growth in combat capacity, while Pakistan boosted its squadron strength to 20 planes, although it neglected to expand its operational infrastructure substantially.

PAF During Operation Searchlight in 1971

PAF had 20 Canadair Sabres (No 14. Squadron *Tail-choppers*), 3 T-33 trainers and 2 helicopters stationed in East Pakistan, while army aviation squadron No.4 had 8 helicopters present for service. PAF operational effectiveness suffered a little because most Bengali pilots and technicians had been grounded during the political unrest in March 1971. Air Commodore *Mitthy* Masud, AOC East Pakistan was replaced by Air Commodore Enamul Huq in March 1971, because the former officer opposed any form of armed action against civilians. When Operation Searchlight was launched to quell the Awami League led political movement, PAF contribution was crucial to its success.

Pakistan high command had been using 4 C-130 Hercules planes and the entire PIA fleet was employed to transfer troops to East Pakistan and after the war started, two entire infantry division in an operation dubbed Great Fly-In was airlifted to East Pakistan from West Pakistan between March 26 -May 2. The Pakistani airplanes had to make the trip to East Pakistan via Sri Lanka as overflights over India had been banned since February 1971. Moving two entire infantry divisions, which were sorely needed to bolster the army in East Pakistan where it was facing stiff opposition in a span of 2 weeks was a vital factor in sustaining the army operation. Most Pakistani army bases in East Pakistan had been cut off from each other since March 29 and Helicopters and C-130 planes were used to ferry troops and munitions to army bases cut off from supplies and surrounded by the Mukti Bahini, and this proved crucial for the initial survival and ultimate success of the Pakistani troops during the early phases of the battle. Helicopters also evacuated the Pakistani wounded from isolated bases, acted as artillery spotters, flew reconnaissance missions over hostile territory and dropped combat troops off in remote places to outflank and cutoff Mukti Bahini positions. The PAF enjoyed total air supremacy during March– November as the Mukti Bahini lacked both planes and air defense capability to counter their efforts, and flew nearly 100 to 170 sorties between March - November in support of the army. Pakistani forces defeated the Bengali resistance by mid- May 1971 and occupied the province by June, 1971. The PAF had requisitioned and jury-rigged crop dusters and light civilian aircraft to augment its recon and ground attack capabilities during this period.

PAF Preparations for Indian Intervention

Pakistan high command was fully aware that the IAF considerably outnumbered the PAF eastern detachment and they held the qualitative edge as well in the eastern theater. Pakistani planners had anticipated the PAF being neutralized with 24 hours of the IAF commencing combat operations over East Pakistan. There was only one fully functional airbase (at Tejgaon near Dhaka) in East Pakistan, all the satellite air bases in the province lacked the service facilities for sustaining prolonged operations. The PAF had plans to deploy a squadron of Shenyang F-6 planes at Kurmitola (Now Shahjalal International Airport) in 1971, these planes were temporarily deployed but ultimately withdrawn because, although the runway was functional at that base, the base was not fully functional to support the planes. and the lack of infrastructure meant PAF could not deploy additional planes. This marginalization or neglect of East Pakistan defense since 1948 had hamstrung the PAF Eastern contingent in 1971, when its capabilities was put to the test. Pakistan deployed no additional air defence assets other than the one light Ack-Ack regiment and a few batteries to assist the PAF in 1971. The 6th light Ack Ack guarded Dhaka, 46th Light Ack-Ack battery was in Chittagong, and elements of the 43rd Ack-Ack were present in areas around East Pakistan. The caliber of the regiment was not enhanced to *heavy*, and no SAMs were deployed in East Pakistan. The only long range radar (Russian P-35 model) was also taken to West Pakistan along with all the C-130 Hercules planes. Several *Dummies* were deployed at the airbases to deceive the IAF. To augment the short radar cover, which could now provide only a 3-5 minute warning to the planes, observers were deployed around the country armed with radios and telephones. They in turn were exposed to Mukti Bahini attacks, which reduced their effectiveness. The IAF had flown reconnaissance flights over East Pakistan since June 1971 and had engaged their opponents earlier in the east than they did in the west, having clashed with PAF over the Salient of Boyra in West Bengal on 22 November. Between then and 3 December 1971, there were no engagements of the two airforces. Pakistanis had lost 3 planes (2 shot down and 1 damaged) on November 22 over Boyra, so were down to 17 operational Sabres in December 1971 as no replacement aircraft were sent from West Pakistan.

IAF Operations in 1971

The IAF had assembled units from the Central and Eastern Air commands in Eastern command bases for the campaign by December 1971. The Central Air Command HQ was located at Allahabad while the Eastern Command was HQed in Shillong, so Air Marshal P.C Lal created an advanced HQ at Fort William to better coordinate matters after a consultation with Lt. Gen. Jacob, COS Army Eastern Command in addition to redrawing the operational boundaries of the respective commands for the campaign. Several Central Command units were temporarily housed in Eastern Air Command bases for the duration of the campaign.

Eastern Air Command Order of Battle 1971

Location of IAF, PAF and BAF units on December 1971 in and around Bangladesh. Some unit locations are not shown. Map not to exact scale

Western Sector: (Operating on the west of Jamuna river)

- No. 22 Squadron (*Swifts*): Folland Gnat MK 1 Dumdum, then Kalaikudda, then Calcutta (WC Sikand)
- No. 30 Squadron (*Charging Rhinos*): Mig 21 FL - Kalaikudda (WC Chudda) - Fighter Interceptor
- No. 14 Squadron (*Bulls*): Hawker Hunter F. MK 56 - Kalaikudda (WC Sundersan) - Fighter
- No. 16 Squadron (*Rattlers*): Canberra - Kalaikudda - (WC Gautum) - Bomber
- No. 221 Squadron (*Valiants*): Su-7 BMK – Fighter/Bomber
- No. 7 Squadron (*Battle Axes*): Hawker Hunter F. MK 56 and 2 F. MK 1 - Bagdogra (WC Ceolho, then WC Suri). The squadron was moved Chamb after December 12.
- No. 104 (Alluitte 3) and No. 104 (Mi-4) Heli units

North East and North Western Sector: (Areas to the East of Jamuna River)

CO: Air Vice Marshal Devasher **HQ:** Shillong

- No. 17 Squadron (*Golden Arrows*): Hawker Hunter F MK 56 - Hashimara (WC Chatrath)
- No 37 Squadron (*Black Panthers*): Hawker Hunter F MK 10 - Hashimara (WC Kaul)
- No. 4 Squadron (*Oorials*): Mig 21 FL Gauhati (WC JV Gole)
- No. 24 Squadron (*Hunting Hawks*): Folland Gnat Gauhati (WC Bhadwar)
- No. 15 Squadron (*Flying Lancers*): Folland Gnat - Gauhati then Agortala (WC Singh)
- No. 28 Squadron (*First Supersonics*): Mig 21FL Gauhati (WC Bishnu)
- No. 105 (Mi-4) and 121 (Alouette III) Helicopter Squadrons - Agartola

Mukti Bahini airforce: Kilo Flight

The Indian Army was helping the Mukti Bahini through Operation Jackpot since May 1971, while the Indian navy had helped set up the Bengali Naval commando unit and had provided command staff for the Bengali gunboats which were busy mining riverine crafts and harassing merchant marine operations in East Pakistan. The IAF could not come to grips with the PAF until formal hostilities commenced, but the Bengali airmen joined the act when 9 Bengali pilots and 50 technicians, formally of the PAF and serving with the Mukti Bahini in various capacity were gathered for a special mission on 28 September 1971 at Dimapur in Nagaland. A number of Bengali civilian pilots from the PIA later joined this group. Indian civilian authorities and the IAF donated 1 DC-3 Dakota (gifted by the Maharaja of Jodhpor), 1 Twin Otter plane and 1 Alouette III helicopter for the new born Bangladesh Air Force, which was to take advantage of the lack of night fighting capability of the PAF to launch hit and run attacks on sensitive targets inside Bangladesh from the air. The Bengali rank and file fixed up the WWII vintage runway at Dimapur, then added began rigging the aircraft for combat duty. The Dakota was modified to carry 5,000 lb bombs, but for technical reasons it was used to ferry Bangladesh government personnel, Captain Abdul Khalek, Captain Alamgir Satter and Captain Abdul Mukit, all destined to earn the *Bir Pratik* award, piloted the Dakota. The Helicopter was rigged to fire 14 rockets from pylons attached to its side and had .303 Browning machine guns attached to it, in addition to having 1 inch steel plate welded to its floor for extra protection. Squadron Leader Sultan Mahmood, Flight Lieutenant Bodiul Alam and Captain Shahabuddin, all of whom later won the *Bir Uttam* award, operated the helicopter. The Otter boasted 7 rockets under each of its wings and could launch ten 25 pound bombs. The bombs were rolled out by hand through a makeshift door. Flight Lt. Shamsul Alam, along with Captains Akram Ahmed and Sharfuddin Ahmad flew the Otter, all three were later awarded *Bir Uttam* for their service in 1971. This tiny force was dubbed *Kilo Flight*, the first fighting formation of Bangladesh Air force.

Under the command of Group Captain A.K. Khandkar and Squadron Leader Sultan Mahmood, intense training took place in night flying and instrumental navigation. After 2 months of training, the formation was activated for combat. The first sortie was scheduled to take place on November 28, but was moved back 6 days to December 2, 1971. The Otter (Flown by Flight Lt. Shamsul Alam , co pilot FL Akram) was moved to Kailashsahar, and was prepared for a mission against targets in Chittagong. The Helicopter (Pilot Flight Lt. Sultan Mahmood and Fl. Lt. Bodiul Alam) was to hit Narayangang, flying from Teliamura, near Agartola.

In the early hours of December 3, 1971, the twin otter and the helicopter took off from their respective bases and hit the oil depots at Naryanganj and Chittagong, which the Mukti Bahini guerrillas had been unable to sabotage due to the tight security. Ironically, the PAF initiated Operation Chengis Khan on the same night, and the IAF commenced offensive operations in the East from December 3, 1971. Kilo flight would in total fly 12 missions in 1971, hitting various targets in Chittagong, Naryanganj and Bhairab. The formation base was moved from Dimapur to Shamshernagar after it was liberated in December 4, then finally was moved to Agartala before the end of the war. the BAF contingent was present in Dhaka when the surrender ceremony took place in December 16, 1971.

IAF Commences Operations: December 3, 1971

Following the preemptive strike by the PAF on its airfields in the western sector, the IAF went into action on the midnight of 3 December 1971. However, the western air campaign was, at least in the initial days, limited to striking PAF forward bases and providing ground support, but was not aimed at achieving air supremacy. In the east, however, faced with only the No. 14 Squadron defending the whole sector, the Eastern Air Command was given the task to achieve total air dominance, which ultimately it did.

3–4 December

Canberra bombers struck Tejgaon repeatedly on the night of 3 December. The PAF No. 14 operated only Sabres which lacked night fighting capability, so the bombers were opposed only by the guns of the Pakistani light ack-ack regiment. By the morning of 4 December, however, strike missions against Tejgaon were assigned to Hunters of the No. 7, No. 14 sqn, No. 17 sqn and No.37 sqn, Su-7s (No. 221 Sqn) and MiG-21s (No. 28 sqn).

The first daytime raids in East Pakistan were flown by Hunters of No.17 Sqn and these were given top cover by four MiG-21s from No.28 Sqn. It proved unnecessary, the Hunters shot down one Sabre when intercepted before the rendezvous took place. No. 14 sqn also struck Kurmitola AFB, hitting the Hangars and Installations with rockets. By the afternoon, Hunter's would strike Narayangunj fuel depots. Hunters from No. 14 Sqn also struck Chittagong Harbour on the morning of 4 December. In an afternoon strike on Tejgaon by MiGs from 28 Sqn, a Twin otter was destroyed on the ground.

For the interceptors sent up to challenge the strikes, PAF was to suffer the loss of three Sabres in dog fights over Dhaka, two to Hunters striking Kumitola. Of these, Wg Cdr S M Ahmed and Flt. Lt. Saeed ejected safely over the village of Ghazipur, but were not found by search parties and were listed as "missing" for the duration of the war. Later reports would suggest that both pilots were killed by hostile local populace.

Though not programmed or required to fly, Ahmad had insisted - in keeping with the PAF's tradition of its seniors leading in combat - and was soon in the thick of battle with 4 Hunters, joined minutes later by some MiG-21s and Su-7s. In the melee, the Hunters' leader shot down Ahmad's F-86, forcing him to eject 5 miles from Kurmitola; despite an air and ground search he was never found. Rashidi, in the meanwhile, successfully extricated himself from the 'one-versus-several' situation just as another pair of PAF F-86s, comprising Sdn. Ldr. Afzaal and Flt. Lt. Saeed, was engaging 3 Hunters, a few miles away. Both Afzaal and Saeed were immediately set upon by another Hunter and was himself shot down. Only minutes later Afzaal had avenged this loss by chasing a MiG-21 and shooting it down. Although Saeed had ejected safely, he too was never found; reportedly both Saeed and Ahmad were taken away by Mukti supporters.

The last of the Sabres lost that day was to an afternoon strike on Narayangunj, Fg Off Sajjad Noor was shot down while attempting to engage a strike by Hunters from No. 14Sqn. Noor ejected safely over the village of Zinjira and was later rescued.

The IAF also suffered some of its heaviest losses on these missions, losing six Hunters and one Su-7. No. 7 sqn, on a strike mission against an ammunition train at Lal Munir Hat, would suffer one Pilot- Flt Lt A R Da Costa KIA, along with the loss of two Hunters- both hit by fierce ground fire and crashing in Indian territory. One of the pilots of the stricken planes, Sqn Ldr S K Gupta safely ejected at Bagdogra. No. 14 Sqn also lost two Hunters on the day to ack ack. Both the pilots, Sqn Ldr K D Mehra and Flt Lt K C Tremenhere, ejected safely . Tremenhere was taken POW while Mehra managed to evade capture and get back to Indian territory. The highest price of the day was however, paid by No. 37 Sqn, which suffered the death of two pilots- Sqn Ldr S B Samanta and Fg Off S G Khonde. No. 221 Sqn was to suffer one Su-7 shot down with the pilot, Sqn Ldr V. Bhutani taken POW.

IAF Canberra planes had also struck Chittagong airport, oil tanks and refinery on December 4, and lost 2 planes but managed to damage the installations. In total the PAF had flown 32 operational sorties against IAF incursions on December 4 and had expanded 30,000 rounds of ammunition, while the ground based weapons had fired 70,000 rounds, the highest expenditure per day per aircraft of ammunition in the history of the PAF. Pakistani authorities claimed between 10 to 12 IAF planes destroyed, and took measures to conserve ammunition in anticipation of a long war.

5–7 December

People of Dhaka witnessed thrilling low-level dogfights throughout 4 and 5 December. The IAF concentrated in attacking the aircraft on the ground. However, for the dear price paid, it failed to cause significant damage to the PAF assets in well-dispersed and camouflaged locations. IAF also flew ground support missions, and the lessening pressure meant that the PAF managed to fly some ground support missions over Comilla and other areas. In total 20 operational sorties were flown by the Sabres, and 12,000 rounds of ammunition were used up during December 5 by the PAF. By the evening of 5 December the IAF realised that a change of tactic was necessary. The Ack-Ack regiment managed to defend the airbase during 5 December and the night of the early hours of the 6th against Indian attacks successfully.

On the morning of 6 December four MiG-21s (No. 28 Sqn), flying from Gauhati at very low level, climbed up tu 5,000 m and dived at 900 kmh, hitting Tejgaon airstrip with 500 kg bombs, scoring several hits on the runway, and rendering it unusable for operations. The airport was without air cover at that time, as a PAF ground support mission had just landed and the duty flight had not taken off. Two craters, ten meters deep and twenty meters wide, separated by 1200 meters had rendered the runway unusable (the bombs were BETAB-500, anti-airstrip ordnance). However, Kurmitola was to remain operational till the morning of 7 December, when Mig-21s of No. 28 Sqn again hit that runway. No. 7 Sqn was pulled out of the eastern ops on the 6 December to help the army in the west. Repeated attack by MiG-21s and Hunters of No. 14 and No.28 however, kept the runway cratered. An aviation website noted:

> *"A notable fact remains that the MiG-21FL was neither as easy to fly nor to operate in combat under conditions the IAF had to expect in the case of a new war with Pakistan. It was designed as simple point-defence fighter-interceptor that was to operate under close GCI-control and attack its targets from the rear hemisphere with R-3S (ASCC-Code AA-2 Atoll) heat-seeking missiles. However, pleased with the speed and handling of the MiGs during operational conversions, Indian pilots trained intensively and gained not only considerable confidence, but also expertise. The Indians were to use it as an air superiority fighter as well as fighter bomber*

over extended ranges and well inside the enemy airspace, with minimal or no GCI-support at all."

Effectively, MiG-21 had success as interdiction-strike aircraft, taking-out an important air base with only eight sorties. The results of the IAF's assault was that by 7 December, the PAF in the East was effectively grounded. The IAF also bombed other airfields including the abandoned WWII airfields of Comilla, Lal Munir Hat and Shamsher Nagar throughout the war, denying their use to PAF planes that may be moved by road, as well as to any external aerial reinforcement. Jessore Airfield had come under Mitro Bahini control by this time, so it was spared. Pakistani authorities made repeated attempts to repair the runways. Airforce and army engineers, helped by civilian workers, worked round the clock during Dec 6-7, and by 4:50 AM Dec 7, only 8 hours of respite was needed to regain fully operational status at Tejgaon, However, the IAF hit the base on the 7th, and it was estimated 36 hours of work without further damage was needed to make the base operational again. The IAF ensured no such respite took place. In desperation, it was suggested that the broad streets at second capital be used as runways, but technical problems ruled out that possibility - grounding the PAF Sabres forever in East Pakistan.

PAF fighter pilots were sent to West Pakistan via Burma on 8 December and 9 December when it became clear at least 36 hours of uninterrupted work was needed to fix the runways and the ack-ack units were unable to keep the IAF away. Pakistani authorities claimed that between 4–15 December the IAF had lost 22 to 24 aircraft, 7 to the PAF and the rest to ack-ack units. The IAF records 19 aircraft lost in East Pakistan, 3 in air combat, 6 to accidents and the rest to ack-ack while 5 Sabres were shot down by IAF planes. After the liberation of Dhaka, 13 airframes were found at the Tejgaon airport by the Mitro Bahini in various states of sabotage. 2 T-33 trainers were inoperable, but 8 Sabres were made operational later. 5 of them were incorporated in the Bangladesh Air Force in 1972. The Pakistan HQ had issued orders to blow up the aircraft, but Air Commodore Enam had pointed out that the sight of burning planes would demoralize the Pakistani troops defending Dacca. PAF personnel destroyed the ammunition stocks and sabotaged the electric and hydraulic systems of the aircraft on 15 December.

The PAF continued to use helicopters at night to fly reinforcements to remote bases and airlift munitions. Prior to the surrender of Pakistan Eastern Command on 16 December the Army Aviation squadron, commanded by Lt. Col. Liaquat Bokhari, escaped to Burma with selected personnel, including Maj. Gen. Rahim Khan (GOC 39th Ad Hoc division).

Operations in Support of Ground Forces

With the PAF in the east effectively neutralised, the IAF could now concentrate in supporting their advancing army. Movements of Pakistani troops during day time came to a virtual halt due to relentless IAF air attack. Ferries across major river crossings were sunk by the IAF thus denying the Pak army its line of retreat to Dhaka. On 7 December, INS Vikrant, the navy's sole aircraft carrier at the time, joined the operation. Sea Hawks operating from the deck of *Vikrant* struck Chittagong harbour, Cox's Bazar and Barisal. Whatever remained of the Pakistani Navy was destroyed or sunk. The airfields in Cox's Bazar, Chiringa and Feni were made inoperative.

On 10 December IAF helilifted troops of the IV Corps from Ashuganj to Raipura and Narsingi in what came to be termed the *Operation Cactus-Lilly* (also known as the *Helibridge over Meghna*). Entire Brigade strengths were lifted over the River Meghna, allowing the Indian Army to continue their advance in-spite of stiff resistance at Ashuganj, where the retreating Pakistani Army also blew up the Bridge.

To the south of this area near Chandpur, the 39 division (CO: General Rahim Khan) HQ at had requested evacuation by river on December 8. Under the escort of a gunboat, the flotilla, made up of local launches sailed in the early hours of December 10. The IAF spotted and bombed the ships, which were either sunk or beached themselves and failed to reach Dhaka. The survivors later were evacuated by ships operating at night and by helicopters.

On 11 December, India airdropped Para Bn Gp 130 in the now famous Tangail airdrop. The operation involved An-12, C-119s, 2 Caribous and Dakotas from 11 sqn and 48 Sn. In total, about 1000 troops were airdropped. The only hitch was one paratrooper who a static line hangup. Gnats from No. 22 sqn provided top cover for the operation, which ultimately went unhindered. Also on the 11th of December three converted An-12s from the No.44 Squadron struck the Jaydebpur Ordnance factory in East Pakistan.

On the morning of 14 December, a message was intercepted by Indian Intelligence of a high-level meeting of the civilian administration in East Pakistan and a decision was made to mount an attack. Within 15 minutes interception of the message, a strike was launched against Dhaka. Armed with tourist guide maps of the city, four Mig 21s of No. 28 Sqn got Airborne. A few minutes had passed after the meeting had started, when the IAF MIG's came screaming & blasted the Governors House with 57 mm rockets in the first, thereby ripping the massive roof of the main hall and turning the building into a smouldering wreck. The Governor of East Pakistan, Mr. A H Malik, was so shocked with the incident that he resigned on the spot by writing on a piece of paper and thereby renouncing all ties with the West Pakistani administration, to take refuge at the Red Cross Center in Dhaka.

Fate of Pakistan Navy in East Pakistan

Pakistan Forces GHQ had declined a substantial naval contingent for the defense of East Pakistan for two reasons: they had inadequate ships to challenge the Indian navy on both fronts and the PAF in the east was not deemed strong enough to protect the ships from Indian airpower (The IAF and Indian Navy air arm). The fate of Pakistani naval vessels in December was ample proof of the soundness of this decision and the repercussion of neglecting East Pakistan defense infrastructure (the reason PAF could only station 1 squadron of planes there). Pakistan Eastern Command had planned to fight the war without the navy and faced with a hopeless task against overwhelming odds, the navy planned to remain in the ports when war broke out.

The Pakistan Navy had 4 Gunboats (PNS *Jessore, Rajshahi, Comilla,* and *Sylhet*), all 345 ton vessels capable of attaining a maximum speed of 20 knots, were crewed by 29 sailors and fitted with 40/60 mm cannons and machine guns in East Pakistan. 1 patrol boat ("Balaghat") and 17 armed boats (armed with 12.7mm/20mm guns and/or .50 or.303 Browning machine guns) in addition to various civilian owned Pakistan forces requisitioned and jury rigged boats armed with various weapons were also part of the Pakistan naval contingent. The improvised armed boats were adequate for patrolling and anti-insurgency ops but hopelessly out of place in conventional warfare. Before the start of hostilities in December PNS *Jessore* was in Khulna with 4 other boats, PNS *Rajshahi, Comilla* and *Balaghat* was at Chittagong. PNS *Sylhet* was undergoing repairs at a dry-dock near Dhaka. The outbreak of hostilities in December 3 found most of the boats scattered around the province.

Indian aircraft attacked the *Rajshahi* and *Comilla* near Chittagong on the 4 December, the *Rajshahi* was damaged and the *Comilla* sunk. The *Balaghat,* which was not attacked, rescued the Comilla crew and the surviving ships returned to Chittagong. On December 5, Indian planes sank two patrol boats in Khulna. The PNS *Sylhet* was destroyed on December 6 and the *Balaghat* on December 9 by Indian aircraft. PNS *Jessore,* which had withdrawn from Khulna to Dacca, was destroyed on December 11 while escorting boats evacuating Pakistani troops from Chandpur. PNS *Rajshahi* was repaired, and under the command of Lt. Commander Shikder Hayat managed to evade the Indian blockade and reach Malaysia before the surrender on December 16. From there it sailed to Karachi and continued to serve in the Pakistan navy.

Tragedy Near Khulna

Indian Army Eastern Command had ordered Bangladesh Navy gunboats BNS *Palash* and BNS *Padma,* accompanied by INS *Panvel* under the overall command of Commander M.N Samant, to sail to Chalna port. These ships, carrying Bengali seamen and Indian command crew, had been operating against Pakistani shipping since November, and under the advise of Indian Eastern Air command, had painted their superstructure yellow to avoid misidentification, which had been reported back to Eastern air-command. This task force sailed on December 6, entered Mangla at 7:30 Am on December 10 and took over the port facility. Commander Samant knew that Khulna was a IAF target but decided to push on anyway. Around 11:30 AM, when the 3 ships were closing in on Khulna dockyard, 3 airplanes dived on them. Commander Samant recognized the IAF planes and ordered the ships to hold fire; all 3 ships were strafed and sunk by the planes. 3 Bengali Naval commandos and 7 Bengali sailors were killed, 6 naval commandos, 1 BSF JCO, 3 Indian officers and 7 Bengali seamen were injured. Indian Navy gave 14 awards (including 3 Mahavir Chakras, and 6 Vir Chakras) to the Indian rank and file involved in this incident. Bengali Seaman Ruhul Amin, who tried to save MV Palash despite being wounded and ordered to abandon ship, and later had died under torture, was awarded 'Bir Shershtra" by Bangladesh government. 21 Indian and Bengali sailors became POWs.

The IAF was to continue flying interdiction missions for the remainder of the war in, shooting up ammunition dumps and other fixed installations. Gnats and Sukhoi Su-7s flew many missions in support of army units as they moved swiftly towards Dhaka, delivering ordnance such as iron bombs to take out enemy bunkers which occasionally posed an obstacle to advancing infantry. Canberras repeatedly struck Jessore forcing the enemy to abandon this strategic city. The IAF also was prepared to hit any Chinese incursions into Indian territory in the eastern Himalayas. As it turned out, the Chinese did not stir.

Surrender of Pakistani Forces in East Pakistan

The *Instrument of Surrender* of Pakistani forces stationed in East Pakistan was signed at Ramna Race Course in Dhaka at 16.31 IST on 16 December 1971, by Lieutenant General Jagjit Singh Aurora, General Officer Commanding-in-chief of Eastern Command of the Indian Army and Lieutenant General A. A. K. Niazi, Commander of Pakistani forces in East Pakistan. As Aurora accepted the surrender, the surrounding crowds on the race course began shouting anti-Niazi and anti-Pakistan slogans.

India took approximately 90,000 prisoners of war, including Pakistani soldiers and their East Pakistani civilian supporters. 79,676 prisoners were uniformed personnel, of which 55,692 were Army, 16,354 Paramilitary, 5,296 Police, 1000 Navy and 800 PAF. The remaining prisoners were civilians - either family members of the military personnel or collaborators (razakars). The Hamoodur Rahman Commission report instituted by Pakistan lists the Pakistani POWs as follows:

Branch	Number of captured Pakistani POWs
Army	54,154
Navy	1,381
Air Force	833
Paramilitary including police	22,000
Civilian personnel	12,000
Total	90,368

American and Soviet Involvement

The United States supported Pakistan both politically and materially. President Richard Nixon and his Secretary of State Henry Kissinger feared Soviet expansion into South and Southeast Asia. Pakistan was a close ally of the People's Republic of China, with whom Nixon had been negotiating a *rapprochement* and where he intended to visit in February 1972. Nixon feared that an Indian invasion of West Pakistan would mean total Soviet domination of the region, and that it would seriously undermine the global position of the United States and the regional position of America's new tacit ally, China. In order to demonstrate to China the *bona fides* of the United States as an ally, and in direct violation of the US Congress-imposed sanctions on Pakistan, Nixon sent military supplies to Pakistan, routing them through Jordan and Iran, while also encouraging China to increase its arms supplies to Pakistan. The Nixon administration also ignored reports it received of the "genocidal" activities of the Pakistani Army in East Pakistan, most notably the Blood telegram. This prompted widespread criticism and condemnation both by Congress and in the international press.

When Pakistan's defeat in the eastern sector seemed certain, Nixon ordered the USS *Enterprise* into the Bay of Bengal. The *Enterprise* arrived on station on 11 December 1971. It has been documented that Nixon even persuaded Iran and Jordan to send their F-86, F-104 and F-5 fighter jets in aid of Pakistan. On 6 December and 13 December, the Soviet Navy dispatched two groups of ships and a submarine, armed with nuclear missiles, from Vladivostok; they trailed U.S. Task Force 74 into the Indian Ocean from 18 December 1971 until 7 January 1972. The Soviets also had a nuclear submarine to help ward off the threat posed by USS *Enterprise* task force in the Indian Ocean.

The Soviet Union sympathized with the Bangladeshis, and supported the Indian Army and Mukti Bahini during the war, recognizing that the independence of Bangladesh would weaken the position of its rivals the United States and China. The USSR gave assurances to India that if a confrontation with the United States or China developed, it would take counter-measures. This assurance was enshrined in the Indo-Soviet friendship treaty signed in August 1971.

Aftermath

India

The war stripped Pakistan of more than half of its population and with nearly one-third of its army in captivity, clearly established India's military dominance of the subcontinent. In spite of the magnitude of the victory, India was surprisingly restrained in its reaction. Mostly, Indian leaders seemed pleased by the relative ease with which they had accomplished their goals the establishment of Bangladesh and the prospect of an early return to their homeland of the 10 million Bengali refugees who were the cause of the war. In announcing the surrender to the Indian Parliament, Prime Minister Indira Gandhi declared:

> *"Dacca is now the free capital of a free country. We hail the people of Bangladesh in their hour of triumph. All nations who value the human spirit will recognize it as a significant milestone in man `s quest for liberty."*

Pakistan

For Pakistan it was a complete and humiliating defeat, a psychological setback that came from a defeat at the hands of intense rival India. Pakistan lost half its territory, significant portion of its economy and its geo-political role in South Asia. Pakistan feared that the two-nation theory was disproved and that the Islamic ideology had proved insufficient to keep Bengalis part of Pakistan. Also, the Pakistani military suffered further humiliation by having their 90,000 prisoners of war (POWs) released by India only after the negotiation and signing of the Simla Agreement on July 2, 1972. In addition to repatriation of prisoners of war also, the agreeement established an ongoing structure for the negotiated resolution of future conflicts between India and Pakistan (referring to the remaining western provinces that now composed the totality of Pakistan). In signing the agreement, Pakistan also, by implication, recognized the former East Pakistan as the now independent and sovereign state of Bangladesh.

The Pakistani people were not mentally prepared to accept defeat, the state-controlled media in West Pakistan had been projecting imaginary victories. When the surrender in East Pakistan was finally announced, people could not come terms with the magnitude of defeat, spontaneous demonstrations and mass protests erupted on the streets of major cities in West Pakistan. Also, referring to the remaining rump Western Pakistan as simply "Pakistan" added to the effect of the defeat as international acceptance of the secession of the eastern half of the country and its creation as the independent state of Bangladesh developed and was given more credence. The cost of the war for Pakistan in monetary and human resources was very high. Demoralized and finding himself unable to control the situation, General Yahya Khan surrendered power to Zulfiqar Ali Bhutto who was sworn-in on 20 December 1971 as President and as the (first civilian) Chief Martial Law Administrator. A new and smaller western-based Pakistan emerged on 16 December 1971.

The loss of East Pakistan had shattered the prestige of the Pakistani military. Pakistan lost half its navy, a quarter of its air force and a third of its army. The popularized myth that one Muslim had the fighting prowess of five Hindus no longer held any legitimacy. The war also exposed the shortcoming of Pakistan's declared strategic doctrine that the "defence of East Pakistan lay in West Pakistan". Hussain Haqqani, in his book *Pakistan: Between Mosque and Military* notes,

> *"Moreover, the army had failed to fulfill its promises of fighting to the last man. The eastern command had laid down arms after losing only 1,300 men in battle. In West Pakistan 1,200 military deaths had accompanied lack luster military performance."*

In his book *The 1971 Indo-Pak War: A Soldier's Narrative* Pakistani Major General Hakeem Arshad Qureshi a veteran of this conflict noted,

> *"We must accept the fact that, as a people, we had also contributed to the bifurcation of our own country. It was not a Niazi, or a Yahya, even a Mujib, or a Bhutto, or their key assistants, who alone were the cause of our break-up, but a corrupted system and a flawed social order that our own apathy had allowed to remain in place for years. At the most critical moment in our history we failed to check the limitless ambitions of individuals with dubious antecedents and to thwart their selfish and irresponsible behaviour.*

> *It was our collective 'conduct` that had provided the enemy an opportunity to dismember us."*

Bangladesh

Bangladesh became an independent nation, the world's third most populous Muslim state. Mujibur Rahman was released from a West Pakistani prison, returned to Dhaka on 10 January 1972 and to become first President of Bangladesh and later its Prime Minister.

On the brink of defeat around 14 December, the Pakistani Army, and its local collaborators, systematically killed a large number of Bengali doctors, teachers and intellectuals, part of a pogrom against the Hindu minorities who constituted the majority of urban educated intellectuals. Young men, especially students, who were seen as possible rebels were also targeted. The extent of casualties in East Pakistan is not known. R.J. Rummel cites estimates ranging from one to three million people killed. Other estimates place the death toll lower, at 300,000. Bangladesh government figures state that Pakistani forces aided by collaborators killed three million people, raped 200,000 women and displaced millions of others. In 2010 Bangladesh government set up a tribunal to prosecute the people involved in alleged war crimes and those who collaborated with Pakistan. According to the Government, the defendants would be charged with Crimes against humanity, genocide, murder, rape and arson.

Hamoodur Rahman Commission

In aftermath of war Pakistan Government constituted the Hamoodur Rahman Commission headed by Justice Hamoodur Rahman in 1971 to investigate the political and military causes for defeat and the Bangladesh atrocities during the war. The commission's report was classified and its publication banned by Bhutto as it put the military in poor light, until some parts of the report surfaced in Indian media in 2000.

When it was declassified, it showed many failings from the strategic to the tactical levels. It confirmed the looting, rapes and the killings by the Pakistan Army and their local agents. It lay the blame squarely on Pakistani generals, accusing them of war crimes and neglect of duty. Though no actions were ever taken on commissions findings, the commission had recommended public trial of Pakistan Army generals.

Simla Agreement

In 1972 the Simla Agreement was signed between India and Pakistan, the treaty ensured that Pakistan recognized the independence of Bangladesh in exchange for the return of the Pakistani POWs. India treated all the POWs in strict accordance with the Geneva Convention, rule 1925. It released more than 90,000 Pakistani PoWs in five months. Further, as a gesture of goodwill, nearly 200 soldiers who were sought for war crimes by Bengalis were also pardoned by India.

The accord also gave back more than 13,000 km^2 of land that Indian troops had seized in West Pakistan during the war, though India retained a few strategic areas. But some in India felt that the treaty had been too lenient to Bhutto, who had pleaded for leniency, arguing that the fragile democracy in Pakistan would crumble if the accord was perceived as being overly harsh by Pakistanis and that he would be accused of losing Kashmir in addition to the loss of East Pakistan.

Long Term Consequences

- Steve Coll, in his book *Ghost Wars*, argues that the Pakistan military's experience with India, including Pervez Musharraf's experience in 1971, influenced the Pakistani government to support jihadist groups in Afghanistan even after the Soviets left, because the jihadists were a tool to use against India, including bogging down the Indian Army in Kashmir.
- After the war, Zulfikar Ali Bhutto came to power. Pakistan launched Project-706, a secret nuclear weapon development program, to defend itself from India. A vast majority of

Pakistani nuclear scientists who were working at the International Atomic Energy Agency and European and American nuclear programs immediately came to Pakistan and joined Project-706.

Important Dates

- **7 March 1971:** Sheikh Mujibur Rahman declares that, "The current struggle is a struggle for independence", in a public meeting attended by almost a million people in Dhaka.
- **25 March 1971:** Pakistani forces start Operation Searchlight, a systematic plan to eliminate any resistance. Thousands of people are killed in student dormitories and police barracks in Dhaka.
- **26 March 1971:** Sheikh Mujibur Rahman signed an official declaration of independence and sent it through a radio message on the night of 25 March (the morning of 26 March). Later Major Ziaur Rahman and other Awami League leaders announced the declaration of independence on behalf of Sheikh Mujib from Kalurghat Radio Station, Chittagong. The message is relayed to the world by Indian radio stations.
- **17 April 1971:** Exiled leaders of Awami League form a provisional government.
- **3 December 1971:** War between India and Pakistan officially begins when West Pakistan launches a series of preemptive air strikes on Indian airfields.
- **6 December 1971:** East Pakistan is recognized as Bangladesh by India.
- **14 December 1971:** Systematic elimination of Bengali intellectuals is started by Pakistani Army and local collaborators.
- **16 December 1971:** Lieutenant-General A. A. K. Niazi, supreme commander of Pakistani Army in [East Pakistan, surrenders to the Allied Forces (Mitro Bahini) represented by Lieutenant General Jagjit Singh Arora of Indian Army at the surrender. Bangladesh gains victory.
- **12 January 1972:** Sheikh Mujibur Rahman comes to power.

Military Awards

For bravery, a number of soldiers and officers on both sides were awarded the highest military award of respective countries. Following is a list of the recipients of the Indian award Param Vir Chakra, Bangladeshi award Bir Sreshtho and the Pakistani award Nishan-E-Haider:

India

Recipients of the Param Vir Chakra:

- Lance Naik Albert Ekka (Posthumously)
- Flying Officer Nirmal Jit Singh Sekhon (Posthumously)
- Major Hoshiar Singh
- Second Lieutenant Arun Khetarpal (Posthumously)

Bangladesh

Recipients of the Bir Sreshtho

- Captain Mohiuddin Jahangir (Posthumously)
- Lance Naik Munshi Abdur Rouf (Posthumously)
- Sepoy Hamidur Rahman (Posthumously)
- Sepoy Mostafa Kamal (Posthumously)
- ERA Mohammad Ruhul Amin (Posthumously)
- Flight Lieutenant Matiur Rahman (Posthumously)
- Lance Naik Nur Mohammad Sheikh (Posthumously)

Pakistan

Recipients of the Nishan-E-Haider:

- Major Muhammad Akram (Posthumously)
- Pilot Officer Rashid Minhas (Posthumously)
- Major Shabbir Sharif (Posthumously)
- Sowar Muhammad Hussain (Posthumously)
- Lance Naik Muhammad Mahfuz (Posthumously)

Dramatization

Films

- *Border*, a 1997 Bollywood war film directed by J.P.Dutta. This movie is an adaptation from real life events that happened at the Battle of Longewala fought in Rajasthan (Western Theatre) during the 1971 Indo-Pak war. *Border* at the Internet Movie Database
- *Hindustan Ki Kasam*, a 1973 Bollywood war film directed by Chetan Anand. The aircraft in the film are all authentic aircraft used in the 1971 war against Pakistan. These include MiG-21s, Gnats, Hunters and Su-7s. Some of these aircraft were also flown by war veterans such as Samar Bikram Shah (2 kills) and Manbir Singh. *Hindustan Ki Kasam* at the Internet Movie Database
- *1971 - Prisoners of War*, a 2007 Bollywood war film directed by Sagar Brothers. Set against the backdrop of a prisoners' camp in Pakistan, follows six Indian prisoners awaiting release after their capture in the 1971 India-Pakistan war.

3

Kargil War
Conflict and Destruction

Kargil War

The Kargil War, also known as the Kargil conflict, was an armed conflict between India and Pakistan that took place between May and July 1999 in the Kargil district of Kashmir and elsewhere along the Line of Control (LOC). The conflict is also referred to as **Operation Vijay** (Victory in Hindi) which was the name of the Indian operation to clear the Kargil sector.

The cause of the war was the infiltration of Pakistani soldiers and Kashmiri militants into positions on the Indian side of the LOC, which serves as the *de facto* border between the two states. During the initial stages of the war, Pakistan blamed the fighting entirely on independent Kashmiri insurgents, but documents left behind by casualties and later statements by Pakistan's Prime Minister and Chief of Army Staff showed involvement of Pakistani paramilitary forces, led by General Ashraf Rashid. The Indian Army, later on supported by the Indian Air Force, recaptured a majority of the positions on the Indian side of the LOC infiltrated by the Pakistani troops and militants. With international diplomatic opposition, the Pakistani forces withdrew from the remaining Indian positions along the LOC.

The war is one of the most recent examples of high altitude warfare in mountainous terrain, which posed significant logistical problems for the combating sides. This was only the second direct ground war between any two countries after they had developed nuclear weapons; it is also the most recent. (India and Pakistan both test-detonated fission devices in May 1998, though the first Indian nuclear test was conducted in 1974.) The conflict led to heightened tension between the two nations and increased defence spending by India.

Location

Before the Partition of India in 1947, Kargil was part of the Baltistan district of Ladakh, a sparsely populated region with diverse linguistic, ethnic and religious groups, living in isolated valleys separated by some of the world's highest mountains. The First Kashmir War (1947–48) concluded with the LOC bisecting the Baltistan district, with the town and district of Kargil lying on the Indian side in the Ladakh subdivision of the Indian state of Jammu and Kashmir. After Pakistan's defeat in the Indo-Pakistani War of 1971, the two nations signed the Simla Agreement promising not to engage in armed conflict with respect to that boundary.

The town of Kargil is located 205 km (120 miles) from Srinagar, facing the Northern Areas across the LOC. Like other areas in the Himalayas, Kargil has a temperate climate. Summers are cool with frigid nights, while winters are long and chilly with temperatures often dropping to -48 °C (-54 °F).

An Indian national highway (NH 1D) connecting Srinagar to Leh cuts through Kargil. The area that witnessed the infiltration and fighting is a 160 km long stretch of ridges overlooking this only road linking Srinagar and Leh. The military outposts on the ridges above the highway were generally around 5,000 metres (16,000 ft) high, with a few as high as 5,485 metres (18,000 ft). Apart from the district capital, Kargil, the populated areas near the front line in the conflict included the Mushko Valley and the town of Drass, southwest of Kargil, as well as the Batalik sector and other areas, northeast of Kargil.

One of the reasons why Kargil was targeted was that the terrain surrounding it, lent itself to pre-emptive seizure of unoccupied military positions. With tactically vital features and well-prepared defensive posts atop the peaks, a defender of the high ground would enjoy advantages akin to a fortress. Any attack to dislodge a defender from high ground in mountain warfare requires a far higher ratio of attackers to defenders, and the difficulties would be exacerbated by the high altitude and freezing temperatures.

Kargil is just 173 km (108 mi) from the Pakistani-controlled town of Skardu, which was capable of providing logistical and artillery support to Pakistani combatants.

Background

After the Indo-Pakistani War of 1971, there had been a long period with relatively few direct armed conflicts involving the military forces of the two neighbors - notwithstanding the efforts of both nations to control the Siachen Glacier by establishing military outposts on the surrounding mountains ridges and the resulting military skirmishes in the 1980s. During the 1990s, however, escalating tensions and conflict due to separatist activities in Kashmir, some of which were supported by Pakistan, as well as the conducting of nuclear tests by both countries in 1998, led to an increasingly belligerent atmosphere. In an attempt to defuse the situation, both countries signed the Lahore Declaration in February 1999, promising to provide a peaceful and bilateral solution to the Kashmir conflict.

During the winter of 1998 -1999, some elements of the Military of Pakistan were covertly training and sending Pakistani troops and paramilitary forces, some allegedly in the guise of mujahideen, into territory on the Indian side of the LOC. The infiltration was code named "Operation Badr";

its aim was to sever the link between Kashmir and Ladakh, and cause Indian forces to withdraw from the Siachen Glacier, thus forcing India to negotiate a settlement of the broader Kashmir dispute. Pakistan also believed that any tension in the region would internationalise the Kashmir issue, helping it to secure a speedy resolution. Yet another goal may have been to boost the morale of the decade-long rebellion in Indian Administered Kashmir by taking a proactive role. Some writers have speculated that the operation's objective may also have been as a retaliation for India's Operation Meghdoot in 1984 that seized much of Siachen Glacier.

According to India's then army chief Ved Prakash Malik, and many other scholars, much of the background planning, including construction of logistical supply routes, had been undertaken much earlier. On several occasions during the 1980s and 1990s, the army had given Pakistani leaders (Zia ul Haq and Benazir Bhutto) similar proposals for infiltration into the Kargil region, but the plans had been shelved for fear of drawing the nations into all-out war.

Some analysts believe that the blueprint of attack was reactivated soon after Pervez Musharraf was appointed chief of army staff in October 1998. After the war, Nawaz Sharif, Prime Minister of Pakistan during the Kargil conflict, claimed that he was unaware of the plans, and that he first learned about the situation when he received an urgent phone call from Atal Bihari Vajpayee, his counterpart in India. Sharif attributed the plan to Musharraf and "just two or three of his cronies", a view shared by some Pakistani writers who have stated that only four generals, including Musharraf, knew of the plan. Musharraf, however, asserted that Sharif had been briefed on the Kargil operation 15 days ahead of Vajpayee's journey to Lahore on February 20.

War Progress

There were three major phases to the Kargil War. First, Pakistan infiltrated forces into the Indian-controlled section of Kashmir and occupied strategic locations enabling it to bring

NH1 within range of its artillery fire. The next stage consisted of India discovering the infiltration and mobilizing forces to respond to it. The final stage involved major battles by Indian and Pakistani forces resulting in India recapturing some territory held by Pakistani forces and the subsequent withdrawal of Pakistani forces back across the Line of Control after international pressure.

Occupation by Pakistan

During the winter season, due to extreme cold in the snow-capped mountainous areas of Kashmir, it was a common practice for both the Indian and Pakistan Armies to abandon some forward posts on their respective sides of the LOC and to reduce patrolling of areas that may be avenues of infiltration. When weather conditions became less severe, forward posts would be reoccupied and patrolling resumed.

During February 1999, the Pakistan Army began to re-occupy the posts it had abandoned on its side of the LOC in the Kargil region, but also sent forces to occupy some posts on the Indian side of the LOC. Troops from the elite Special Services Group as well as four to seven battalions of the Northern Light Infantry (a paramilitary regiment not part of the regular Pakistani army at that time) covertly and overtly set up bases on the vantage points of the Indian-controlled region. According to some reports, these Pakistani forces were backed by Kashmiri guerrillas and Afghan mercenaries.

Pakistani intrusions took place in the heights of the lower Mushkoh Valley, along the Marpo La ridgeline in Dras, in Kaksar near Kargil, in the Batalik sector east of the Indus River, on the heights above of the Chorbatla sector where the LOC turns North and in the Turtok sector south of the Siachen area.

India Discovers Infiltration and Mobilizes

Initially, these incursions were not detected for a number of reasons: Indian patrols were not sent into some of the areas infiltrated by the Pakistani forces and heavy artillery fire by Pakistan in some areas provided cover for the infiltrators. But by the second week of May, the ambushing of an Indian patrol team led by Capt Saurabh Kalia, who acted on a tip-off by a local shepherd in the Batalik sector, led to the exposure of the infiltration. Initially, with little knowledge of the nature or extent of the infiltration, the Indian troops in the area assumed that the infiltrators were jihadis and claimed that they would evict them within a few days. Subsequent discovery of infiltration elsewhere along the LOC, and the difference in tactics employed by the infiltrators, caused the Indian army to realize that the plan of attack was on a much bigger scale. The total area seized by the ingress is generally accepted to between 130 km^2 - 200 km^2; Musharraf, however, stated that 500 square miles (1,300 km^2) of Indian territory was occupied.

The Government of India responded with Operation Vijay, a mobilisation of 200,000 Indian troops. However, because of the nature of the terrain, division and corps operations could not be mounted; subsequent fighting was conducted mostly at the regimental or battalion level. In effect, two divisions of the Indian Army, numbering 20,000, plus several thousand from the Paramilitary forces of India and the air force were deployed in the conflict zone. The total number of Indian soldiers that were involved in the military operation on the Kargil-Drass sector was thus close to 30,000. The number of infiltrators, including those providing logistical backup, has been put at approximately 5,000 at the height of the conflict. This figure includes troops from Pakistan-administered Kashmir who provided additional artillery support.

The Indian Air Force launched Operation Safed Sagar in support of the mobilization of Indian land forces, but its effectiveness during the war was limited by the high altitude and weather conditions, which in turn limited bomb loads and the number of airstrips that could be used.

The Indian Navy also readied itself for an attempted blockade of Pakistani ports (primarily Karachi port) to cut off supply routes. Later, the then-Prime Minister of Pakistan Nawaz Sharif disclosed that Pakistan was left with just six days of fuel to sustain itself if a full-fledged war had broken out.

India Attacks Pakistani positions

The terrain of Kashmir is mountainous and at high altitudes; even the best roads, such as National Highway 1D from Leh to Srinagar, are only two lanes. The rough terrain and narrow roads slowed traffic, and the high altitude, which affected the ability of aircraft to carry loads, made control of NH 1D (the actual stretch of the highway which was under Pakistani fire) a priority for India. From their observation posts, the Pakistani forces had a clear line-of-sight to lay down indirect artillery fire on NH 1D, inflicting heavy casualties on the Indians. This was a serious problem for the Indian Army as the highway was its main logistical and supply route. The Pakistani shelling of the arterial road posed the threat of Leh being cut off, though an alternative (and longer) road to Leh existed via Himachal Pradesh.

The infiltrators, apart from being equipped with small arms and grenade launchers, were also armed with mortars, artillery and anti-aircraft guns. Many posts were also heavily mined, with India later stating to having recovered more than 8,000 anti-personnel mines according to an ICBL report. Pakistan's reconnaissance was done through unmanned aerial vehicles and AN/TPQ-36 Firefinder radars supplied by the US. The initial Indian attacks were aimed at controlling the hills overlooking NH 1D, with high priority being given to the stretches of the highway near the town of Kargil. The majority of posts along the Line of Control were adjacent to the highway, and therefore the recapture of nearly every infiltrated post increased both the territorial gains and the security of the highway. The protection of this route and the recapture of the forward posts were thus *ongoing objectives* throughout the war.

The Indian Army's first priority was to recapture peaks that were in the immediate vicinity of NH 1D. This resulted in Indian troops first targeting the Tiger Hill and Tololing complex in Dras, which dominated the Srinagar-Leh route. This was soon followed by the Batalik-Turtok sub-sector which provided access to Siachen Glacier. Some of the peaks that were of vital strategic importance to the Pakistani defensive troops were Point 4590 and Point 5353. While 4590 was the nearest point that had a view of NH 1D, point 5353 was the highest feature in the Dras sector, allowing the Pakistani troops to observe NH 1D. The recapture of Point 4590 by Indian troops on June 14 was significant, notwithstanding the fact that Point 4590 resulting in the Indian Army suffering the most casualties in a single battle during the conflict. Though most of the posts in the vicinity of the highway were cleared by mid-June, some parts of the highway near Drass witnessed sporadic shelling until the end of the war.

The tail of an Indian air force MiG-21 fighter shot down by a Pakistani missile. The pilot Squadron Leader Ajay Ahuja was killed.

Once India regained control of the hills overlooking NH 1D, the Indian Army turned to driving the invading force back across the Line of Control. The Battle of Tololing, among other assaults, slowly tilted the combat in India's favor. The Pakistani troops at Tololing were aided by Pakistani fighters from Kashmir. Some of the posts put up a stiff resistance, including Tiger Hill (Point 5140) that fell only later in the war. Indian troops found well-entrenched Pakistani soldiers at Tiger Hill, and both sides suffered heavy casualties. After a final assault on the peak in which 10 Pakistani soldiers and 5 Indian soldiers were killed, Tiger Hill finally fell. A few of the assaults occurred atop hitherto unheard of peaks - most of them unnamed with only Point numbers to differentiate them which witnessed fierce hand to hand combat.

As the operation was fully underway, about 250 artillery guns were brought in to clear the infiltrators in the posts that were in the line-of-sight. The Bofors field howitzer (infamous in India due to the Bofors scandal) played a vital role, with Indian gunners making maximum use of the terrain that assisted such an attack. However, its success was limited elsewhere due to the lack of space and depth to deploy the Bofors gun.

It was in this type of terrain that aerial attacks were used with limited effectiveness. The IAF lost a MiG-27 strike aircraft which it attributed to an engine failure as well as a MiG-21 fighter which was shot down by Pakistan; initially Pakistan said it shot down both jets after they crossed into its territory and one Mi-8 helicopter to Stinger SAMs. Years later, a retired Pakistani Officer confirmed that the MiG-27 was lost to technical failure. During attacks the IAF used laser-guided bombs to destroy well-entrenched positions of the Pakistani forces.

On May 27, 1999, Flt. Lt. Nachiketa developed engine trouble in the Batalik sector and bailed out of his craft. Sqn Ldr Ajay Ahuja went out of his way to locate his comrade but was shot down using a shoulder-fired Stinger missile. According to reports, he had bailed out of his stricken plane safely but was apparently killed by his captors as his body was returned riddled with bullet wounds.

In many vital points, neither artillery nor air power could dislodge the outposts manned by the Pakistani soldiers, who were out of visible range. The Indian Army mounted some direct frontal ground assaults which were slow and took a heavy toll given the steep ascent that had to be made on peaks as high as 18,000 feet (5,500 m). Since any daylight attack would be suicidal, all the advances had to be made under the cover of darkness, escalating the risk of freezing. Accounting for the wind chill factor, the temperatures were often as low as -11 °C to -15 °C (12 °F to 5 °F) near the mountain tops. Based on military tactics, much of the costly frontal assaults by the Indians could have been avoided if the Indian Military had chosen to blockade the supply route of the opposing force, virtually creating a siege. Such a move would have involved the Indian troops crossing the LoC as well as initiating aerial attacks on Pakistan soil, a manoeuvre India was not willing to exercise fearing an expansion of the theatre of war and reducing international support for its cause.

Two months into the conflict, Indian troops had slowly retaken most of the ridges that were encroached by the infiltrators; according to official count, an estimated 75%–80% of the intruded area and nearly all high ground was back under Indian control.

Withdrawal and Final Battles

Following the outbreak of armed fighting, Pakistan sought American help in de-escalating the conflict. Bruce Riedel, aide to then President Bill Clinton reported that the US intelligence had imaged Pakistani movements of nuclear weapons to forward deployments for fear of the Kargil hostilities escalating into a wider conflict between the two countries. However, President Clinton refused to intervene until Pakistan had removed all forces from the Indian side of the Line of Control. Following the Washington accord on July 4, where Sharif agreed to withdraw Pakistani troops, most of the fighting came to a gradual halt, but some Pakistani forces remained in positions on the Indian side of the LOC. In addition, the United Jihad Council (an umbrella for extremist groups) rejected Pakistan's plan for a climb-down, instead deciding to fight on.

The Indian army launched its final attacks in the last week of July; as soon as the Drass subsector had been cleared of Pakistani forces, the fighting ceased on July 26. The day has since been marked as *Kargil Vijay Diwas* (Kargil Victory Day) in India. By the end of the war, India had resumed control of all territory south and east of the Line of Control, as was established in July 1972 as per the Simla Agreement.

However it had failed to occupy strategic peak Point 5353, Bunker Ridge, Saddle Ridge and Dalu Nag. Point 5353 is the highest peak in the region which has a clear view of the National Highway 1 D that connects the Kashmir valley with Kargil; it remains occupied by Pakistan even a decade after the battle.

World Opinion

Pakistan was criticised by other countries for allowing its paramilitary forces and insurgents to cross the Line of Control. Pakistan's primary diplomatic response, one of plausible deniability linking the incursion to what it officially termed as "Kashmiri freedom fighters", was in the end not successful. Veteran analysts argued that the battle was fought at heights where only seasoned troops could survive, so poorly equipped "freedom fighters" would neither have the ability nor the wherewithal to seize land and defend it. Moreover, while the army had initially denied the involvement of its troops in the intrusion, two soldiers were awarded the Nishan-E-Haider (Pakistan's highest military honour). Another 90 soldiers were also given gallantry awards, most of them posthumously, confirming Pakistan's role in the episode. India also released taped phone conversations between the Army Chief and a senior Pakistani general where the latter is recorded saying: "the scruff of [the militants] necks is in our hands," although Pakistan dismissed it as a "total fabrication". Concurrently, Pakistan made several contradicting statements, confirming its role in Kargil, when it defended the incursions saying that the LOC itself was disputed. Pakistan also attempted to internationalize the Kashmir issue, by linking the crisis in Kargil to the larger Kashmir conflict but, such a diplomatic stance found few backers on the world stage.

As the Indian counter-attacks picked up momentum, Pakistani prime minister Nawaz Sharif flew to meet U.S. President Bill Clinton on July 4 to obtain support from the United States. Clinton rebuked Sharif, however, and asked him to use his contacts to rein in the militants and withdraw Pakistani soldiers from Indian territory. Clinton would later reveal in his autobiography that "Sharif's moves were perplexing" since the Indian Prime Minister had travelled to Lahore to promote bilateral talks aimed at resolving the Kashmir problem and "by crossing the Line of Control, Pakistan had wrecked the [bilateral] talks." On the other hand, he applauded Indian restraint for not crossing the LoC and escalating the conflict into an all-out war.

G8 nations supported India and condemned the Pakistani violation of the LOC at the Cologne summit. The European Union also opposed Pakistan's violation of the LOC. China, a long-time ally of Pakistan, insisted on a pullout of forces to the pre-conflict positions along the LoC and settling border issues peacefully. Other organizations like the ASEAN Regional Forum too supported India's stand on the inviolability of the LOC.

Faced with growing international pressure, Sharif managed to pull back the remaining soldiers from Indian territory. The joint statement issued by Clinton and Sharif conveyed the need to respect the Line of Control and resume bilateral talks as the best forum to resolve all disputes.

Gallantry Awards

A number of Indian soldiers earned awards for gallantry during the campaign.

- Grenadier Yogendra Singh Yadav, 18 Grenadiers, Param Vir Chakra,
- Lieutenant Manoj Kumar Pandey, 1/11 Gorkha Rifles, Param Vir Chakra, Posthumous
- Captain Vikram Batra, 13 JAK Rifles, Param Vir Chakra, Posthumous
- Squadron Leader Ajay Ahuja, Indian Air Force, Vir Chakra, Posthumous
- Rifleman Sanjay Kumar, 13 JAK Rifles, Param Vir Chakra

Two Pakistani soldiers received the Nishan-e-Haider.

- Captain Karnal Sher Khan, Nishan-e-Haider, Posthumous
- Havaldaar Lalak Jan, Northern Light Infantry, Nishan-e-Haider, Posthumous

Impact and Influence of Media

The Kargil War was significant for the impact and influence of the mass media on public opinion in both nations. Coming at a time of exploding growth in electronic journalism in India, the Kargil news stories and war footage were often telecast live on TV, and many websites provided in-depth analysis of the war. The conflict became the first "live" war in South Asia; it was given such detailed media coverage that one effect was the drumming up of jingoistic feelings.

The conflict soon turned into a news propaganda war, in which press briefings given by government officials of each nation produced conflicting claims and counterclaims. The Indian government placed a temporary news embargo on information from Pakistan, banning the telecast of the state-run Pakistani channel PTV and blocking access to online editions of the *Dawn* newspaper. The Pakistani media criticized this apparent curbing of freedom of the press in India, while India media claimed it was in the interest of national security. The Indian government ran advertisements in foreign publications including *The Times* and *The Washington Post* detailing Pakistan's role in supporting extremists in Kashmir in an attempt to garner political support for its position.

As the war progressed, media coverage of the conflict was more intense in India than in Pakistan. Many Indian channels showed images from the battle zone in a style reminiscent of CNN's coverage of the Gulf War (one of the shells fired by Pakistan troops even hit a Doordarshan transmission centre in Kargil while coverage continued). Reasons for India's increased coverage included the greater number of privately owned electronic media in India compared to Pakistan and relatively greater transparency in the Indian media. At a seminar in Karachi, Pakistani journalists agreed that while the Indian government had taken the press and the people into its confidence, Pakistan had not.

The print media in India and abroad was largely sympathetic to the Indian cause, with editorials in newspapers based in the west and other neutral countries observing that Pakistan was largely responsible for the conflict. Some analysts believe that Indian media, which was both larger in number and more credible, may have acted as a force multiplier for the Indian military operation in Kargil and served as a morale booster. As the fighting intensified, the Pakistani version of events found little backing on the world stage. This helped India gain valuable diplomatic recognition for its position.

WMDs and the Nuclear Factor

Since Pakistan and India each had weapons of mass destruction, many in the international community were concerned that if the Kargil conflict intensified, it could lead to nuclear war. Both countries had tested their nuclear capability in 1998 (India conducted its first test in 1974 while it was Pakistan's first-ever nuclear test). Many pundits believed the tests to be an indication of the escalating stakes in the scenario in South Asia. When the Kargil conflict started just a year after the nuclear tests, many nations desired to end it before it intensified.

International concerns increased when Pakistani foreign secretary Shamshad Ahmad made a statement on May 31 warning that an escalation of the limited conflict could lead Pakistan to use "any weapon" in its arsenal. This was immediately interpreted as a threat of nuclear retaliation by Pakistan in the event of an extended war, and the belief was reinforced when the leader of Pakistan's senate noted, "The purpose of developing weapons becomes meaningless if they are not used when they are needed." Many such ambiguous statements from officials of both countries were viewed as warnings of an impending nuclear crisis where the combatants would consider use of their limited nuclear arsenals in 'tactical' nuclear warfare in the belief that it would not have ended in mutual assured destruction, as could have occurred in a nuclear conflict between the United States and the USSR. Some experts believe that following nuclear tests in 1998, the Pakistani military was emboldened by its nuclear deterrent to markedly increase coercion against India.

The nature of the India-Pakistan conflict took a more sinister turn when the U.S. received intelligence that Pakistani nuclear warheads were being moved towards the border. Bill

Clinton tried to dissuade Pakistan prime minister Nawaz Sharif from nuclear brinkmanship, even threatening Pakistan of dire consequences. According to a White House official, Sharif seemed to be genuinely surprised by this supposed missile movement and responded that India was probably planning the same. In an article in May 2000 Dr Sanjay Badri-Maharaj claimed that India too had readied at least five nuclear-tipped ballistic missiles, but could not back up this claim with any official proof.

Sensing a deteriorating military scenario, diplomatic isolation, and the risks of a larger conventional and nuclear war, Sharif ordered the Pakistani army to vacate the Kargil heights. He later claimed in his official biography that General Pervez Musharraf had moved nuclear warheads without informing him. Recently however, Pervez Musharraf revealed in his memoirs that Pakistan's nuclear delivery system was not operational during the Kargil war; something that would have put Pakistan under serious disadvantage if the conflict went nuclear.

The threat of WMD included chemical and even biological weapons. Pakistan accused India of using chemical weapons and incendiary weapons such as napalm against the Kashmiri fighters. India, on the other hand, showcased a cache of gas masks, among other firearms, as proof that Pakistan may have been prepared to use non-conventional weapons. US official and the Organisation for the Prohibition of Chemical Weapons determined that Pakistani allegations of India using banned chemicals in its bombs were unfounded.

Aftermath

India

From the end of the war until February 2000, the Indian stock market rose by over 30%. The next Indian national budget included major increases in military spending.

There was a surge in patriotism, with many celebrities expressing their support for the Kargil cause. Indians were angered by media reports of the death of pilot Ajay Ahuja, especially after Indian authorities reported that Ahuja had been murdered and his body mutilated by Pakistani troops. The war had produced higher than expected fatalities for the Indian military, with a sizeable percentage of them including newly commissioned officers. One month after conclusion of the Kargil war, the Atlantique Incident - where a Pakistan Navy plane was shot down by India - briefly reignited fears of a conflict between the two countries.

After the war, the Indian government severed ties with Pakistan and increased defence preparedness. India increased its defence budget as it sought to acquire more state of the art equipment. Media reported about military procurement irregularities and criticism of intelligence agencies like Research and Analysis Wing, which failed to predict the intrusions or the identity/number of infiltrators during the war. An internal assessment report by the armed forces, published in an Indian magazine, showed several other failings, including "a sense of complacency" and being "unprepared for a conventional war" on the presumption that nuclearism would sustain peace. It also highlighted the lapses in command and control, the insufficient troop levels and the dearth of large-calibre guns like the Bofors. In 2006, retired Air Chief Marshal, A.Y. Tipnis, alleged that the Indian Army did not fully inform the government about the intrusions, adding that the army chief Ved Prakash Malik, was initially reluctant to use the full strike capability of the Indian Air Force, instead requesting only helicopter gunship support. Soon after the conflict, India also decided to complete the project - previously stalled by Pakistan - to fence the entire LOC.

The end of the Kargil conflict was followed by the 13th Indian General Elections to the Lok Sabha, which gave a decisive mandate to the National Democratic Alliance (NDA) government. It was re-elected to power in September–October 1999 with a majority of 303 seats out of 545 in the Lok Sabha. On the diplomatic front, Indo-U.S. relations improved, as the United States appreciated Indian attempts to restrict the conflict to a limited geographic area. Relations with Israel which had discreetly aided India with ordnance supply and materiel such as unmanned aerial vehicles and laser-guided bombs, as well as satellite imagery also were bolstered.

Kargil Review Committee

Soon after the war the Atal Behari Vajpayee government set up an inquiry into its causes and to analyze perceived Indian intelligence failures. The high-powered committee was chaired by eminent strategic affairs analyst K. Subrahmanyam and given powers to interview anyone with current or past associations with Indian security, including former Prime Ministers. The committee's final report (also referred to as the 'Subrahmanyam Report') led to a large-scale restructuring of Indian Intelligence. It, however, came in for heavy criticism in the Indian media for its perceived avoidance of assigning specific responsibility for failures over detecting the Kargil intrusions. The Committee was also embroiled in controversy for indicting Brigadier Surinder Singh of the Indian Army for his failure to report enemy intrusions in time, and for his subsequent conduct. Many press reports questioned or contradicted this finding and claimed that Singh had in fact issued early warnings that were ignored by senior Indian Army commanders and, ultimately, higher government functionaries.

Pakistan

Faced with the possibility of international isolation, the already fragile Pakistani economy was weakened further. The morale of Pakistani forces after the withdrawal declined as many units of the Northern Light Infantry suffered heavy casualties. The government refused to accept the dead bodies of many officers, an issue that provoked outrage and protests in the Northern Areas. Pakistan initially did not acknowledge many of its casualties, but Sharif later said that over 4,000 Pakistani troops were killed in the operation and that Pakistan had lost the conflict. Responding to this, Pakistan President Pervez Musharraf said, "It hurts me when an ex-premier undermines his own forces," and claimed that Indian casualties were more than that of Pakistan.

Many in Pakistan had expected a victory over the Indian military based on Pakistani official reports on the war, but were dismayed by the turn of events and questioned the eventual retreat.The military leadership is believed to have felt let down by the prime minister's decision to withdraw the remaining fighters. However, some authors, including ex-CENTCOM Commander Anthony Zinni, and ex-PM Nawaz Sharif, state that it was General Musharraf who requested Sharif to withdraw the Pakistani troops. With Sharif placing the onus of the Kargil attacks squarely on the army chief Pervez Musharraf, there was an atmosphere of uneasiness between the two. On October 12, 1999, General Musharraf staged a bloodless *coup d'état*, ousting Nawaz Sharif.

Benazir Bhutto, an opposition leader and former prime minister, called the Kargil War "Pakistan's greatest blunder". Many ex-officials of the military and the Inter-Services Intelligence (Pakistan's principal intelligence agency) also believed that "Kargil was a waste of time" and "could not have resulted in any advantage" on the larger issue of Kashmir. A retired Pakistani Army General, Lt Gen Ali Kuli Khan, lambasted the war as "a disaster bigger than the East Pakistan tragedy", adding that the plan was "flawed in terms of its conception, tactical planning and execution" that ended in "sacrificing so many soldiers." The Pakistani media criticized the whole plan and the eventual climbdown from the Kargil heights since there were no gains to show for the loss of lives and it only resulted in international condemnation.

Despite calls by many, no public commission of inquiry was set up in Pakistan to investigate the people responsible for initiating the conflict. The Pakistan Muslim League (N) (PML(N)) published a white paper in 2006, which stated that Nawaz Sharif constituted an inquiry committee that recommended a court martial for General Pervez Musharraf, but Musharraf "stole the report" after toppling the government, to save himself. The report also claims that India knew about the plan 11 months before its launch, enabling a complete victory for India on military, diplomatic and economic fronts. A statement in June, 2008 by a former army corps commander of Pakistan that Sharif "was never briefed by the army" on the Kargil attack, reignited the demand for a probe of the episode by legal and political groups.

Though the Kargil conflict had brought the Kashmir dispute into international focus which was one of the aims of Pakistan it had done so in negative circumstances that eroded its credibility, since the infiltration came just after a peace process between the two countries was underway. The sanctity of the LOC too received international recognition. President Clinton's move to ask Islamabad to withdraw hundreds of armed militants from Indian-administered Kashmir was viewed by many in Pakistan as indicative of a clear shift in US policy against Pakistan.

After the war, a few changes were made to the Pakistan army. In recognition of the Northern Light Infantry's performance in the war - which even drew praise from a retired Indian Lt. General the regiment was incorporated into the regular army. The war showed that despite a tactically sound plan that had the element of surprise, little groundwork had been done to gauge the politico-diplomatic ramifications. And like previous unsuccessful infiltrations attempts, such as *Operation Gibraltar*, which sparked the 1965 war, there was little coordination or information sharing among the branches of the Pakistan military. One U.S. Intelligence study is reported to have stated that Kargil was yet another example of Pakistan's (lack of) grand strategy, repeating the follies of the previous wars.

Casualties

Casualties for both sides were heavy. Pakistani claims gave two figures. The figure of 357 soldiers dead was challenged by some Pakistani officials, who claimed that 4,000 Pakistani soldiers were killed in the conflict. Pakistan also confirmed that more than 665 Pakistani troops were wounded and 8 were captured. According to India, Indian losses stand at 527 soldiers killed, 1,363 wounded, and 1 captured.

Pakistan army losses have been difficult to determine, partly because Pakistan has not published an official casualties list. The US Department of State had made an early, partial estimate of close to 700 fatalities. According to numbers stated by Nawaz Sharif there were over 4,000 fatalities. His PML (N) party in its "white paper" on the war mentioned that more than 3,000 Mujahideens, officers and soldiers were killed. Another major Pakistani political party, the Pakistan Peoples Party, also says that "thousands" of soldiers and irregulars died. Indian estimates stand at 1,042 Pakistani soldiers killed. Musharraf, in his Hindi version of his memoirs, titled "Agnipath", differs from all the estimates stating that 357 troops were killed with a further 665 wounded. Apart from General Musharraf's figure on the number of Pakistanis wounded, the number of people injured in the Pakistan camp is not yet fully known. One Indian Pilot was officially captured during the fighting, while there were eight Pakistani soldiers who were captured during the fighting, and were repatriated on 13 August 1999;

Kargil War in the arts

The brief conflict provided considerable dramatic material for filmmakers and authors in India. Some documentaries which were shot on the subject were used by the ruling party coalition, led by Bharatiya Janata Party (BJP), in furthering its election campaign that immediately followed the war. The following is a list of the major films and dramas on the subject.

- *LOC: Kargil* (2003), a Hindi movie which depicts many incidents from the war was one of the longest in Indian movie history, running for more than four hours.
- *Lakshya* (2004), another Hindi movie portraying a fictionalised account of the conflict. Movie critics have generally appreciated the realistic portrayal of characters. The film also received good reviews in Pakistan because it portrays both sides fairly.

Administered by	Area	Population	% Muslim	% Hindu	% Buddhist	% Other
India	Kashmir valley	~4 million	95%	4%	-	-
	Jammu	~3 million	30%	66%	-	4%
	Ladakh	~0.25 million	46% (Shia)	-	50%	3%
Pakistan	Northern Areas	~1 million	99%	-	-	-
	Azad Kashmir	~2.6 million	100%	-	-	-
China	Aksai Chin	-	-	-	-	-

- Statistics from the BBC In Depth report.
- There are roughly 1.5 million Refugees from Indian-administered Kashmir in Pakistan administered Kashmir and Pakistan UNHCR
- About 300,000 Hindus in Indian Administered Kashmir valley are internally displaced due to militancy in Kashmir. - CIA
- Muslims are majority in Poonch, Rajouri, Kishtwar and Doda districts in Jammu region. Shia Muslims make for majority in Kargil district in Ladakh region.

- *Sainika* (2002) the Kannada film directed by Mahesh Sukhdhare depicted the life of a soldier with Kargil war as one of the events. Starring C.P.Yogishwar and Sakshi Shivanand.
- *Dhoop* (2003), directed by national award winner Ashwini Chaudhary, which depicted the life of Anuj Nayyar's parents after his death. Anuj Nayyar was a captain in the Indian army and was awarded Maha Vir Chakra posthumously. Om Puri plays the role of S.K. Nayyar, Anuj's father.
- *Mission Fateh - Real Stories of Kargil Heroes*, a TV series telecast on Sahara channel chronicling the Indian Army's missions.
- *Fifty Day War* - A theatrical production on the war, the title indicating the length of the Kargil conflict. This was claimed to be the biggest production of its kind in Asia, involving real aircraft and explosions in an outdoor setting.
- *Kurukshetra*(2008) - A Malayalam film directed by a former Indian Army Major - major Ravi (Retd) based on his actual experience of Kargil War.

Many other movies like *Tango Charlie* drew heavily upon the Kargil episode, which still continues to be a plot for mainstream movies with a Malayalam movie *Keerthi Chakra*. The impact of the war in the sporting arena was also visible during the India-Pakistan clash in the 1999 Cricket World Cup, which coincided with the Kargil timeline. The game witnessed heightened passions and was one of the most viewed matches in the tournament.

Reasons behind the dispute

The Kashmir Conflict arises from the Partition of India in 1947 into modern India and Pakistan. Both the countries have made claims to Kashmir, based on historical developments and religious affiliations of the Kashmiri people. The state of Jammu and Kashmir, which lies strategically in the Northwest of the subcontinent, bordering China and the former Soviet

Union, was a princely state ruled by Maharaja Hari Singh, under the paramountcy of British India. In geographical and legal terms, the Maharaja could have joined either of the two new Dominions. Although urged by the Viceroy, Lord Mountbatten of Burma, to determine the future of his state before the transfer of power took place, Hari Singh demurred. In October 1947, incursions and counter-incursions by Pakistan and India took place leading to a war, as a result of which the state of Jammu and Kashmir remains divided between the two countries.

Two-thirds of the former princely state (known as the Indian state of Jammu and Kashmir), comprising Jammu, the Kashmir Valley, and the sparsely populated Buddhist area of Ladakh are controlled by India; one-third is administered by Pakistan. The latter includes a narrow strip of land called Azad Kashmir and the Northern Areas compromising the Gilgit Agency, Baltistan and the former kingdoms of Hunza and Nagar. Attempts to resolve the dispute through political discussions were unsuccessful. In September 1965, war broke out again between Pakistan and India. The United Nations called for a yet another cease-fire, and peace was restored once again following the Tashkent Declaration in 1966, by which both nations returned to their original positions along the demarcated line. After the 1971 war and the creation of independent Bangladesh, under the terms of the 1972 Simla Agreement between Prime Minister Indira Gandhi of India and Zulfiqar Ali Bhutto of Pakistan, it was agreed that neither country would seek to alter the cease-fire line in Kashmir, which was renamed as the Line of Control, "unilaterally, irrespective of mutual differences and legal interpretations".

Numerous violations of the Line of Control have occurred, including the infamous incursions by insurgents and Pakistani armed forces at Kargil leading to the Kargil war. There are also sporadic clashes on the Siachen Glacier, where the Line of Control is not demarcated and both countries maintain forces at altitudes rising to 20,000 ft (6,100 m).

Indian View

Indian viewpoint is succinctly summarized by Ministry of External affairs, Government of India –

- India holds that the Instrument of Accession of the State of Jammu and Kashmir to India, signed by the Maharaja Hari Singh (erstwhile ruler of the State) on 26 October 1947, was completely valid in terms of the Government of India Act (1935), Indian Independence Act (1947) and international law and was total and irrevocable.
- The Constituent assembly of Jammu and Kashmir had unanimously ratified the Maharaja's Instrument of Accession to India and had adopted a constitution for the state that called for a perpetual merger of the state with the Union of India. India claims that this body was a representative one, and that its views were those of the Kashmiri people at the time.
- United Nations Security Council Resolution 1172 tacitly accepts India's stand regarding all outstanding issues between India and Pakistan and urges the need to resolve the dispute through mutual dialogue and does not call for a plebiscite.
- United Nations Security Council Resolution 47 cannot be implemented since Pakistan failed to withdraw its forces from Kashmir which was the first step in implementing the resolution. Now the resolution is obsolete since the geography and demographics of the region have been permanently altered. The resolution was passed by United Nations Security Council under Chapter VI of the United Nations Charter. Resolutions passed under Chapter VI of UN charter are considered non binding and have no mandatory enforceability as opposed to the resolutions passed under Chapter VII.
- India does not accept the two-nation theory that forms the basis of Pakistan and argues that Kashmir, despite being a Muslim-majority state, is in many ways an "integral part" of secular India.

- The state of Jammu and Kashmir was provided significant autonomy in the Article 370 of the Constitution of India.
- All differences between India and Pakistan including Kashmir need to be settled through bilateral negotiations as agreed to by the two countries when they signed the Simla Agreement on 2 July 1972.

Additional Indian viewpoint regarding the broader debate over the Kashmir conflict include:

- India believes that the insurgency and terrorism in Kashmir is deliberately being fueled by Pakistan to create instability in the region. The Government of India has repeatedly asked the international community to declare Pakistan as a sponsor of terrorism.
- Pakistan is trying to raise anti-India sentiment among the people of Kashmir by spreading false propaganda against India. According to the state government of Jammu and Kashmir, Pakistani radio and television channels deliberately spread "hate and venom" against India to alter Kashmiri opinion.
- In a diverse country like India, disaffection and discontent are not uncommon. Indian democracy has the necessary resilience to accommodate genuine grievances within the framework of our sovereignty, unity and integrity. Government of India has expressed its willingness to accommodate the legitimate political demands of the people of the state of Jammu and Kashmir.
- India has asked United Nations that it should not be leave unchallenged or unaddressed claims of moral, political and diplomatic support for terrorism, which were clearly in contravention of United Nations Security Council Resolution 1373 which is a Chapter VII resolution that makes it mandatory for member states to not provide active or passive support to terrorist organizations. Specifically, it has pointed out that the Pakistani government continues to support various terrorist organizations, such as Jaish-e-Mohammad and Lashkar-e-Taiba, in direct violation of this resolution.

- India points out at various reports by human rights organizations condemning Pakistan for the lack civic liberties in Pakistan-administered Kashmir. According to India, most regions of Pakistani Kashmir, especially Northern Areas, continue to suffer from lack of political recognition, economic development and basic fundamental rights.

Pakistani View

Pakistan's claims to the disputed region are based on the rejection of Indian claims to Kashmir, namely the Instrument of Accession. Pakistan insists that the Maharaja was not a popular leader, and was regarded as a tyrant by most Kashmiris, Pakistan also maintains that the Maharaja used brute force to suppress the population. Pakistan also accuses India of hypocrisy, as it refused to recognize the accession of Junagadh to Pakistan and Hyderabad's independence, on the grounds that those two states had Hindu majorities (in fact, India occupied and forcibly integrated those two territories). Furthermore, as he had fled Kashmir due to Pakistani invasion, Pakistan asserts that the Maharaja held no authority in determining Kashmir's future. Additionally, Pakistan argues that even if the Maharaja had any authority in determining the plight of Kashmir, he signed the Instrument of Accession under duress, thus invalidating the legitimacy of his actions.

Pakistan also claims that Indian forces were in Kashmir before the Instrument of Accession was signed with India, and that therefore Indian troops were in Kashmir in violation of the Standstill Agreement, which was designed to maintain the status quo in Kashmir (although India was not signatory to the Agreement, signed between Pakistan and the Hindu ruler of Jammu and Kashmir).

From 1990 to 1999 some organizations report that Indian Armed Forces, its paramilitary groups, and counter-insurgent militias have been responsible for the deaths 4,501 of Kashmiri civilians. Also from 1990 to 1999, there are records of 4,242 women between the ages of 7-70 that have been raped. Similar allegations were also made by some human rights organizations.

In short, Pakistan holds that:

- The popular Kashmiri insurgency demonstrates that the Kashmiri people no longer wish to remain within India. Pakistan suggests that this means that either Kashmir wants to be with Pakistan or independent.
- According to the two-nation theory which is one of the theories that is cited for the partition that created India and Pakistan, Kashmir should have been with Pakistan, because it has a Muslim majority.
- India has shown disregard to the resolutions of the UN Security Council, and the United Nations Commission in India and Pakistan by failing to hold a plebiscite to determine the future allegiance of the entire state.
- The Kashmiri people have now been forced by the circumstances to rise against the alleged repression of the Indian army and uphold their right of self-determination through militancy. Pakistan claims to give the Kashmiri insurgents moral, ethical and military support.
- Recent protests in Indian administered Kashmir show a large number of people showing increased anger over Indian rule with massive rallies taking place to oppose Indian control of the state.
- Pakistan also points to the violence that accompanies elections in Indian Kashmir and the anti Indian sentiments expressed by some people in the state.
- Pakistan has noted the wide spread use of extrajudicial killings in Indian-administered Kashmir carried out by Indian security forces while claiming they were caught up in encounters with militants. These fake encounters are common place in Indian-administered Kashmir and the perpetrators are spared criminal prosecution. These fake encounters go largely uninvestigated by the authorities.
- Pakistan points towards reports from the United Nations which condemn India for its human rights violations against Kashmiri people.

- Pakistan President Asif Ali Zardari stated in October 2008 that Kashmiri 'freedom fighters' were terrorists. However his remarks met with widespread condemnation across Pakistan and Kashmir, including prominent politicians.
- The Chenab formula - This was proposed in 1960's, in which Kashmir valley and other Muslim dominated areas north of Chenab river will go to Pakistan, and Jammu and other Hindu dominated region will go to India.
- Pakistan points towards the numerous Human rights violations which occur within Indian-administered Kashmir and the many reports by Human rights organization strongly condemning Indian troops for widespread rape and murder of innocent civilians accusing these civilians of being killed in encounters.

Chinese View

- China did not accept boundaries of the princely state of Kashmir and Jammu north of the Aksai Chin and the Karakoram proposed by the British.
- China settled its border disputes with Pakistan in the Trans Karakoram Tract in 1963 with the proviso that the settlement was subject to the final solution of the Kashmir dispute.

4

Insurgency in Jammu and Kashmir

Introduction

Insurgency in Kashmir has existed in various forms, both on the Indian administrated side of the disputed territory of Jammu and Kashmir and Pakistan-administered Kashmir. Kashmir has been the target of a campaign of militancy by all sides in the conflict. Thousands of lives have been lost since 1989 due to the intensified insurgency 1989, a widespread armed insurgency started in Kashmir with the disputed 1987 election; since after 1987 rigged State elections some of the 'states legislative assembly' 'formed militant wings' later on after the disputed rigged election and furthermore that had started a catalyst for the insurgency. Casualties include civilians, Kashmiri, and Indian Armed Forces and foreign militants.

The Inter-Services Intelligence of Pakistan has been accused by India of supporting and training mujahideen to fight in Jammu and Kashmir. While, International Human Right Groups have accused Indian army of committing grave Human rights violations in Indian-administered Jammu and Kashmir.

According to official figures released in Jammu and Kashmir assembly(Indian controlled), there were 3,400 disappearance cases and the insurgency has left more than 47,000 people dead till July 2009. However, the number of insurgency-related deaths in the state have fallen sharply since the start of a slow-moving peace process between India and Pakistan.

Militancy and military : Though there had been instances of sporadic conflict in many regions for many years, intensified attacks occurred in the late 1980s, when the 1987 state elections were rigged although disputed ; had resulted in some of the 'states legislative assembly' 'formed militant wings' later on after the election forming and creating the catalyst for the insurgency. However Indian Government believes Mujahideen fighters from Afghanistan slowly infiltrated the region, with Pakistan's help, following the end of the Soviet-Afghan War in 1989. Since then, violence has increased significantly in strength. Many separatists have carried out attacks on local Hindus, Indian civilians and Indian army installations in response to what they see as Indian army occupation.

India frequently asserts that most of the separatist militant groups are based in Pakistan and Pakistan-administered Kashmir (also known as Azad Kashmir). Some like the All Parties Hurriyat Conference and the Jammu and Kashmir Liberation Front, demand an independent Kashmir. Other militant groups such as Lashkar-e-Toiba and Jaish-e-Mohammed favour a Pakistani-Kashmir. These groups have contacts with Taliban and Bin Laden. Both the organisations no longer operate under these names after they were banned by the Indian and Pakistani government, and by other countries including the US and UK. Of the larger militant groups, the Hizbul Mujahideen, a militant organisation based in Indian administered Kashmir, unlike other groups, has only kept its name. Despite casualties, the militants are still believed to number thousands rather than hundreds. Several new separatist organizations have also emerged. According to US Intelligence, Al-Qaeda also has a main base in Pakistani Kashmir and is helping to foment terrorism in Jammu and Kashmir. However India, Pakistan and the separatist organizations call this as hoax. Inspector General Police, Kashmir range also referred this as a hoax.

It is hard to determine the total number of casualties. According to a report by the Government of India in the year 2000, 31,000 Indian civilians had lost their lives due to the insurgency. Human rights groups and local NGOs put the total figure at more than 84,000 (2005 figure). Militancy had reached its peak in 1994 when the region saw more than 6,043 incidents and has since declined. However, Kashmir continues to remain as the most volatile region in the world with an average of 2,500 incidents every year. According to an Indian estimate in 2005 there were about 2,000 militants in the Kashmir valley alone; 1,200 of them belong to the Hizbul Mujahideen. Not all Kashmiri separatists and militant organizations share the same ideology. Some fight in the name of religion, some are openly pro-Pakistan and some favour an independent Kashmir.

Due to the presence of these numerous anti-India insurgent groups India has been compelled to deploy massive number of troops in the Indian administered *Jammu and Kashmir* for the task of counter insurgency. New Delhi has never made an official count, but military analysts estimate that anywhere from 30,000 to nearly 33,000 security personnel are most likely involved, supported by thousands of Indian paramilitary groups such as the Rashtriya rifles, and the Romeo Force (all a part of Indian army). Stimson.org notes of the Indian Armed forces in Kashmir that:

Some reports estimate that India deploys approximately 400,000 combined army and paramilitary forces in Kashmir, most of which are stationed in the interior, 80,000 of which are deployed along the LoC. Pakistani forces deployed along the LoC are reported to number in the 40,000-50,000 range Times Online reports that around 250,000 Indian troops are stationed in Kashmir, while Pravda.RU, a widely read Russian News source notes that 350,000-600,000 troops may be deployed in Kashmir.

In a 'Letter to American People' written by Osama bin Laden in 2002 he stated that one of the reasons he was fighting America is because of her support to India on the Kashmir issue. In 2002 U.S. Secretary of Defense Donald Rumsfeld on a trip to Delhi suggested that Al-Qaeda was active in Kashmir. An investigation in 2002 unearthed evidence that Al-Qaeda and its affiliates were prospering in Pakistan-administered Kashmir with tacit approval of Pakistan's National Intelligence agency Inter-Services Intelligence. Also US Intelligence agencies believe that Al-Qaeda and Taliban are helping organize a terror campaign in Kashmir to foment conflict between India and Pakistan. A 2001 report 'Pakistan's Role in the Kashmir Insurgency' of US Think tank RAND corporation noted that 'More intrinsically, the nature of the Kashmir conflict has been transformed from what was originally a secular, locally- based struggle (conducted via the Jammu Kashmir Liberation Front - JKLF) to one that is now largely carried out by foreign militants and rationalised in pan-Islamic religious terms.' In July 2006 Al-Qaeda stated that it had established a wing in Kashmir.

Militant Groups

Over the last two years, a militant group, Lashkar-e-Toiba has split into two factions: *Al Mansurin* and *Al Nasirin*. Another new group reported to have emerged is the Save Kashmir Movement. Harkat-ul-Mujahideen (formerly known as Harkat-ul-Ansar) and Lashkar-e-Toiba are believed to be operating from Muzaffarabad, Azad Kashmir and Muridke, Pakistan respectively. Other less well known groups are the Freedom Force and Farzandan-e-Milat. A smaller group, Al-Badr, has been active in Kashmir for many years and is still believed to be functioning. All Parties Hurriyat Conference, an organization that uses moderate means to press for the rights of the Kashmiris, is often considered as the *mediator* between New Delhi and insurgent groups.

Not much is known about collaboration between the various groups, but most say they are members of an alliance known as the United Jihad Council (UJC). The two groups which India says were behind the December 2001 attack on the Indian parliament in New Delhi known then as Jaish-e-Mohammed and Lashkar-e-Toiba are believed to be members of the *UJC*. India says that it was Jaish-e-Mohammed that attacked the Jammu and Kashmir State Assembly in Srinagar in October 2001. It is also known that the Jaish-e-Mohammed was responsible for the hijacking of Indian Airlines Flight IC-814 to Kandahar, which forced the Government of India to release Maulana Masood Azhar, the chief of the Jaish-e-Mohammed. Recruits from various parts of the world have been sent to Pakistan-administered Kashmir for training and advice.

In 2008, Richard Benkin compared the Islamist militants in Kashmir to Palestinian militants, stating that Kashmir is a transitory goal in the Islamist goal to control India:

> *"Kashmir is South Asia`s West Bank. Just as Pakistan and its Islamist allies ultimately seek to turn all of India into an Islamic state; so, too, the Arabs have tried again and again to destroy the Israel and even had that as their stated policy. After their colossal failure to do so in 1967, they tried once more to invade Israel with national armies only to fail again. So they changed tactics and stopped talking about their ultimate goal. Instead they focused on "the occupation" (West Bank and Gaza). Their real aim-to destroy Israel and turn it into an Islamic state-never changed. This tactic successfully distracted a gullible Europe which supported Arab calls for their temporary goal. Similarly, South Asian Islamists still want more than Kashmir. Kashmir, like the West Bank, is a transitory goal, but a critical one."*

India and Pakistan

A 1994 report by Human Rights Watch group lends support to both Indian and Pakistani charges. In support of Indian claims, it states that:

> *There is compelling evidence that elements of the Pakistani government have sponsored a significant flow of arms to Kashmiri*

> *militants [from arms bazaars in the North West Frontier Province], as well as an extensive training program.*

While in support of Pakistani claims, its states that "*the human rights record of the Indian government in Punjab and Kashmir is appalling. Abuses in Kashmir are clearly on the rise.*" The US government has also supported the claim that anti-India terror groups exist in India. India claims that there are also other Afghan, Egyptian, Yemeni and Bangladeshi terrorists active in Jammu and Kashmir. The Council on Foreign Relations states that Pakistan's military and Inter-Services Intelligence (ISI) both include personnel who sympathize with or even assist Islamist militants adding that "ISI has provided covert but well-documented support to terrorist groups active in Kashmir, among other outfits." In a recent infiltration bid, a Pakistan Army officer was shot dead, with India citing that this was clear and conclusive evidence of Pakistani involvement in the insurgency. The UN Security Council has also confirmed the existence of terrorist groups based in [Pakistani] Kashmir and urged Pakistan to crack down on terrorist groups which had been operating in Kashmir and killing innocent people.

Pakistan describes the separatists as "freedom fighters" and says that it supports their effort for the cause of the Kashmiris only morally and diplomatically. Pakistan however admits that there has been 'cross border infiltration of militants' across the Line of Control. In 2008, Pakistani President Asif Ali Zardari said India has never been a threat to Pakistan, and that militants in Kashmir are terrorists. In 2002, Pakistani president Pervez Musharraf tried to clamp down on the militants operating from Pakistan. India, however, claims that Islamabad supports these groups financially and militarily. Sources have maintained that Pakistan's intelligence organisation, Inter Services Intelligence, is the main supplier of funds and arms to these groups; a claim that Islamabad has dismissed. According to the Indian news site Rediff.com, British Government had stated in 2002 that there is a 'clear link' between Pakistan's Inter Services Intelligence and three major militant groups. An article in The Guardian had uncovered evidence that Pakistani militants were openly raising funds and training new recruits and that the ISI's Kashmir Cell was instrumental in funding and controlling the militant outfits. Richard Bennett, a British military and intelligence analyst states that the ISI has armed and trained generations of Islamist extremists and has directed many of their attacks both within the Kashmir and in India's major cities.

Indian sources also allege that there are between 2,600 to 3,000 militants receiving training in camps across Pakistan and Pakistan Administered Kashmir. During a peace summit between former Pakistani President Pervez Musharraf and Indian former-Prime Minister Atal Bihari Vajpayee in January 2004, Islamabad assured India that it would do everything possible to curb the activities any training camps on its territory. However, violence has continued in Kashmir despite a 3 year long peace process between India and Pakistan. There were as many as 166 incidents in June 2005 alone in which some 201 people have died.

According to Indian sources there are about 37 training camps in Pakistan, 49 in Azad Kashmir and 22 in Afghanistan. The FBI also has produced images of camps operating in Pakistan. India claims that every year thousands of armed insurgents infiltrate into Indian-administered Kashmir and carry out attacks against Indian Security Forces and Kashmiri civilians. In June 2005, the Indian Army had foiled at least 72 infiltration attempts along the Line of Control in Kashmir. India alleges that despite the commitments made by Pervez Musharraf, Islamabad has done little to stop the training camps on its soil. According to India, most of the militants in Kashmir come from Pakistan, Afghanistan, Egypt, Yemen and Bangladesh. Not all Kashmiri separatists and militant organizations share the same ideology. Some fight in the name of religion, some are pro-Pakistan and some favour an independent Kashmir. While the vast majority of militants are Muslims, one report indicated a minority of fighter (40 to 50) are Hindu militants who have either taken up arms or provided safe cover for militants.

Indian Claims

The following statistics were compiled by Indian Army:

- Number of civilians killed in Kashmir since 1988: 65,000 to 1,00,000
- Number of Youth disappeared during turmoil : 3429
- Number of Kashmiri militant camps in Pakistan-administered Kashmir: 49
- Total number of Kashmir militant camps in Pakistan: 37
- Number of Kashmiri militant camps in Afghanistan: 22 (During Taliban rule)
- Number of militants* operating in Jammu and Kashmir: 800 (2009 estimate)
- Number of Kashmiri Militants in Indian jails: 125
- Total number of Kashmiri Pandits displaced from the state: over 750,000
- Amount of explosives recovered from Kashmiri Militants* in India: 60 tons or 30,000 kg (estimate)
- Major Kashmiri Militant training camps:

Location of Major Militant* Camps

Muridke (near Lahore)	Punjab, Pakistan
Kotli	Pakistan-administered Kashmir
Muzaffarabad	Pakistan-administered Kashmir
Skardu	Northern Areas, Pakistan
Gultari	Northern Areas, Pakistan
Tarkuti	Northern Areas, Pakistan
Batrasi	North West Frontier Province, Pakistan
Sufaida	North West Frontier Province, Pakistan
Tanda Allabyar	Sindh, Pakistan
Note: Pakistan denies the existence of such training camps on their territory, and the existence of such camps is a matter of controversy.	

Human Rights Violations

Human Rights Violations by Militants: Militants are accused of violence against the Kashmir populace. Thousands of civilian Kashmiris (Hindus, Sikhs, Buddhists and Muslims have been killed in Kashmir over the past 10 years by militants organisations. Human rights organizations put the figure of the number of civilians killed between 1 January 1999 and 31 December 1999 at about 9,733. According to official figures released in 2009, Indian Health and Family Welfare Minister Ghulam Nabi Azad, a Kashmiri himself and former chief minister of Jammu and Kashmir said 14,808 Muslims lost their lives while 1,748 Hindus and 115 Sikhs were killed during the rein of militancy in the state since 1989 by militants.

Tens of thousands of Kashmiri Pandits have emigrated as a result of the violence. Estimates of the displaced varies from 170,000 to 700,000. Thousands of Pandits have to move to Jammu because of terrorism. On 15 February 2006 United States Congressman Frank Pallone introduced a resolution in United States House of Representatives condemning the violation of Human rights of Kashmiri Pandits. He stated that an ethnic cleansing campaign was being run by Islamic terrorists to convert Kashmir into a Muslim state and 400,000 Kashmiri Pandits had either been murdered or displaced from their homes. The resolution was passed by the House (with Senate concurring) and stated that (1) Congress condemns the human rights violations committed against Kashmiri Pandits in the strongest terms (2) it is the sense of Congress that the Government of the Republic of India and the State Government of Jammu and Kashmir should take immediate steps to remedy the situation of the Kashmiri Pandits and should act to ensure the physical, political, and economic security of this embattled community; and (3) Congress supports mutual discussions between the Government of India and the State Government of Jammu and Kashmir to achieve a peaceful and equitable solution to the Kashmiri conflict that is acceptable to the Kashmiri Pandits while ensuring that they are a part of the ongoing dialogue.

Human Rights violations by Pakistan: Human rights violations have also been reported in Pakistan-administered Kashmir. A 2-day conference on Gilgit Baltistan was held on April 8–9, 2008 at the European Parliament in Brussels under the auspices of International Kashmir Alliance. Here several members of the European Parliament (MEPs) expressed concern over the human rights violation in Gilgit Baltistan and urged the government of Pakistan to establish democratic institutions and rule of law in this area of northern Kashmir. Abdul Hamid Khan, Chairman Balawaristan National Front speaking at the same conference said "no democratically elected representative (from Gilgit Baltistan) was included when Karachi Agreement was signed between Pakistan and Muslim Conference leaders in 1949." On 25 April 2007 European Union published a report entitled 'on Kashmir: present situation and future prospects'. Section 2 of the noted the absence of democracy in Gilgit Baltistan region and in section 32 deplored the human rights violations in this region. A 2008 report by the United Nations High Commissioner for Refugees determined that Pakistan administered Kashmir, was 'Not Free'. It also criticized the Pakistani Government saying 'The appropriation of land in the Northern Areas by non-Kashmiri migrants from elsewhere in Pakistan, with the tacit encouragement of the federal government and army, has led to dwindling economic opportunities for the local population and an increase in sectarian tension between the majority Shia Muslims and a growing number of Sunnis.' The same report determined that the Indian administered Jammu and Kashmir was 'Partly Free'. Parties like Balawaristan National Front are fighting for independence of Pakistan-administered Kashmir from Pakistan.

Human Rights Violations by India: A 1996 Human Rights Watch report accuses the Indian military and Indian-government backed paramilitaries of "committing serious and widespread human rights violations in Kashmir." One such alleged massacre occurred on 6 January 1993 in the town of Sopore. *TIME Magazine* described the incident as such: "In retaliation for the killing of one soldier, paramilitary forces rampaged through Sopore's market setting buildings ablaze and shooting bystanders. The Indian government pronounced the event 'unfortunate' and claimed that an ammunition dump had been hit by gunfire, setting off fires that killed most of the victims." In addition to this, there have been claims of disappearances by the police or the army in Kashmir by several human rights organizations.

Many human rights organizations such as Amnesty International and the Human Rights Watch (HRW) have condemned human rights abuses in Kashmir by Indians such as "extra-judicial executions", "disappearances", and torture; the "Armed Forces Special Powers Act", which "provides impunity for human rights abuses and fuels cycles of violence. The Armed Forces Special Powers Act (AFSPA) grants the military wide powers of arrest, the right to shoot to kill, and to occupy or destroy property in counterinsurgency operations. Indian officials claim that troops need such powers because the army is only deployed when national security is at serious risk from armed combatants. Such circumstances, they say, call for extraordinary measures." Human rights organizations have also asked Indian government to repeal the Public Safety Act, since "a detainee may be held in administrative detention for a maximum of two years without a court order." A 2008 report by the United Nations High Commissioner for Refugees determined that Indian Administered Kashmir, was only 'partly Free'. The Indian government forces and allied paramilitaries have also been accused of widespread sexual violence against Kashmiri women.

Militant Acts in J&K

- **July and August 1989:** 3 CRPF personnel and politician Mohd. Yusuf Halwai of NC/F were killed.
- **1989 kidnapping of Rubaiya Sayeed** daughter of the then Home Minister of India Mufti Sayeed.
- **1995 kidnapping** of western tourists in Jammu and Kashmir 6 foreign trekkers from Anantnag district were kidnapped by Al Faran, One was beheaded later, one escaped and other four remain untraced presumable killed.
- **1997 Sangrampora massacre:** On 21 March 1997, 7

Kashmiri Pandits were killed in Sangrampora village in the Budgam district.

- **Wandhama Massacre:** In January 1998, 24 Kashmiri Pandits living in the village of Wandhama were massacred by Pakistani militants. According to the testimony of one of the survivors, the militants dressed themselves as officers of the Indian Army, entered their houses and then started firing blindly. The incident was significant because it coincided with former US president Bill Clinton's visit to India and New Delhi used the massacre to present a case against the alleged Pakistan-supported terrorism in Kashmir.
- **1998 Prankote massacre:** 26 Hindu villagers of Udhampur district were killed by militants.
- **1998 Champanari massacre:** 25 Hindu villagers killed on 19 June 1998 by Islamic militants.
- **2001 terrorist attack on Jammu and Kashmir** legislative assembly On 1 October 2001, a bombing at the Legislative Assembly in Srinagar killed 38.
- **2002 Qasim Nagar massacre:** 29 Hindu labourers were killed in Jammu by militants on July 13, 2002.
- **2003 Nadimarg Massacre:** 24 Hindus killed in Nadimarg, Kashmir on 23 March 2003 by Lashkar-e-Taiba militants.
- **Qasim Nagar Attack:** On 13 July 2003, armed militants believed to be a part of the Lashkar-e-Toiba threw hand grenades at the Qasim Nagar market in Srinagar and then fired on civilians standing nearby killing 27 and injuring many more.
- **20 July 2005 Srinagar Bombing:** A car bomb exploded near an armoured Indian Army vehicle in the famous Church Lane area in Srinagar killing 4 Indian Army personnel, one civilian and the suicide bomber. Militant group Hizbul Mujahideen, claimed responsibility for the attack.
- **Budshah Chowk attack:** A militant attack on 29 July 2005 at Srinigar's city centre, Budshah Chowk, killed 2 and left

more than 17 people injured. Most of those injured were media journalists.

- **Assassination of Ghulam Nabi Lone:** On 18 October 2005 suspected Kashmiri militants killed Jammu and Kashmir's then education minister Ghulam Nabi Lone. Militant group called Al Mansurin claimed responsibility for the attack. Abdul Ghani Lone, a prominent All Party Hurriyat Conference leader, was assassinated by unidentified gunmen during a memorial rally in Srinagar. The assassination resulted in wide-scale demonstrations against the Indian forces for failing to provide enough security cover for Mr. Lone.
- **On 3 May 2006** militants massacred 35 Hindus in Doda and Udhampur districts in Jammu and Kashmir.
- **On 12 June 2006** one person was killed and 31 were wounded when terrorists hurled three grenades on Vaishnodevi shrine-bound buses at the general bus stand here this morning.
- **2 June 2009:** 17-year-old Nigeen Awan was shot and killed at her residence by Militants.
- **16 June 2009:** 45-year-old Rashma Jan died when terrorists barged into her house at Sopore on 16 June and fired indiscriminately.

Recent Developments

Violent activities in the region declined in 2004. There are two main reasons for this: warming of relations between New Delhi and Pakistan which consequently lead to a ceasefire between the two countries in 2003 and the fencing of the LOC being carried out by the Indian Army. Moreover, coming under intense international pressure, Islamabad was compelled to take actions against the militants' training camps on its territory. In 2004, the two countries also agreed upon decreasing the number of troops present in the region.

Under pressure, Kashmiri militant organisations have made an offer for talks and negotiations with New Delhi, which was accepted by India. India's Border Security Force blamed the Pakistani military for providing cover-fire for the militants whenever they infiltrated into Indian territory from Pakistan. However, ever since the ceasefire has come into action, the militants have received no back-up from Pakistani Military, which has contributed significantly to the decline in *cross-border terrorism* in the state. Even the recently elected Pakistani President, Asif Ali Zardari admitted that the militants operating in Kashmir were indeed terrorists""

2008

According to Govt. of India Home Ministry, 2008 marks the lowest civilian casualties in 20 years with 89 deaths, compared to highest of 1,413 in 1996. 85 security personnel died in 2008 compared to 613 in 2001. Human right situation improved with only 1 custodial death and no custodial disappearance.

2009

- Hizbul Mujahideen founder, considered founder of terrorism in Kashmir, Ahsan Dar was arrested on 14 January.
- **February 21, 2009:** Bomai Killing: Army kills two devotees in an indiscriminate firing incident by 22nd Battalion of Rashtriya Rilfes in Bomai, Sopore. Which results in a massive valley wide protests.
- **6 March 2009:** Nowhatta Killing: A CRPF vehicle killed one youth and crushed another at Nawhatta during a protest. The killing triggered violent protests across the city. Authorities clamed curfew for continuously for four days.
- Separatists and workers of a political party were believed to be behind stone pelting incidents which generally leads to retaliatory fire by the police. Autorickshaw laden with stones meant for distribution was seized by the police in 11 March 2009.
- **18 March 2009:** Rajpora killing: Barely a few hours after the union home minister, P Chidambaram, assured action

against troopers found guilty for Bomai killings, 181 bn of paramilitary CRPF troopers shot dead a carpenter, Ghulam Mohiudin Malik son of Muhammad Akbar Malik, at Khaigam Pakherpora in south Kashmir's Pulwama district.

- **31 May 2009:Shopian rape and murder case:** Protests over rape and murder of two young women allegedly by Indian Armed Forces. Pro-freedom leaders arrested and police and paramilitary forces resorted to firing at protesters in several places, including Shopian, Baramulla and Srinagar killing one person and injuring hundreds.
- **18 August 2009**: Government stated there had been 3429 youth missing since 1990 - till date. However local and international rights groups have suggested over 8,000 people have disappeared in the region.
- **9 September 2009**: An Indian army major and three militants were killed in an encounter in the Mendhar area of Poonch district in Jammu and Kashmir. Indian army had earlier pointed out that there has been an increase in the activity on the western border. Anti-India militant outfits have been trying to push in as much men, money and weapons on to the Indian side before snow blocks their passage.
- **2 December 2009**: A Kashmir based group, International People's Tribunal on Human Rights and Justice, said that it had found 2600 bodies in unmarked graves during a three year survey. While the group did not who was the buried were, it alleged that some could be innocent people killed by security force, and called for an investigation.
- **18 December 2009**: India withdraws 30,000 troops from Kashmir in one of the largest troop withdrawals in response to dramatic improvement in security situation.

2010

- **6 January 2010**: A militant attack on a police station in Srinagar triggers a 20 hour gun battle between Lashkar-e-

Taiba militants and Indian police. Two militants, one police officer, and one civilian were reported killed.

- **29 January 2010**: Rebel attack kills 2 Indian soldiers in Kashmir.

5

Cross Border Trouble

Introduction

The border and the Line of Control separating Indian and Pakistani Kashmir passes through some exceptionally difficult terrain. The world's highest battleground, the Siachen Glacier is a part of this difficult-to-man boundary. Even with 200,000 military personnel, India maintains that it is infeasible to place enough men to guard all sections of the border throughout the various seasons of the year. Pakistan has indirectly acquiesced its role in failing to prevent "cross border terrorism" when it agreed to curb such activities after intense pressure from the Bush administration in mid 2002.

The Government of Pakistan has repeatedly claimed that by constructing a fence along the line of control, India is violating the Shimla Accord. However, India claims the construction of the fence has helped decrease armed infiltration into Indian-administered Kashmir.

In 2002 Pakistani President and Army Chief General Pervez Musharraf promised to check infiltration into Jammu and Kashmir.

Water Dispute

Another reason behind the dispute over Kashmir is water. Kashmir is the origin point for many rivers and tributaries of the Indus River basin. They include Jhelum and Chenab which primarily flow into Pakistan while other branches - the Ravi, Beas and the Sutlej irrigate northern India. Pakistan has been apprehensive that in a dire need, India (under whose portion of Kashmir lies the origins and passage of the said rivers) would use its strategic advantage and withhold the flow and thus choke the agrarian economy of Pakistan. The Boundary Award of 1947 meant that the headwaters of Pakistani irrigation systems were in Indian Territory. The Indus Waters Treaty signed in 1960 resolved most of these disputes over the sharing of water, calling for mutual cooperation in this regard. But this treaty faced issues raised by Pakistan over the construction of dams on the Indian side which limit water to the Pakistani side.

Human Rights Abuse

Indian administered Kashmir: In Jammu and Kashmir, India, the violent Islamic insurgency has specifically targeted the Hindu Kashmiri Pandit minority, violated their human rights and 400,000 have either been murdered or displaced. US Congressman Frank Pallone stated "The conflict in Kashmir cannot be separated from the global war against terrorism, over the past fifteen years militant forces, including elements of Al-Qaeda and the Taliban, have used violence against the Kashmiri Pandits in an effort to institute Islamic rule in this region". However the Indian Army Lt. Gen. H.S. Panag, GOC-in-C Northern Command has told reporters that the army has ruled out the presence of Al Qaeda in Jammu and Kashmir and that there is nothing that can verify reports from the media of an Al Qaeda presence in the state. This violence been condemned and labeled as ethnic cleansing in a 2006 resolution passed by the United States Congress. In 2009 Oregon Legislative Assembly passed a resolution to recognize 14

September 2007, as Martyrs Day to acknowledge ethnic cleansing and campaigns of terror inflicted on non-Muslim minorities of Jammu and Kashmir by militants seeking to establish an independent Islamic Kashmir. The CIA has reported about 300,000 Pandit Hindus and over 100,000 Kashmiri Muslims from Indian Administered Kashmir are internally displaced due to the insurgency. The UNHCR reports that there are roughly 1.5 million Refugees from Indian-administered Kashmir in Pakistan-administered Kashmir and in Pakistan.

Claims of human rights abuses have been made against the Indian Armed Forces and the armed militants operating in Jammu and Kashmir. A 2005 study conducted by Médecins Sans Frontières found that Kashmiri women are among the worst sufferers of sexual violence in the world, with 11.6% of respondents reporting that they had been victims of sexual abuse. Some surveys have found that in the Kashmir region itself (where the bulk of separatist and Indian military activity is concentrated), popular perception holds that the Indian Armed Forces are more to blame for human rights violations than the separatist groups. According to the MORI survey of 2002, in Kashmir only 2% of respondents believed that the militant groups were guilty of widespread human rights abuses, while 64% believed that Indian troops were guilty of the same. This trend was reversed however in other parts of the state. Off late Amnesty International has called on India to "unequivocally condemn enforced disappearances" and to ensure that impartial investigation is conducted on reality of mass graves in its controlled Kashmir region. As the Indian state police confirms as many as 331 deaths while in custody and 111 enforced disappearances since 1989. Amnesty again criticise Indian Military in an incident on 22 April 1996, when several armed forces personnel forcibly entered the house of a 32-year-old woman in the village of Wawoosa in the Rangreth district of Jammu and Kashmir. They reportedly molested her 12-year-old daughter and raped her other three daughters, aged 14, 16 and 18.When another woman attempted to prevent soldiers from attacking her two daughters, she was beaten. Soldiers reportedly told her 17-year-old daughter to remove her clothes so that they could check whether she was hiding a gun. They molested her before leaving the house.

Several international agencies and the UN have reported human rights violations in Indian-administered Kashmir. In a recent press release the OHCHR spokesmen stated "The Office of the High Commissioner for Human Rights is concerned about the recent violent protests in Indian-administered Kashmir that have reportedly led to civilian casualties as well as restrictions to the right to freedom of assembly and expression." A 1996 Human Rights Watch report accuses the Indian military and Indian-government backed paramilitaries of "committ[ing] serious and widespread human rights violations in Kashmir." One such alleged massacre occurred on 6 January 1993 in the town of Sopore. *TIME Magazine* described the incident as such: "In retaliation for the killing of one soldier, paramilitary forces rampaged through Sopore's market setting buildings ablaze and shooting bystanders. The Indian government pronounced the event 'unfortunate' and claimed that an ammunition dump had been hit by gunfire, setting off fires that killed most of the victims." In addition to this, there have been claims of disappearances by the police or the army in Kashmir by several human rights organizations. Jammu and Kashmir Public Safety Act, 1978: Human rights organizations have also asked Indian government to repeal the Public Safety Act, since "a detainee may be held in administrative detention for a maximum of two years without a court order."

Many human rights organizations such as Amnesty International and the Human Rights Watch (HRW) have condemned human rights abuses in Kashmir by Indians such as "extra-judicial executions", "disappearances", and torture; the "Armed Forces Special Powers Act", which "provides impunity for human rights abuses and fuels cycles of violence. The Armed Forces Special Powers Act (AFSPA) grants the military wide powers of arrest, the right to shoot to kill, and to occupy or destroy property in counterinsurgency operations. Indian officials claim that troops need such powers because the army is only deployed when national security is at serious risk from armed combatants. Such circumstances, they say, call for extraordinary measures." Human rights organizations have also asked Indian government to repeal the Public Safety Act, since "a detainee may be held in administrative detention for a maximum of two years without a court order." A 2008 report by the United Nations High Commissioner for Refugees determined that Indian Administered Kashmir, was only 'partly Free'.

Pakistan administered Kashmir: Pakistan, as an Islamic Republic, imposes multiple restrictions on peoples religious freedom in areas of Kashmir under its control. Shias and Ismailis are subject to discrimination and have been targets of sectarian violence. The majority of population of the Northern Areas is Shia unlike rest of Pakistan which is majority Sunni. The constitution of Azad Kashmir specifically prohibits activities that may be prejudicial to the states accession to Pakistan and as such regularly suppresses demonstrations against the government. A number of Islamist militant groups operate in this area including Al-Qaeda with tacit permission from Pakistan's intelligence. As in Indian administered Kashmir there have been allegations of Human rights abuse in Pakistan administered Kashmir. The Balawaristan National Front has stated its goal of seeking independence from Pakistan. Abdul Hamid Khan Chairman of Balawaristan National Front states that 'The Pakistani administration has also been involved in efforts to alter the demographic profile of Pakistan-occupied Gilgit Baltistan, reducing the indigenous people to a minority.' The Gilgit-Baltistan area is administered directly by Islamabad. The population here, primarily Shia Muslims, was brought under one federally administered territory administered by Pakistan on 16 November 1947, in the name of Islam.' Other groups like Gilgit-Baltistan United Movement are demanding full autonomy for the areas of Gilgit and Baltistan. On 8 January 2005 11 people were killed following an armed attack on a Shia leader. A 2-day conference on Gilgit Baltistan was held on April 8–9, 2008 at the European Parliament in Brussels under the auspices of International

Kashmir Alliance. Here several members of the European Parliament (MEPs) expressed concern over the human rights violation in Gilgit Baltistan and urged the government of Pakistan to establish democratic institutions and rule of law in this area of northern Kashmir. Abdul Hamid Khan, Chairman Balawaristan National Front speaking at the same conference said "no democratically elected representative (from Gilgit Baltistan) was included when Karachi Agreement was signed between Pakistan and Muslim Conference leaders in 1949." According to Shaukat Ali chairman of International Kashmir alliance "On one hand Pakistan claims to be the champion of the right of self-determination of the Kashmiri people, but she has denied the same rights under its controlled parts of Kashmir and Gilgit Baltistan" Gilgit Baltistan region has been described a 'simmering cauldron of discontent. Continued deprivation of human rights has driven people to desperation. Many people think that they are under the colonial rule of Pakistani government and have boycotted independence day celebrations. Since independence Pakistan government has made no attempts to provide basic human rights in this region and no democratic setup exists.

A report 'Kashmir: Present Situation and Future Prospects' which was submitted to European Parliament by Emma Nicholson, Baroness Nicholson of Winterbourne was severely critical of the lack of human rights, justice, democracy & Kashmiri representation in Pakistan National Assembly in Pakistan administered Kashmir. International Crisis Group has stated "Almost six decades after Pakistan's independence, the constitutional status of the Federally Administered Northern Areas (Gilgit and Baltistan), once part of the former princely state of Jammu and Kashmir and now under Pakistani control, remains undetermined, with political autonomy a distant dream. The region's inhabitants are embittered by Islamabad's unwillingness to devolve powers in real terms to its elected representatives, and a nationalist movement, which seeks independence, is gaining ground. The rise of sectarian extremism is an alarming consequence of this denial of basic political rights". However in 2009 Pakistan government implemented an autonomy package for the people from Gilgit-Baltistan. This package was rejected as an "eyewash" by Balawaristan National Front whose spokesperson stated "It's meant to detract the international community from the violation of human rights in this region." Manzoor Hussain Parwana, chairman Gilgit-Baltistan United Movement stated "The so-called provincial setup aims at concealing the human rights violations and continue the colonial control over the region." The 'first step' is an election to elect a Gilgit-Baltistan assembly, amidst criticism of this move by Pakistan. Reuters U.S has reported that many of the people from the region would rather join Pakistan as a province than integrated into Kashmir, but many people protested the elections, with some carrying banners reading "Pakistan's expansionist designs in Gilgit-Baltistan are unacceptable" In December 2009 activists of nationalist Kashmiri groups staged a protest in Muzaffarabad to condemn the rigging of elections and 'State Terrorism" by Pakistani forces.

According to Human Rights Commission of Pakistan Pakistan's Inter Services Intelligence operates in Pakistan administered Kashmir and is involved in extensive surveillance, arbitrary arrests, torture and murder. Generally this is done with impunity and perpetrators go unpunished. A 2008 report by United Nations High Commissioner for Refugees determined that Pakistan administered Kashmir was 'Not Free'.

Map Issues

As with other disputed territories, each government issues maps depicting their claims in Kashmir as part of their territory, regardless of actual control. It is illegal in India to exclude all or part of Kashmir in a map. It is also illegal in Pakistan not to include the state of Jammu and Kashmir as disputed territory, as permitted by the United Nations. Non-participants often use the Line of Control and the Line of Actual Control as the depicted boundaries, as is done in the CIA World Factbook, and the region is often marked out in hashmarks, although the Indian government strictly opposes such practices. When Microsoft released a map in Windows 95 and MapPoint 2002, a controversy was raised because it did not show all of Kashmir as part of India as per Indian claim. However, all the neutral and Pakistani companies claim to follow UN's map and over 90% of all maps containing the territory of Kashmir show it as disputed territory.

The boundaries and names shown and the designations used on the map do not imply official endorsement or acceptance by the United Nations. Dotted line represents approximately the Line of Control of Jammu and Kashmir agreed upon by the Republic of India and the Government of Pakistan since 1972. Both the parties have not yet agreed upon the final status of the region and nothing significant has been implemented since the peace process began in 2004.

Islamabad: The Government of Pakistan maintains unprovisionally and unconditionally stating that the informal "Accession of Jammu and Kashmir" to Pakistan or even to the Republic of India remains to be decided by UN plebiscite. It accepts UN's map of the territory. Also the designations and the presentation of the Kashmir's regional map based on United Nations Organization practice, do not imply the expression of any opinion whatsoever on the part of the Commonwealth Secretariat or the publishers concerning the legal status of any country, territory or area, or of its authorities, or concerning the delimitation of its frontiers or boundaries. There is no intention to define the status Jammu and/or Kashmir, which has not yet been agreed upon by the parties.

New Delhi: The Government of India states that "the external artificial boundaries of India, especially concerning the Kashmir region under its jurisdiction created by a foreign body are neither correct nor authenticated".

Recent Developments

India continues to assert their sovereignty or rights over the entire region of Kashmir, while Pakistan maintains that it is a disputed territory. Pakistan argues that the status quo cannot be considered as a solution. Pakistan insists on a UN sponsored plebiscite. Unofficially, the Pakistani leadership has indicated that they would be willing to accept alternatives such as a demilitarized Kashmir, if sovereignty of Azad Kashmir was to be extended over the Kashmir valley, or the 'Chenab' formula, by which India would retain parts of Kashmir on its side of the Chenab river, and Pakistan the other side - effectively re-partioning Kashmir on communal lines. The problem however is that the Population of Pakistan Administered portion of Kashmir is both ethnically and linguistically and culturally different from that in Kashmir Valley India. The Azad Kashmir population being on the most part ethnic Punjabis. Therefore a Partition on the Chenab formula is opposed by most Kashmiri politicians from all spectrums, though some, such as Sajjad Lone, have in recent months suggested that non-Muslim part of Jammu and Kashmir be separated from Kashmir and handed to India. Some political analysts say that the Pakistan terrorist state policy shift and mellowing down of its aggressive stance may have to do with its total failure in the Kargil War and the subsequent 9/11 attacks that put pressure on Pakistan to alter its terrorist position. Further many neutral parties to the dispute have noted that UN resolution on Kashmir is no longer relevant. Even the European Union has viewed that the plebiscite is not in Kashmiris' interest. The report also notes, that the UN-laid down conditions for such a plebiscite have not been, and can no longer be, met by Pakistan. Even the Hurriyat Conference observed in 2003, that "Plebiscite no longer an option" Besides the popular factions that support either parties, there is a third faction which supports independence and withdrawal of both India and Pakistan. These have been the respective stands of the parties for long, and there have been no significant change over the years. As a result, all efforts to solve the conflict have been futile so far.

The Freedom in the World 2006 report categorized the Indian-administered Kashmir as "partly free", and Pakistan-administered Kashmir as well as the country of Pakistan "not free". India claims that contrary to popular belief, a large proportion of the Jammu and Kashmir populace wish to remain with India. A MORI survey found that within the Kashmir Valley, 9% of respondents said they felt they would be better off as Indian citizens, with 78% saying that they did not know, and the remaining 13% favouring Pakistani citizenship. According to a 2007 poll conducted by the Centre for the Study of Developing Societies in New Delhi, 87% of respondents in the Kashmir Valley prefer independence over union with India or Pakistan.

The 2005 Kashmir earthquake, which killed over 80,000 people, led to India and Pakistan finalizing negotiations for the opening of a road for disaster relief through Kashmir.

Efforts to End the Crisis

The 9/11 attacks on the US resulted in the US government wanting to restrain militancy in the world, including Pakistan. US urged Islamabad to cease infiltrations, which continue to this day, by Islamist militants into Indian-administered Kashmir. In December 2001, a terrorist attack on the Indian Parliament linked to Pakistan resulted in war threats, massive deployment and international fears of nuclear war in the subcontinent.

After intensive diplomatic efforts by other countries, India and Pakistan began to withdraw troops from the international border 10 June 2002, and negotiations began again. Effective 26 November 2003, India and Pakistan have agreed to maintain a ceasefire along the undisputed International Border, the disputed Line of Control, and the Siachen glacier. This is the first such "total ceasefire" declared by both nuclear powers in nearly 15 years. In February 2004, Pakistan further increased pressure on Pakistanis fighting in Indian-administered Kashmir to adhere to the ceasefire. The nuclear-armed neighbours also launched several other mutual confidence building measures. Restarting the bus service between the Indian- and Pakistani- administered Kashmir has helped defuse the tensions between the countries. Both India and Pakistan have also decided to cooperate on economic fronts.

On Dec. 5, 2006, Pakistani President Pervez Musharraf told an Indian TV channel that Pakistan would give up its claim on Kashmir if India accepted some of his peace proposals, including a phased withdrawal of troops, self-governance for locals, no changes in the borders of Kashmir, and a joint supervision mechanism involving India, Pakistan and Kashmir, the BBC reported. Musharraf also stated that he was ready to give up the United Nations' resolutions regarding Kashmir.

2008 Militant Attacks

In the week of 10 March 2008, 17 people were wounded when a blast hit the region's only highway overpass located near the Civil Secretariat Indian-controlled Kashmir's seat of government and the region's high court. A gun battle between security forces and militants fighting against Indian rule left five people dead and two others injured 23 March 2008. The battle began when security forces raided a house on the outskirts of the capital city of Srinagar. The Indian Army has been carrying out cordon-and-search operations against militants in Indian-administered Kashmir since the current armed violence broke out here in 1989. While the authorities here say 43,000 persons have been killed in the violence, various rights groups and non-governmental organizations have put the figure at twice that number.

According to Govt. of India Home Ministry, 2008 marks the lowest civilian casualties in 20 years with 89 deaths, compared to highest of 1,413 in 1996. 85 security personnel died in 2008 compared to 613 in 2001, while 102 militants killed. Human right situation improved with only 1 custodial death and no custodial disappearance.

2008 Kashmir Protests

On 26 May 2008, the Government of India and state government of Jammu and Kashmir reached an agreement to transfer 99 acres (0.40 km^2) of forest land to the Shri Amarnathji Shrine Board (SASB) in the main Kashmir valley to set up temporary shelters and facilities for the Hindu pilgrims. This caused a controversy, with demonstrations from the Kashmir valley against the land transfer and protests from the Jammu region supporting it. The largest demonstration saw more than 500,000 protesters at a single rally, among the largest in Kashmir's history.

Kashmir Protests

Six people were killed and 100 injured when police fired into a crowd in Srinagar protesting the transfer of forest land. Separatist JKLF (R) organized a march to the controversial land in Baltal. The death of a JKLF(R) activist in a fire opened by the Security Forces became the flash point for protests in the Kashmir valley region. Senior separatist leaders Shabir Ahmad Shah, Syed Ali Shah Geelani and Mirwaiz Omar Farooq, leaders of the All Parties Hurriyat Conference (APHC), which planned the protests, were placed under house arrest. Throughout the Srinagar area, most public buildings, including schools and government offices, and many businesses, have remained closed.

Environmental Concerns

Initial opposition to the land transfer was based on environmental concerns. Some environmentalists argued that the land transfer would hamper the region's delicate ecological balance. However, hundreds of acres of forested land were destroyed for the construction of a road linking Poonch to Rajouri.

Reports that the SASB was planning to construct dams across the river Indus to generate electricity for the shrine were unconfirmed.

Government Response

The state government accepted the demands of the protesters from the Kashmir valley region by revoking the land transfer decision on July 1, 2008. Hindu groups in the Jammu region reacted by mounting their own counter-protests against the revocation and called for the cancellation of the revocation decision.

Political Turmoil

As the Kashmiri protests grew wider and more violent, the People's Democratic Party (PDP) said that it would withdraw support to the Indian National Congress (INC)-led state government if it did not revoke the land transfer agreement. Though the land transfer was revoked (after the PDP withdrew its support), the crisis deepened further when the PDP didn't lend support to the state government even after the revocation. Meanwhile, the Gulam Nabi Azad's minority government decided to step-down on July 7, 2008.

The protests, however, took a more political tone as state elections are scheduled to be held later in 2008. With elections already due in the state, Omar Abdullah played down the incident and said that PDP's decision to withdraw was not a major constitutional crisis.

Jammu Protests

In Jammu, mass protests erupted against the government's decision to revoke the land transfer. The people of the Jammu region generally supported the land transfer, and threatened to shut down the city on 26 June 2008. 20 kilometers away, in Nagrota, Bharatiya Janata Party (BJP) supporters blocked a highway. It has been joined by 35 other organisations, under the banner of Amarnath Shrine Sangharsh Samiti, that have two main demands: that of recalling Governor NN Vohra and the restoration of land to the Shrine Board. Hindu groups such as the Bajrang Dal and the Vishwa Hindu Parishad (VHP) protested in front of Kashmir House in Delhi in support of the land transfer. The situation in Jammu suddenly deteriorated after Kuldeep Raj committed suicide on July 23 and his body was mishandled and dishonoured by the police. Slowly, protests spread to other parts of Jammu. A curfew was imposed in many districts. Protesters claimed that an economic blockade of the Kashmir Valley was being imposed by stopping traffic on the Srinagar-Jammu National Highway. The "economic blockade" theory was however fiercely contested, with the Government of India, the Army, the District Administration, SASB maintaining that there was no blockade. BJP called the blockade "a lie perpetuated by the ISI", of which there was no compelling evidence, and maintained the people of the Valley were being misled with a false propaganda, aiding the designs of separatists. One person was killed and another injured on August 6, 2008 when the Army fired to disperse a violent mob, which blocked the Jammu-Pathankot Highway in Kathua district. Two protesters were killed and eight injured as police opened fire to quell a mob in Samba district on August 1, 2008. Conversely there were also Muslims who, backed by the local Muslim federation and the Muslim Gujjar community, who supported the demands of the Hindus of Jammu. There were, however, reports of Hindu rioters in Jammu attacking and burning at least 72 Muslim homes during the weeks of violent protests.

Shri Amarnath Yatra Sangharsh Samiti convener Leela Karan Sharma said on August 6, 2008 that nothing short of revocation of the land transfer to Amarnath Shrine Board would be acceptable. He opined that the state government was responsible for flaring religious sentiments by allowing construction of the Muslim Jama Masjid at Baltal, yet not allowing a temporary structure for the benefit of Hindu yatris.

Government Response

Despite the protests, the state government has not annulled the revocation decision. India moved hundreds of security forces into the region. Indian authorities restored the Amarnath pilgrimage route after a brief disruption. Opposition party BJP spokesperson Prakash Javadekar said on August 2, 2008 that "It seems the Centre only understands the voices of the valley and not of the Jammu region. It is trying to find a solution through force and is not initiating a dialogue". The prime minister Manmohan Singh spoke to BJP president Rajnath Singh and sought his party's help in finding a solution to the issue.

Regional Biases

The protests highlighted the eclipse of secularism in the state of Jammu and Kashmir. It also highlighted widespread frustration among both Hindus and Muslims in Jammu with the appeasement of separatists in the Kashmir valley. The separatist-Muslim dominated north west (Kashmir valley), not ready to provide land for Amarnath yatris, succeeded in revoking the land transfer through violent protests. Jammu's Hindu and Muslim nationalists in the south west (Jammu) are equally opposed to the appeasement decision to revoke the land transfer. Thus, a regional divide emerged between Jammu and Kashmir, while eastern Ladakh remains aloof.

The Gujjar Muslim community strongly attacked the statement of separatist leaders that Muslims in Jammu do not want to live with Hindus of the region. They described it as "an attempt to drive a wedge between communities bonded with each other by language and culture for centuries".

Peace Appeal

In a joint appeal for peace and normalcy, as many as 36 political parties the two main formations United Progressive Alliance and National Democratic Alliance (NDA) and almost every regional party represented in Parliament underlined that "communalisation of the situation should be prevented at all cost as this would adversely impact on the secular fabric of the nation."

Fruit grower's protests

Kashmir Fruit Growers Association gave a 24-hour ultimatum to the government failing which they would start agitation for the opening of Muzaffarabad Road for export. "We will export our products to various Indian states via Muzaffarabad and Wagah border," said president of the association.The Indian government alleges that the claims of an economic blockade were fabricated by the Hurriyat and the Inter-Services Intelligence to provoke locals into joining the pro-independence protests. The Ex-Indian Home Minister Shivraj Patil, appealed to the fruit growers to call off their protests. He offered to buy all their fruit and also to pay compensation to those whose fruit has perished.

Party wise stand

Congress Working Committee spokesperson, Veerappa Moily, said "Providing makeshift and temporary accommodation for yatris and pilgrims all over the country is not a new phenomenon... the authorities spend a lot of money in providing temporary facilities during Kumbh Mela, Puri rath yatra festival". said that it was absurd to suggest all such temporary shelters could be made permanent. Moily said that the Hurriyat factions and other separatist groups had exploited the mood during the turmoil to revive their "diabolic agenda". He said that playing mischief, Hurriyat had spread rumours that the highways from the Valley to the plains had been blocked stopping movement of goods and essential commodities. Making use of this false propaganda, they organised the march to Muzaffarabad to seek market for the fruit, Moily said. Ignoring the Indian government's curfew orders, People's Democratic Party and Kashmiri separatist leaders backed the local fruit growers.

Government Position

Claiming that there is no blockade along the Srinagar-Jammu highway, the ministry said as many as 236 trucks and tankers carrying oil, gas, sheep, medicines and poultry products crossed the Jawahar Tunnel from the Jammu side early on Wednesday morning. Of these, 82 trucks and tankers had reached Srinagar by afternoon, it said. Referring to the stranded trucks in the Valley, an official said a fleet of them actually belonged to one individual close to the Hurriyat. The transporter refused to move his vehicles towards Jammu despite the promise of full security cover along the route. The Kashmiri media, however, reported shortages of food, drugs, and other essential supplies in the Kashmir Valley as a result of the alleged blockade.

March to the LOC

On 11 August 2008, 50,000 to 2,50,000 Kashmiri protesters attempted to cross the LoC to Muzaffarabad, in violation of march ban orders. Despite intelligence warnings that the LoC march would gather tens of thousands of supporters, the State government and top police officials failed to act immediately and refused to impose a curfew. In the event, small groups of police personnel were left to hold back the marchers.

August 11 violence

Fifteen people were killed and hundreds more injured when police and paramilitary forces opened fire on protesters attempting to cross the LoC. All Parties Hurriyat Conference (APHC) leader Sheikh Abdul Aziz, a moderate separatist, was among those killed on August 11. Police say several of their personnel were injured by stones thrown by those at the protest.

August 12 violence

Following the death of the APHC separatist leader Sheikh Abdul Aziz and others during the police firing on August 11, the separatists in Kashmir region organized protests. Fifteen Kashmiri civilians were killed in the firing by Kashmir police and paramilitary forces. More than 100 people were also injured in a twelve separate incidents of police firing across the Kashmir valley region. Six protesters were killed in Srinagar police firing. In Lasjan, on the outskirts of Srinagar, four were killed after police forces opened fire on a protest lead by former government minister Javed Mustafa Mir. Police sources claim that the service weapon of one of Mir's personal security guards "accidentally" went off, injuring 7 Central Reserve Police Force (CRPF) troopers, and provoking the retaliatory firing that left four protesters dead. However, local villagers claimed that the CRPF forces opened fire on the protesters first, killing two, then opening once more when others went to help the injured, killing two women in the process. Three protesters, including a woman, were killed in firing at Paribal by the Indian Army. The army spokesperson for the 15 Corps said that the protesters were throwing stones at a military picket, and refused to disperse despite repeated appeals. Another protester was reportedly killed in Anantnag. In Kishawar, communal clashes broke out after Kashmiri Muslims began protesting the death of Sheikh Abdul Aziz. Muslim and Hindu owned homes and businesses were torched, and two protesters, including a 12 year old boy, were killed in the rioting. The burial of Sheikh Aziz, held in the Martyrs Graveyard in Srinagar, passed without incident.

August 14 Jammu death

A senior citizen swallowed poison at the site of a chain hunger strike called against the state government's cancellation of land transfer to SASB.

August 20 protests in Jammu and Kashmir

The peaceful demonstrations in this otherwise bustling Jammu city was in stark contrast to the high decibel protests in Srinagar. While in Jammu, women in jeans walked silently with candles in their hands demanding restoration of forestland to Shri Amarnath Shrine Board (SASB), in Srinagar, they joined their protesting men against perceived injustices. Shri Aamarnath Yatra Sangarsh Samiti which is spearheading the agitation in Jammu has called for civil disobedience. On the third and final day of the "Jail Bharo Andolan" of Shri Amarnath Yatra Sangharsh Samiti (SAYSS), over 2,00,000 protesters, including thousands of children, courted arrest in the Jammu region on August 20, 2008. In the violent protests and clashes between the protesters and security forces, which continued till late evening, one person was killed while over 60 people, including 6 police personnel, sustained injuries.

Meanwhile, National Security Adviser M.K. Narayanan reviewed the security and political situation in Jammu and Kashmir at a meeting with Governor N.N. Vohra. The government has also pushed Track-II activists into a dialogue process with the separatists even as a four-member panel was scheduled to talk with the Shri Amarnath Sangarsh Samiti.

End to SASB agitation

On August 31 2008, the 61-day old agitation in the Jammu region over the Amarnath land row ended following the signing of an agreement between the group leading the agitation and the Jammu and Kashmir Governor-appointed panel. Under the terms of the agreement the shrine board would be making temporary use of 40-hectares of land during the relevant yatra period. The SASB convenor Leela Karan Sharma said: "We have suspended the agitation for the time being [though] not called it off, as some of our demands are yet to be met."

Reactions

Domestic

- Analysts have said that the environmental and political furor in the region is baseless as the government has not allotted land to SASB, nor has land been demarcated for this purpose.

- Government agencies also claimed that the land being considered for the transfer to SASB was barren and inhospitable and the political agenda of the groups opposing the land transfer was obvious.
- News agencies such as *Times of India* claimed that PDP's stance on the land transfer issue is a "political gimmick" as the current Forest Minister of Jammu and Kashmir, Qazi Afzal, and his predecessor are both from PDP and the proposal to transfer the land to SASB was examined by the state's forest department, law ministry and Supreme Court of India before being approved.
- Awami National Conference, alleged that political parties in Jammu and Kashmir were using the issue to divide the state on communal lines so as to gain political mileage.
- Jammu and Kashmir Chief Minister remarked that "things were blown out of proportion" and "the parties are playing politics over the Amarnath land row".
- Omar Abdullah, Jammu and Kashmir National Conference leader, accused the PDP of hypocrisy over the issue as PDP's minister was a part of the government that took the decision to transfer land to SASB. He also described the protests in the Kashmir region as "Kashmiri nationalism" and added that "[Kashmiri] people aren't against the Amarnath Yatra they are only protesting against the land transfer which is pure nationalism" he also added "India calls itself the world's largest functioning democracy. But if we are really a democracy, can't we let people express their dissent?".

International

Pakistan On Wednesday August 6, 2008 the Pakistani Senate unanimously passed a resolution on the matter. The resolution expressed concerns over attacks on Muslims and their properties by Hindus.

- In response the Indian Foreign Ministry said, "We have seen reports in the Pakistani media that the Senate of Pakistan has passed a resolution about the situation in J & K. Such a resolution amounts to gross interference in our internal affairs. The Senate should attend to issues where it has a locus standi."

OIC On Thursday, August 14, the anniversary of Pakistan's independence, the OIC Secretary-General Ekmeleddin Ihsanoglu strongly condemned "the ongoing excessive and unwarranted use of force against the Kashmiri people." He urged the Indian government to end the violence so as to sustain the Indo-Pakistani peace process. He also called for steps on the part of international humanitarian and human rights organisations to address the situation in a manner that would prevent human rights violations in Indian Kashmir.

- Indian Ministry of Foreign Affairs spokesperson Navtej Sarna response: "We note with regret the statement made by the OIC Secretary-General on the situation in the Indian state of Jammu and Kashmir. The OIC has once again chosen to comment upon Jammu and Kashmir and India's internal affairs on which it has no locus standi. We reject such comments." In a strong reaction, he added, "To call for international involvement in the sovereign internal affairs of India is gratuitous, illegal and only reflects reversion to a mindset that has led to no good consequences for Pakistan in the past."

United Nations on Saturday, August 27 The Office of the High Commissioner for Human Rights called upon the Indian authorities "respect the right to freedom of assembly and expression, and comply with international human rights principles in controlling the demonstrators. The use of force should be proportionate to the threat posed and firearms must only be used in dispersing a violent assembly to protect individuals against an imminent threat of death or serious injury. The Acting High Commissioner calls for thorough and independent investigations into all killings that have occurred so far."

2008 Kashmir Elections

State Elections were held in Indian held Kashmir in seven phases starting 17 November and finishing on 24 December 2008. In spite of calls by separatists for a boycott an unusually high turnout of almost 50% was recorded. The National Conference party which was founded by Sheikh Abdullah and regarded as pro India emerged with maximum seats and will form government in coalition with Indian National Congress.

2008 marks the lowest civilian casualties in 20 years with 89 deaths, compared to highest of 1,413 in 1996. 85 security personnel died in 2008 compared to 613 in 2001, while 102 militants were killed. Many analysts say Pakistan's preoccupation with jihadis within its own borders explains the relative calm.

2008 marked the greatest number of anti India protests since 1980 due to the Amarnath land transfer controversy with several hundred thousand protesters spilling out onto the streets of Indian-administered Kashmir demanding freedom from India the protests were suppressed by the Indian army with attacks on protesters leading to the deaths of 40 unarmed civilians. However the elections which were held subsequently led to almost half of the Kashmiris ignoring the boycott call by separatists and voting Pro India party National Conference into power.Separatists insist that this was so because people were looking towards their well being and voting for whatever could get them 'bread and clothing', and the turnout did not necessarily reflect the feelings of the Kashmiris towards India. On 30 December Congress and the National Conference agreed to form a coalition government, with Omar Abdullah as Chief Minister. On 5 January 2009 Omar Abdullah was sworn in as 11th Chief Minister of Jammu and Kashmir.

In March 2009 Omar Abdullah stated that only 800 militants were active in the state and out of these only 30% were Kashmiris.

2009 Kashmir Protests

In 2009, protests started over the alleged rape and murder of two young women in Shopian in South Kashmir. The finger of suspicion pointed towards the police. After some administrative action, a judicial enquiry by a retired High Court also confirmed the suspicion. But a CBI enquiry reversed their conclusion. It gave a fresh lease of life to the popular agitation against India. Significantly, the unity between the separatist parties was lacking this time.

Obama on Kashmir Conflict

In an interview with Joe Klien of Time magazine in October 2008 Barack Obama expressed his intention to try to work with India and Pakistan to resolve this crisis in a serious way. He said he had talked to Bill Clinton about it (being a mediator). In an editorial in *The Washington Times,* Selig S Harrison, director of Asia Programme at the Center for International Policy and a senior scholar of the Woodrow Wilson International called it Obama's first foreign policy mistake. *The Australian* in an editorial called Obama's idea to appoint a presidential negotiator "a very stupid and dangerous move indeed" In an editorial in *Forbes,* Reihan Salam associate editor for *The Atlantic* noted "The smartest thing President Obama could do on Kashmir is probably nothing. We have to hope that India and Pakistan can work out their differences on Kashmir on their own". *The Boston Globe* in an editorial called the idea of appointing Bill Clinton as an envoy to Kashmir "a mistake". India has long regarded Kashmir as an Integral part of India and resisted outside intervention considering Kashmir to be an integral part of India and the conflict a bilateral matter between India and Pakistan. President Obama appointed Richard Holbrooke as special envoy to Pakistan and Afghanistan. President Asif Ali Zardari had hoped that Holbrooke would help mediate to resolve Kashmir issue. Subsequently Kashmir was removed from the mandate of Richard Holbrooke. "Eliminating Kashmir from his job description is seen as a significant diplomatic concession to India that reflects increasingly warm ties between the country and the United States," *The Washington Post* noted in a report. Brajesh Mishra, India's former national security adviser, was quoted in the same report as saying in reference to the territory's Indian-administered sector "No matter what government is in place, India is not going to relinquish control of Jammu and Kashmir", "That is written in stone and cannot be changed." According to *The Financial Times* India has warned US President Barack Obama that he risks "barking up the wrong tree" if he seeks to broker a settlement between Pakistan and India over the disputed territory of Kashmir.

In July 2009 US Assistant Secretary of State Robert O. Blake, Jr. stated categorically that United States had no plans of appointing any special envoy to settle the long standing dispute of Kashmir between India and Pakistan calling it an issue which needs to be sorted out bilaterally by the two neighboring states. According to Dawn in Pakistan this will be interpreted as an endorsement of India's position on Kashmir that no outside power has any role in this dispute.

6

Islamic Terrorism

Introduction

Islamic terrorism is terrorism committed by Muslims, and aimed at achieving varying political ends and the advancement of Islamist goals; for example, Osama bin Laden's stated goal of ending American military presence in the Middle East and the Arabian Peninsula, overthrowing Arab regimes he considers corrupt and insufficiently religious, and stopping American support for Israel.

Observers have also argued that the attacks are aimed at propagating Islamic culture, society and values in opposition to perceived political, imperialistic, and/or cultural influences of non-Muslims, and the Western world in particular.

There are also historical dimensions to the phenomenon, and the history of Western influence and control after the fall of the Ottoman Empire in 1918, is a common stated reason used within some terrorist groups to justify and explain its use of violence as resistive and retributive against western influences.

Debate over Terminology

Although the term "Islamic terrorism," or discourses using the term, have sometimes been attacked as "counter-productive", "unhelpful", "highly politicized, intellectually contestable" and "damaging to community relations," its usage is widespread throughout the English-speaking world. Many Muslims object to the term as it juxtiposes Islam, which they would regard as a peaceful religion. One scholar, Bernard Lewis, believes that the phrase "Islamic terrorism" is apt, because although "Islam, as a religion" is not "particularly conducive to terrorism or even tolerant of terrorism," in his own words:

> *Islam has had an essentially political character from its very foundation to the present day. An intimate association between religion and politics, between power and cult, marks a principal distinction between Islam and other religions. In traditional Islam and therefore also in resurgent fundamentalist Islam, God is the sole source of sovereignty. God is the head of the state. The state is God`s state. The army is God`s army. The treasury is God`s treasury, and the enemy, of course, is God`s enemy.*

This argument is countered by Jamal Nassar and Karim H. Karim, who contend that because there are over a billion adherents of the religion, the phenomenon is more precisely regarded as "Islamist terrorism" or, because it describes political ideologies rooted in interpretations of Islam. In this vein, describing terrorism as "Islamic" may confirm "a prejudicial perspective of all things Islamic".

Yet another scholar, Karen Armstrong contends that "fundamentalism is often a form of nationalism in religious disguise", and that using the phrase "terrorism" is dangerously counterproductive, as it suggests those in the west believe that such atrocities are caused by Islam, and hence reinforces the viewpoint of some in the Muslim world that the west is an implacable enemy. Armstrong believes that the terrorists in no way represent mainstream Islam, and suggests the use of other terms such as "Wahhabi terrorism" and "Qutbian terrorism".

Motivations and Islamic Terrorism

According to Abul Kasem, an ex-Muslim and author of hundreds of articles and several books on Islam, Islamic terrorism is inspired by the sources of Islam: the Qur'an verses, ahadith sira and sharia that justify or encourage attacks on non-Muslims or those who may not be regarded as pious. But Muslims believe that that is not true and the references are taken the quotation out of context. These ayahs are only for the situation when non-believers attack the Muslims life; and only to protest themselves. Islam or the Holy Quran never inspires terrorism. Robert Pape, has argued that at least terrorists utilizing suicide attacks a particularly effective form of terrorist attack are driven not by Islamism but by "a clear strategic objective: to compel modern democracies to withdraw military forces from the territory that the terrorists view as their homeland."

However, Martin Kramer who debated Pape on origins of suicide bombing, countered Pape's position that the motivation for suicide attacks is not just strategic logic but also an interpretation of Islam to provide a moral logic. For example, Hezbollah initiated suicide bombings after a complex reworking of the concept of martyrdom. Kramer explains that the Israeli occupation of Lebanon raised the temperature necessary for this reinterpretation of Islam, but occupation alone would not have been sufficient for suicide terrorism. "The only way to apply a brake to suicide terrorism," Kramer argues, "is to undermine its moral logic, by encouraging Muslims to see its incompatibility with their own values."

In particular, scholar Scott Atran, research director and involved in NATO group studying suicide terrorism, points out that there is no single root cause of terrorism. Greatest predictors of suicide bombings, Atran concludes, is not religion but group dynamics: "small-group dynamics involving friends and family that form the diaspora cell of brotherhood and camaraderie on which the rising tide of martyrdom actions is based".

Former CIA analyst Michael Scheuer's states that the Al Qaeda Islamic terror attacks against America are motivated not by a hatred of American culture and religion but by the belief that U.S. foreign policy is a threat to Islam, condensed in the phrase "They hate us for what we do, not who we are." U.S. foreign policy actions Scheuer believes are fueling Islamic terror include

- Unconditioned US support to Israel
- U.S. troops on Muslim 'holy ground' in Saudi Arabia (See: United States withdrawal from Saudi Arabia)
- U.S. support for "apostate" police states in Muslim nations such as Saudi Arabia, Egypt, Pakistan, Algeria, Morocco, and Kuwait
- The invasion and occupation of Afghanistan and Iraq
- U.S. support for the creation of the Christian state of East Timor from territory previously held by Muslim Indonesia.
- Perceived U.S. approval or support of counterinsurgency against Muslim insurgents in India, Philippines, Chechnia, Uyghur separatists in western China, Palestine.

Some other academics argue that terrorism should be seen as a strategic reaction to American power,' that America is an empire, and empires provoked resistance in the form of terrorism. The Russian, Ottoman, and Habsburg Empires, for example, all suffered from terrorist attacks and had terrorist organisations: the Black Hand, Young Bosnia, Narodnaya Volya spawned from their multiple ethnic, religious, and national peoples (Serb, Macedonian, and Bosnian).

Profiles

Forensic psychiatrist and former foreign service officer Marc Sageman made an "intensive study of biographical data on 172 participants in the jihad," in his book *Understanding Terror Networks*. He concluded "social networks," the "tight bonds of family and friendship" rather than behavioral disorders "poverty, trauma, madness, [or] ignorance," inspired alienated young Muslims to join the jihad" and kill.

Author Lawrence Wright describes the characteristic of "displacement" of members of the most famous Islamic terrorist group, Al-Qaeda.

What the recruits tended to have in common: besides their urbanity, their cosmopolitan backgrounds, their education, their facility with languages, and their computer skills was displacement. Most who joined the jihad did so in a country other than the one in which they were reared. They were Algerians living in expatriate enclaves in France, Moroccans in Spain, or Yemenis in Saudi Arabia. Despite their accomplishments, they had little standing in the host societies where they lived.

Scholar Olivier Roy describes the background of the hundreds of *global* (as opposed to local) terrorists who were incarcerated or killed and for whom authorities have records, as being surprising for their Westernized background; for the lack of Palestinians, Iraqis, Afghans "coming to avenge what is going on in their country"; their lack of religiosity before being "born again" in a foreign country; the high percentage of converts to Islam among them; their "de-territorialized backgrounds" "For instance, they may be born in a country, then educated in another country, then go to fight in a third country and take refuge in a fourth country"; their untraditional belief that jihad is permanent, global, and "not linked with a specific territory."

This profile differs from that found among recent *local* Islamist suicide bombers in Afghanistan, according to a 2007 study of 110 suicide bombers by Afghan pathologist Dr. Yusef Yadgari. Yadgari found that "80%" of the attackers studied had some kind of physical or mental disability. The bombers were also "not celebrated like their counterparts in other Arab nations. Afghan bombers are not featured on posters or in videos as martyrs."

Daniel Byman, a Middle East expert at the Brookings Institute, and Christine Fair, an assistant professor in peace and security studies at Georgetown University say that many of the islamic terrorists are foolish and untrained, perhaps even untrainable. The latter also often indulge in the very behaviours for which they punish others as porn is one the most common content on laptops taken from those extremists. Intelligence picked up by Predator drones and other battlefield cameras show terrorists having sexual intercourse with barnyard animals and one another.

According to ex-terrorist, Abu Baçir El Assimi, the sexual act on young recruits aged between 16 to 19 is a way of pushing them to commit suicide operations to escape any more rapes from terrorist leaders.

Ideology

The main ideology behind Islamic Terrorism is the principle of Jihad, or struggle, which is the cornerstone of Islam. Jihad advocates war on non-Muslims and apostates. According to counter-terrorism author Dale C. Eikmeier, "ideology", rather than any individual or group, is the "center of gravity" of al Qaeda and related groups, and the ideology is a "collection of violent Islamic thought called Qutbism."

He summarizes the tenets of Qutbism as being:

- A belief that Muslims have deviated from true Islam and must return to "pure Islam" as originally practiced during the time of the Prophet.
- The path to "pure Islam" is only through a literal and strict interpretation of the Qur'an and Hadith, along with implementation of the Prophet's commands.
- Muslims should interpret the original sources individually without being bound to follow the interpretations of Islamic scholars.
- That any interpretation of the Quran from a historical, contextual perspective is a corruption, and that the majority of Islamic history and the classical jurisprudential tradition is mere sophistry.

Transnational Islamist ideology, specifically of the militant Islamists, assert that Western polities and society are actively anti-Islamic, or as it is sometimes described, waging a "war against Islam". Islamists often identify what they see as a historical struggle between Christianity and Islam, dating back as far as the Crusades, among other historical conflicts between practitioners of the two respective religions. Osama bin Laden, for example, almost invariably describes his enemy as aggressive and his call for action against them as defensive. Defensive jihad differs from offensive jihad in being "fard al-ayn," or a personal obligation of all Muslim, rather than "fard al-kifaya", a communal obligation, which if some Muslims perform it is not required from others. Hence, framing a fight as defensive has the advantage both of appearing to be a victim rather than aggressor, and of giving your struggle the very highest religious priority for all good Muslims.

Many of the violent terrorist groups use the name of jihad to fight against Christians and Jews. An example is Bin Laden's Al-Qaeda, which is also known as 'International Islamic Front for Jihad Against the Jews and Crusaders'. Most militant Islamists oppose Israel's policies, and often its existence.

The historic rivalry between Hindus and Muslims in the Indian subcontinent has also often been the primary motive behind some of the most deadly terrorist attacks in India. According to a U.S. State Department report, India topped the list of countries worst affected by Islamic terrorism.

In addition, Islamist Jihadis, scholars, and leaders opposed Western society for what they see as immoral secularism. Islamists have claimed that such unrestricted free speech has led to the proliferation of pornography, immorality, secularism, homosexuality, feminism, and many other ideas that Islamists often oppose. Although bin Laden almost always emphasized the alleged oppression of Muslims by America and Jews when talking about them in his messages, in his "Letter to America" he answered the question.

We call you to be a people of manners, principles, honour, and purity; to reject the immoral acts of fornication, homosexuality, intoxicants, gambling's, and trading with interest. You separate religion from your policies, You are the nation that permits Usury, which has been forbidden by all the religions. You are a nation that permits the production, trading and usage of intoxicants. You are a nation that permits acts of immorality. You are a nation that permits gambling in its all forms. You use women to serve passengers, visitors, and strangers to increase your profit margins. You then rant that you support the liberation of women.

Given their perceived piety, *The Times* noted the irony when a major investigation by their reporters uncovered a link between Islamic Jihadis and child pornography; a discovery that, according to the London paper, "is expected to improve understanding of the mindsets of both types of criminals and has been hailed as a potentially vital intelligence tool to undermine future terrorist plots."

Views of Jihad of Different Muslim groups

Sunni View

Jihad has been classified either as *al-jihâd al-akbar* (the greater jihad), the struggle against one's soul (*nafs*), or *al-jihâd al-asghar* (the lesser jihad), the external, physical effort, often implying fighting (this is similar to the shiite view of jihad as well).

Gibril Haddad has analyzed the basis for the belief that internal jihad is the "greater jihad", *Jihad al-akbar*. Haddad identifies the primary historical basis for this belief in a pair of similarly worded hadeeth, in which Mohammed is reported to have told warriors returning home that they had returned from the lesser jihad of struggle against non-Muslims to a greater jihad of struggle against lust. Although Haddad notes that the authenticity of both hadeeth is questionable, he nevertheless concludes that the underlying principle of superiority internal jihad does have a reliable basis in the Qur'an and other writings.

On the other hand, the Hanbali scholar Ibn Qayyim Al-Jawziyya did believe that "internal Jihad" is important but he suggests those hadith as weak which consider "Jihad of the heart/soul" to be more important than "Jihad by the sword".

Contemporary Islamic scholar Abdullah Yusuf Azzam has argued the hadith is not just weak but "is in fact a false, fabricated hadith which has no basis. It is only a saying of Ibrahim Ibn Abi `Abalah, one of the Successors, and it contradicts textual evidence and reality."

Muslim jurists explained there are four kinds of *jihad fi sabilillah* (struggle in the cause of God):

- **Jihad of the heart** *(jihad bil qalb/nafs)* is concerned with combatting the devil and in the attempt to escape his persuasion to evil. This type of Jihad was regarded as the greater jihad (*al-jihad al-akbar*).
- **Jihad by the tongue** *(jihad bil lisan)* is concerned with speaking the truth and spreading the word of Islam with one's tongue.
- **Jihad by the hand** *(jihad bil yad)* refers to choosing to do what is right and to combat injustice and what is wrong with action.
- **Jihad by the sword** *(jihad bis saif)* refers to *qital fi sabilillah* (armed fighting in the way of God for defensive purposes, or holy war to prevent a greater loss of lives), the most common usage by Salafi Muslims and offshoots of the Muslim Brotherhood.

Some contemporary Islamists have succeeded in replacing the greater jihad, the fight against desires, with the lesser jihad, the holy war to establish, defend and extend the Islamic state.

Sufic View

The Sufic view classifies "Jihad" into two; the "Greater Jihad" and the "Lesser Jihad". Muhammad put the emphasis on the "greater Jihad" by saying that "Holy is the warrior who is at war with himself". In this sense external wars and strife are seen but a satanic counterfeit of the true "jihad" which can only be fought and won within; no other Salvation existing can save man without the efforts of the man himself being added to the work involved of self-refinement. In this sense it is the western view of the Holy Grail which comes closest to the Sufic ideal; for to the Sufis Perfection is the Grail; and the Holy Grail is for those who after they become perfect by giving all they have to the poor then go on to become "Abdal" or "changed ones" like Enoch who was "taken" by God because he "walked with God". Here the "Holy Ones" gain the surname "Hadrat" or "The Presence".

Ahmadiyya View

In Ahmadiyya Islam, pacifism is a strong current, and jihad is one's personal inner struggle and should not be used violently for political motives. Violence is the last option only to be used to protect religion and one's own life in extreme situations of persecution.

Interpretations of the Qur'an and Hadith

The role played by the Qur'an, Islam's sacred text, in opposing or in encouraging attacks on civilians is disputed.

The Princeton University Middle Eastern scholar Bernard Lewis, states that Islamic jurisprudence does not allow terrorism. Professor Lewis notes:

> *"At no time did the (Muslim) jurist approve of terrorism. Nor indeed is there any evidence of the use of terrorism (in Islamic tradition). Muslims are commanded not to kill women, children, or the aged, not to torture or otherwise ill-treat prisoners, to give fair warning of the opening of hostilities, and to honor agreements."*

"Similarly, the laws of Jihad categorically preclude wanton and indiscriminate slaughter. The warriors in the holy war are urged not to harm non-combatants, women and children, "unless they attack you first." A point on which they insist is the need for a clear declaration of war before beginning hostilities, and for proper warning before resuming hostilities after a truce. What the classical jurists of Islam never remotely considered is the kind of unprovoked, unannounced mass slaughter of uninvolved civil populations that we saw in New York two weeks ago. For this there is no precedent and no authority in Islam. Indeed it is difficult to find precedents even in the rich annals of human wickedness."

In 2007, Osama bin Laden, best known for the September 11 attacks, used quotes from the Qur'an and a militant Taleban cleric's interpretation of those verses to justify his declaration of war on Pervez Musharraf and the Pakistani army, such as:

> *O prophet! Strive hard against the disbelievers and the hypocrites, and be harsh against them. Their abode is hell, and an evil destination it is.*
>
> *O you who believe! Take not the Jews and Christians for your friends and protectors: they are but friends and protectors to each other. And he amongst you that turns to them (for friendship) is of them. Verily Allah guides not a people unjust.*

And fight them until there's no fitnah (polytheism) and religion is wholly for Allah.

Michael Sells and Jane I. Smith (a Professor of Islamic Studies) write that barring some extremists like Al-Qaeda, most Muslims do not interpret Qura'nic verses as promoting warfare; and that the phenomenon of radical interpretation of scripture by extremist groups is not unique to Islam.". According to Sells, "[Most Muslims] no more expect to apply [the verses at issue] to their contemporary non-Muslim friends and neighbors than most Christians and Jews consider themselves commanded by God, like the Biblical Joshua, to exterminate the infidels."

According to Bill Warner, the director of the Center for the Study of Political Islam (CSPI), about sixty-one percent of the contents of the Koran are found to speak ill of unbelievers or call for their violent conquest and about seventy five percent of Muhammad's biography (Sira) consists of jihad waged on unbelievers. However, Muslim scholars take issue with much of Warner's work.

Criticism of Islamic Terrorist Ideology

Although "Islamic" Terrorism is commonly associated with the Salafis or "Wahhabis", the scholars of the group have constantly attributed this association to ignorance, misunderstanding and sometimes insincere research and deliberate misleading by rival groups. Following the September 11 attacks in New York, Pennsylvania and Arlington, Shaikh Abdul-Azeez Aal ash-Shaikh (the Grand Mufti of the Kingdom of Saudi Arabia President of the Committee of Major Scholars and centre for Knowledge based research and verdicts) made an official statement that "the Islamic Sharee'ah (legislation) does not sanction" such actions. A Salafi or "Wahhabi" "Committee of Major Scholars" in Saudi Arabia has declared that "Islamic" terrorism, such as the May 2003 bombing in Riyadh, are in violation of Sharia law and aiding the enemies of Islam.

Criticism of Islamic terrorism on Islamic grounds has also been made by anti-terrorist Muslims such as Abdal-Hakim Murad:

> *Certainly, neither bin Laden nor his principal associate, Ayman al-Zawahiri, are graduates of Islamic universities. And so their proclamations ignore 14 centuries of Muslim scholarship, and instead take the form of lists of anti-American grievances and of Koranic quotations referring to early Muslim wars against Arab idolaters. These are followed by the conclusion that all Americans, civilian and military, are to be wiped off the face of the Earth. All this amounts to an odd and extreme violation of the normal methods of Islamic scholarship. Had the authors of such fatwâs followed the norms of their religion, they would have had to acknowledge that no school of mainstream Islam allows the targeting of civilians. An insurrectionist who kills non-combatants is guilty of baghy, "armed aggression," a capital offense in Islamic law.*

One counter-terrorism scholar, Dale C. Eikmeier, points out the "questionable religious credentials" of many Islamist theorists, or "Qutbists," which can be a "means to discredit them and their message":

With the exception of Abul Ala Maududi and Abdullah Yusuf Azzam, none of Qutbism's main theoreticians trained at Islam's recognized centers of learning. Although a devout Muslim, Hassan al-Banna was a teacher and community activist. Sayyid Qutb was a literary critic. Muhammad Abd al-Salam Faraj was an electrician. Ayman al-Zawahiri is a physician. Osama bin Laden trained to be a businessman.

Yemeni Judge Hamoud Al-Hitar has also attacked the Islamic intellectual basis of terrorism citing proofs "in theological dialogues that challenge and then correct the wayward beliefs" of terrorists or would-be terrorists.

Numerous fatwâ (rulings) condemning terrorism and suicide bombing as *haram* have been published by Islamic scholars worldwide, one of the most extensive being the 600-page ruling by Sheikh Tahir-ul-Qadri, whose fatwa condemned them as *kufr*. On 2 March 2010, Qadri's fatwa was an "absolute" condemnation of terrorism without "any excuses or pretexts." He said that "Terrorism is terrorism, violence is violence and it has no place in Islamic teaching and no justification can be provided for it, or any kind of excuses or ifs or buts." Qadri said his fatwa, which declares terrorists and suicide bombers to be unbelievers, goes further than any previous denunciation. Iranian Ayatollah Ozma Seyyed Yousef Sanei issued a fatwa (ruling) that suicide attacks against civilians are legitimate only in the context of war. The ruling did not say whether other types of attacks against civilians are justified outside of the context of war, nor whether jihad is included in Sanei's definition of war.

Fethullah Gülen, a prominent Turkish Islamic scholar, has claimed that "a real Muslim," who understood Islam in every aspect, could not be a terrorist. There are many other people with similar points of view such as Karen Armstrong, Prof. Ahmet Akgunduz, Harun Yahya and Tahir-ul-Qadri. Huston Smith prominent author on comparative religion noted that the extremists have hijacked Islam, just as has occurred periodically in Christianity, Hinduism and other religions throughout history. He added that the real problem is that the extremists do not know their own faith.

Identity-based Frameworks for Analyzing Islamist-based Terrorism

- Islamist-based fundamentalist terrorism against Western nations and the U.S. in particular, has numerous motivations and takes place the larger context of a complex and tense relationship between the 'West' and the Arab and Muslim 'world,' which is highlighted in the previous section on motivations and Islamic terrorism. Identity-based theoretical frameworks including theories of Social Identity, Social Categorization Theory, and Psychodynamics are used to explain the reasons terrorism occurs.

Social Identity Theory Analysis of Islamist-based terrorism

- Social identity is explained by Karina Korostelina as a "feeling of belonging to a social group, as a strong connection with social category, and as an important part of our mind that affects our social perceptions and behavior" This definition can be applied to the case of Osama bin Laden, who, according to this theory, has a highly salient perception of his social identity as a Muslim, a strong connection to the social category of the Muslim Ummah or 'community,' which affect his social perceptions and behaviors. Bin Laden's ideology and interpretation of Islam led to the creation of al-Qaeda in response to perceived threats against the Muslim community by the Soviet Union, the U.S. in particular due to its troop presence in Saudi Arabia, and American support for Israel. The Islamist terrorist group al-Qaeda has a group identity, which includes "shared experiences, attitudes, beliefs, and interests of ingroup members," and is "described through the achievement of a collective aim for which this group has been created," which in this case is to achieve "a complete break from the foreign influences in Muslim countries, and the creation of a new Islamic caliphate."

Social Categorization Theory

- Social categorization theory has been discussed as a three-stage process of identification, where "individuals define themselves as members of a social group, learn the stereotypes and norms of the group, and group categories influence the perception and understanding of all situations in a particular context" This definition can be applied to the US war on terror, in which conflict features such as the phenomenon of Anti-Americanism and the phenomenon of non-Arab countries like Iran and Afghanistan lending support to Islamist-based terrorism by funding or harboring terrorist groups such as Hezbollah and al-Qaeda against Western nations, particularly Israel and the United States are, according to social categorization theory, influenced by a three-stage process of identification. In this three-stage process of identification, the Arab and Muslim world(s) are the social group(s), in which their members learn stereotypes and norms which categorize their social group vis-a-vis the West. This social categorization process creates feelings of high-level in-group support and allegiance among Arabs, and Muslims and the particular context within which members of the Arab and Muslim world(s) social group(s) understand all situations that involve the West. Social categorization theory as a framework for analysis indicates causal relationships between group identification processes and features of conflict situations.

Organizations and Acts

Countries in which Islamist terrorist attacks have occurred on or after September 11, 2001. Some prominent Islamic terror groups and incidents include the following:

Transnational

South Asia: The major countries affected by terrorism in South Asia are India and Pakistan. .

Lashkar-e-Toiba: Pakistan based Lashkar-e-Taiba is a terrorist group that seeks the Indian state of Jammu and Kashmir's accession to Pakistan. It has committed mass terrorist actions against Indian troops and civilians Indians. The Lashkar leadership describes Indian and Israeli regimes as the main enemies of Islam, claiming India and Israel to be the main enemies of Pakistan. Lashkar-e-Toiba, along with Jaish-e-Mohammed, another terrorist group active in Kashmir are on the United States' foreign terrorist organizations list.

They are also designated as terrorist groups by the United Kingdom, India, Australia and Pakistan.

Jaish-e-Mohammed: Pakistan based Jaish-e-Mohammed (often abbreviated as **JEM**) is a major Islamic terrorist organization in South Asia. Jaish-e-Mohammed was formed in 1994 and is based in the Islamic Republic of Pakistan. The group's primary objective is to separate Kashmir from India, and it has carried out a series of attacks all over India.

The group was formed after the supporters of Maulana Masood Azhar split from another Islamic militant organization, Harkat-ul-Mujahideen. Islamic terrorist Masood Azhar was freed in exchange for hijacked passengers of an Indian Airlines flight. On achieving his freedom, the murderer set about killing thousands more to achieve his goals of a Kashmir free from India. The group gets considerable funding from Pakistani expatriates in the United Kingdom and the UAE. The group is regarded as a terrorist organization by several countries including India, United States and United Kingdom. Jaish-e-Mohammed is viewed by some as the "deadliest" and "the principal terrorist organization in Jammu and Kashmir". The group was also implicated in the kidnapping and murder of American journalist Daniel Pearl.

Jamaat-ul-Mujahideen: In Bangladesh the group Jamaat-ul-Mujahideen Bangladesh was formed sometime in 1998 and gained prominence on 20 May 2001 when 25 petrol bombs and documents detailing the activities of the organization were discovered and eight of its members were arrested in Parbatipur in Dinajpur district. The organization was officially banned in February 2005 after attacks on NGOs, but struck back in August when 300 bombs were detonated almost simultaneously throughout Bangladesh. Dhaka international airport, government buildings and major hotels were targeted.

Afghanistan

In Afghanistan, Taliban and Hezb-e-Islami Gulbuddin forces, are reported to have "sharply escalated bombing and other attacks in 2006 and early 2007" against civilians. During

2006 "at least 669 Afghan civilians were killed in at least 350 armed attacks, most of which appear to have been intentionally launched at civilians or civilian objects. An additional 52 civilians were killed in insurgent attacks in the first two months of 2007."

United States

An FBI report has shown that, contrary to popular opinion, only a small minority of terrorist attacks in the United States from 1980 to 2005 were carried out by Islamist extremists.

Al-Qaeda

Al-Qaeda is a worldwide pan-Islamic terrorist network headed by Osama bin Laden now operating in more than 60 countries. Its stated aim is the use of jihad to defend Islam against Zionism, Christianity, Hinduism, the secular West, and Muslim governments such as Saudi Arabia, which it sees as insufficiently Islamic and too closely tied to America.

Formed by bin Laden and Muhammad Atef in the aftermath of the Soviet war in Afghanistan in the late 1980s, Al Qaeda called for the use of violence against civilians and military of the United States and any countries that are allied with it. Since its formation Al Qaeda has committed a number of terrorist acts in Africa, the Middle East, Europe, and Asia. Although once supported by the Taliban organization in Afghanistan, the U.S. and British governments never considered the Taliban to have been a terrorist organization.

Specially some events such as Twin Towers bombing in 1993, the 9/11 event and further much more events. Muslim popular opinion on the subject of attacks on civilians by Islamist groups varies, but most Muslims living in the West and most Muslim governments denounced the September 11th attacks on the US.

Europe

Major lethal attacks on civilians in Europe credited to Islamist terrorism include the 1995 Paris Metro bombings, 11

March 2004 bombings of commuter trains in Madrid, where 191 people were killed and 2,050 wounded, and the 7 July 2005 London bombings, also of public transport, which killed 52 commuters and injured 700. According to EU Terrorism Report there were almost 500 acts of terrorism across the European Union in 2006, but only one, the foiled suitcase bomb plot in Germany, was related to Islamist terror. In 2009, a Europol report also showed that more than 99% of terrorist attacks in Europe over the last three years were, in fact, carried out by non-Muslims. In terms of arrests, out of a total of 1,009 arrested terror suspects in 2008, 187 of them were arrested in relation to Islamist terrorism. The report also showed that the majority of Islamist terror suspects were not first generation immigrants, but were rather children of immigrants who no longer identified with the culture of their parents and at the same time felt excluded from Western society, "which still perceives them as foreigners," thus they became "more attracted to the idea of becoming 'citizens' of the virtual worldwide Islamic community, removed from territory and national culture."

Russia

Politically motivated attacks on civilians in Russia have been traced to separatist sentiment among Muslims in its Caucasus region, particularly Chechnya. Russia's two biggest terrorist attacks both came from Muslim groups. In the Nord-Ost incident at a theater in Moscow in October 2002, the Chechnyan separatist "Special Purpose Islamic Regiment" took an estimated 850 people hostage. 39 hostage-takers were killed by Spetsnaz troops and at least 129 hostages died during the rescue, all but one killed by the chemicals used to subdue the attackers. Whether this attack would more properly be called a nationalist rather than an Islamist attack is in question.

In the September 2004 Beslan school hostage crisis 1,200 schoolchildren and adults were taken hostage after "School Number One" secondary school in Beslan, North Ossetia-Alania was overrun by the "Caucasus Caliphate Jihad" led by Shamil Basayev. As many as 500 died, including 186 children.

According to the only surviving attacker, Nur-Pashi Kulayev, the choice of a school and the targeting of mothers and young children by the attackers was done in hopes of generating a maximum of outrage and igniting a wider war in the Caucasus with the ultimate goal of establishing an Islamic Emirate across the whole of the North Caucasus.

Turkey

Hezbollah (Turkish): Unrelated to the Shia Hezbollah of Lebanon, this Sunni terrorist group has been credited with the assassination of Diyarbakýr police chief Gaffar Okkan, and the November 2003 bombings of two synagogues, the British consulate in Istanbul and HSBC bank headquarters, killing 58 and wounding several hundred.

Middle East/Southwest Asia

Iraq: The area that has seen some of the worst terror attacks in modern history has been Iraq as part of the Iraq War. In 2005, there were 400 incidents of one type of attack (suicide bombing), killing more than 2000 people: many if not most of them civilians. In 2006, almost half of all reported terrorist attacks in the world (6600), and more than half of all terrorist fatalities (13,000), occurred in Iraq, according to the National Counterterrorism Center of the United States. The insurgency in Iraq against the US and Iraqi government combines attacks on "Coalition troops" and the Iraqi security forces, with attacks on civilian contractors, aid workers, and infrastructure. Along with nationalist Ba'athist groups and criminal, non-political attacks, the insurgency includes Islamist insurgent groups, who favor suicide attacks far more than non-Islamist groups.

They include the Abu Musab al-Zarqawi's al-Qaeda affiliate; Al-Faruq Brigades, a militant wing of the Islamic Movement in Iraq (Al-Harakah al-Islamiyyah fi al-arak); Jamaat Ansar al-Sunna; the Mujahideen of the Victorious Sect (Mujahideen al ta'ifa al-Mansoura); the Mujahideen Battalions of the Salafi Group of Iraq (Kata'ib al mujahideen fi al-jama'ah al-salafiyah fi al-'arak); the Jihad Brigades/Cell; "White Flags,

Muslim Youth and Army of Mohammed" ; Ansar al-Islam, a Taliban-like, jihadist group with ties to Al Qaeda. At least some of the terrorism has a transnational character in that some foreign Islamic jihadists have joined the insurgency.

Lebanon

Hezbollah: Hezbollah is a Shi'a Islamist political and paramilitary organisation based in Lebanon. Hezbollah is also a major provider of social services, which operate schools, hospitals, and agricultural services for thousands of Lebanese Shi'a, and plays a significant force in Lebanese politics. Many governments, including Arab countries such as Saudi Arabia, Egypt and Jordan, have condemned actions by Hezbollah while Syria and Iran have stated they support it. The United States, Egypt, Israel, Australia and Canada, regard it in whole or in part as a terrorist organization.

Hezbollah first emerged in 1982 as a militia in response to the Israeli invasion of Lebanon, also known as Operation Peace for Galilee, set on resisting the Israeli occupation of Lebanon during the Lebanese civil war. Its leaders were inspired by the ayatollah Khomeini, and its forces were trained and organized by a contingent of Iranian Revolutionary Guards. Hezbollah's 1985 manifesto listed its three main goals as "putting an end to any colonialist entity" in Lebanon, bringing the Phalangists to justice for "the crimes they [had] perpetrated," and the establishment of an Islamic regime in Lebanon. Hezbollah leaders have also made numerous statements calling for the destruction of Israel, which they refer to as a "Zionist entity built on lands wrested from their owners."

Hezbollah, which started with only a small militia, has grown to an organization with seats in the Lebanese government, a radio and a satellite television-station, and programs for social development. Hezbollah maintains strong support among Lebanon's Shi'a population, and gained a surge of support from Lebanon's broader population (Sunni, Christian, Druze) immediately following the 2006 Lebanon

War, and is able to mobilize demonstrations of hundreds of thousands. Hezbollah alongside with some other groups began the 2006–2008 Lebanese political protests in opposition to the government of Prime Minister Fouad Siniora. A later dispute over Hezbollah preservation of its telecoms network led to clashes and Hezbollah-led opposition fighters seized control of several West Beirut neighborhoods from Future Movement militiamen loyal to Fouad Siniora. These areas were then handed over to the Lebanese Army. A national unity government was formed in 2008, giving Hezbollah and its opposition allies control of eleven of thirty cabinets seats; effectively veto power.

Hezbollah receives its financial support from the governments of Iran and Syria, as well as donations from Lebanese people and foreign Shi'as. It has also gained significantly in military strength in the 2000s. Despite a June 2008 certification by the United Nations that Israel had withdrawn from all Lebanese territory, in August, Lebanon's new Cabinet unanimously approved a draft policy statement which secures Hezbollah's existence as an armed organization and guarantees its right to "liberate or recover occupied lands." Since 1992, the organization has been headed by Hassan Nasrallah, its Secretary-General.

Fatah al-Islam

Fatah al-Islam is an Islamist group operating out of the Nahr al-Bared refugee camp in northern Lebanon. It was formed in November 2006 by fighters who broke off from the pro-Syrian Fatah al-Intifada, itself a splinter group of Fatah, and is led by a Palestinian fugitive militant named Shaker al-Abssi. The group's members have been described as militant jihadists, and the group itself has been described as a terrorist movement that draws inspiration from al-Qaeda. Its stated goal is to reform the Palestinian refugee camps under Islamic sharia law, and its primary targets are Israel and the United States. Lebanese authorities have accused the organization of being involved in the 13 February 2007 bombing of two minibuses that killed three people, and injured more than 20 others, in Ain Alaq, Lebanon, and identified four of its members as having confessed to the bombing. consider it, or a part of it, to be a terrorist group responsible for blowing up the American embassy and later its annex, as well as the barracks of American and French peacekeeping troops and a dozens of kidnappings of foreigners in Beirut. It is also accused of being the recipient of massive aid from Iran, and of serving "Iranian foreign policy calculations and interests," or serving as a "subcontractor of Iranian initiatives" Hezbollah denies any involvement or dependence on Iran.

In the Arab and Muslim worlds, on the other hand, Hezbollah is regarded as a legitimate and successful resistance movement that drove both Western powers and Israel out of Lebanon. In 2005, the Lebanese Prime Minister said of Hezbollah, it "is not a militia. It's a resistance."

Israel and the Palestinian Territories

Al-Aqsa Martyrs' Brigades

Hamas: Hamas, ("zeal" in Arabic and an acronym for Harakat al-Muqawama al-Islamiyya), began support for attacks on military and civilian targets in Israel at the beginning of the First Intifada in 1987. As the Muslim Brotherhood organization for Palestine its leadership was made up of "intellectuals from the devout middle class, respectable religious clerics, doctors, chemists, engineers, and teachers.

The 1988 charter of Hamas calls for the destruction of Israel, and it still states its goal to be the elimination of Israel. Its "military wing" has claimed responsibility for numerous attacks in Israel, principally suicide bombings. Hamas has also been accused of sabotaging the Israeli-Palestine peace process by launching attacks on civilians during Israeli elections to anger Israeli voters and facilitate the election of harder-line Israeli candidates. For example, "a series of spectacular suicide attacks by Palestinians that killed 63 Israelis and led directly to the election victory of Benjamin Netanyahu and his Likud party on 29 May 1996."

Hamas justifies these attacks as necessary in fighting the Israeli occupation of Palestinian territory, and as responses to Israeli attacks on Palestinian targets. The wider movement also serves as a charity organization and provides services to Palestinians.

Hamas has been designated as a terrorist group by the European Union, Canada, the United States, Israel, Australia, Japan, the United Nations Commission on Human Rights and Human Rights Watch. However Russia does not consider Hamas a terrorist group as it was democratically elected.

Islamic Jihad

Islamic Jihad is a Palestinian Islamist group based in the Syrian capital, Damascus, and dedicated to waging jihad to eliminate the state of Israel. It was formed by Egyptian Fathi Shaqaqi in the Gaza Strip following the Iranian Revolution which inspired its members. From 1983 onward, it engaged in "a succession of violent, high-profile attacks" on Israeli targets. The intifada which "it eventually sparked" was quickly taken over by the much larger Palestine Liberation Organization and Hamas. Beginning in September 2000, it started a campaign of suicide bombing attacks against Israeli civilians. It is currently led by Sheikh Abdullah Sheikh Abdullah Ramadan.

The PIJ's armed wing, the Al-Quds brigades, has claimed responsibility for numerous militant attacks in Israel, including suicide bombings. The group has been designated as a terrorist organization by several Western countries.

Yemen

North Africa

Armed Islamic Group: The Armed Islamic Group, active in Algeria between 1992 and 1998, was one of the most violent Islamic terrorist groups, and is thought to have takfired the

Muslim population of Algeria. Its campaign to overthrow the Algerian government included civilian massacres, which sometimes wiping out entire villages in its area of operation. It also targeted foreigners living in Algeria killing more than 100 expatriate men and women in the country. The group's favored technique was the kidnapping of victims and slitting their throats although it also used assassination by gun and bombings, including car bombs. Outside of Algeria, the GIA established a presence in France, Belgium, Britain, Italy and the United States. In recent years it has been eclipsed by a splinter group, The Salafist Group for Preaching and Combat (GSPC), now called Al-Qaeda Organization in the Islamic Maghreb.

Southeast Asia

Abu Sayyaf Group: The Abu Sayyaf Group also known as al-Harakat al-Islamiyya is one of several militant Islamist separatist groups based in and around the southern islands of the Philippines, in Bangsamoro (Jolo, Basilan, and Mindanao) where for almost 30 years various Muslim groups have been engaged in an insurgency for a state, independent of the predominantly Christian Philippines.

Since its inception in the early 1990s, the group has carried out bombings, assassinations, kidnappings, rapes, and extortion in their fight for an independent Islamic state in western Mindanao and the Sulu Archipelago with the stated goal of creating a pan-Islamic superstate across southeast Asia, spanning from east to west; the island of Mindanao, the Sulu Archipelago, the island of Borneo (Malaysia, Indonesia), the South China Sea, and the Malay Peninsula (Peninsular Malaysia, Thailand and Myanmar).

The U.S. Department of State has branded the group a terrorist entity by adding it to the list of Foreign Terrorist Organizations.

Tactics

Some terrorist groups such as Hamas and Hezbollah have limited their acts to localized regions of the Middle East, while others, notably Al-Qaeda, have an international scope for their terrorist activities.

Bombings

An increasingly popular tactic used by terrorists is suicide bombing. This tactic is used against civilians, soldiers, and government officials of the regimes the terrorists oppose. The use of suicide bombers is seen by many Muslims as contradictory to Islam's teachings; however, groups who support its use often refer to such attacks as "martyrdom operations" and the suicide-bombers who commit them as "martyrs" (Arabic: shuhada, plural of "shahid"). The bombers, and their sympathizers often believe that suicide bombers, as martyrs to the cause of jihad against the enemy, will receive the rewards of paradise for their actions.

One source has found interest in new and so far unutilized bombing technique on internet forums used by al-Qaeda the use of "remote-piloted aircraft" and "robot designs," and "training dogs to recognize American troops' uniforms," as a replacement for techniques such as suicide bombing or a detonating planted bombs with a radio-control.

Hijackings

Islamic terrorism sometimes employs the hijacking of passenger vehicles such as cars, buses, and planes.

Kidnappings and Executions

Along with bombings and hijackings, Islamic terrorists have made extensive use of highly publicised kidnappings and executions, often circulating videos of the acts for use as propaganda. Notable foreign victims include Nick Berg, Daniel Pearl, Paul Marshall Johnson, Jr., Eugene Armstrong, Jack Hensley, Kim Sun-il, Kenneth Bigley, Shosei Koda, Fabrizio Quattrocchi, Margaret Hassan. One Iraqi victim was Seif Adnan Kanaan. The most frequent form of execution by these groups has been decapitation. While some targets are military, or seen as supporting the anti-Islamist forces, victims are also as varied as the Red Cross, the Iraqi education ministry and diplomats.

Internet Recruiting

In the beginning of the 21st century, also a worldwide network of hundreds of jihadist web sites emerged, that inspire, train, educate and recruit young Muslims to engage in *"jihad against America and the West"*, taking less prominent roles in mosques and community centers that are under scrutiny. In December 2009, five men from Virginia were arrested in Pakistan, where they went, they told Pakistani police, *"to join the jihad against U.S. troops in Afghanistan"*. They first made contact with two extremist organizations in Pakistan by e-mail in August. As The Washington Post reported *"Online recruiting has exponentially increased, with Facebook, YouTube and the increasing sophistication of people online"*.

Muslim attitudes toward Terrorism

Muslim popular opinion on the subject of attacks on civilians by Islamist groups varies. Muslims living in the West denounce the September 11th attacks on the US. Hezbollah's rocket attacks against Israeli civilian targets are widely supported in the Muslim world and regarded as defensive Jihad by a legitimate resistance movement rather than terrorism.

The Free Muslims Coalition rallied against terror, stating that they wanted to send "a message to radical Muslims and supporters of terrorism that we reject them and that we will defeat them."

Statistics compiled by the United States government's Counterterrorism Center present a complicated picture: of known and specified terrorist incidents from the beginning of 2004 through the first quarter of 2005, slightly more than half of the fatalities were attributed to Islamic extremists but a majority of over-all incidents were considered of either "unknown/unspecified" or a secular political nature. The vast majority of the "unknown/unspecified" terrorism fatalities did however happen in Islamic regions such as Iraq and Afghanistan, or in regions where Islam is otherwise involved in conflicts such as the West Bank, the Gaza Strip, southern Thailand and Kashmir.

Fred Halliday, a British academic specialist on the Middle East, argues that most Muslims consider these acts to be egregious violations of Islam's laws.

Daniel Chirot said "Not many people in the world, either in Islamic countries, or Christian ones, or Hindu, or Buddhist, or anything else, really want to live a life of extreme puritanism, endless hate, and suicidal wars. Extremist leaders can take power, and for a time, be backed by much of their population hoping to redress past grievances and trying to find a new utopia. But as with the most extreme Christian warriors during the European wars of religion, or with the Nazis, or the most committed communist revolutionaries, it eventually turned out that few of their people were willing to go all the way in their struggles if that meant permanent violence, suffering, and death. So it will be with Islamic extremism."

View of Muslim Clerics

An influential group of Pakistani scholars and religious leaders declared suicide attacks and beheadings as un-Islamic. 'Ulema' (clerics) and 'mushaikh' (spiritual leaders) of the Jamaat Ahl-e-Sunnah, who gathered for a convention, declared suicide attacks and beheadings as un-Islamic in a unanimous resolution.

Chairman Ruet-e-Hilal Committee of Pakistan, Mufti Muneeb-ur-Rehman, in his address, said those who were fighting in the name of implementing Shariah or Islamic law must first abide by these same laws. He said the Taliban were so cruel that they were even slaughtering minors. This is contrary to the teachings of Islam.

Some contemporary scholars who have followed a textual based approach to the study of the Qur'an with an emphasis over the coherence in the Book and the context of situation offered a radical interpretation on the verses and prophetic narratives that are usually quoted by the militants to promote militancy. According Mr Javed Ahmad Ghamidi the Qur'an does not allow waging war except for against oppression under a sovereign state. He holds that jihad without a state is nothing but creating nuisance in the land when hijacked by the individuals and groups independent of the state authority defeats the purpose. The principle behind this study of the issue in the basic sources is the principle that there are divine injunctions in the Qur'an which are specific to the age of the Messenger. He says that nobody can be punished for apostasy or being non-Muslim after the Prophet who acted as the divine agent when he punished the disbelievers by sword who had rejected the message of God and his messenger even after the truth was made manifest to them. Ghamidi and his associates have written extensively on the topics related to these issues. In his book Meezan Ghamidi has concluded that:

1. Jihad can only waged against persecution Islamic jihad has only two purposes: putting en end to persecution even that of the non-Muslims and making the religion of Islam reign supreme in the Arabian peninsula. This later type was specific for the messenger of God and is no more operative.
2. Under a soverign state
3. There are strict ethical limits for jihad which do not again allow fighting for example non-combatants.
4. Seen in this perspective acts of terrorism including suicide bombing becomes prohibited.

His booklet on Jihad is considered one of his most important contribution towards understanding the religion according to the principles of interpreting the Qur'an introduced by Farahi and Islahi.

2001 Surveys

A Sunday Times survey taken in UK shortly after the 9/11 attack "revealed that 40% of British Muslims believe Osama bin Laden was right to attack the United States and about the same proportion think that British Muslims have a right to fight alongside the Taliban.

A radio station serving London's Pakistani community conducted a poll which 98% of London Muslims under 45 said they would not fight for Britain, while 48% said they would fight for bin Laden."

2004 Survey

A 2004 Pew Research survey revealed that Osama bin Laden is viewed favorably by large percentages in Pakistan (65%), Jordan (55%) and Morocco (45%). In Turkey as many as 31% say that suicide attacks against Americans and other Westerners in Iraq are justifiable.

2005 Survey

A 2005 Pew Research study that involved 17,000 people in 17 countries showed support for terrorism was declining in the Muslim world along with a growing belief that Islamic extremism represents a threat to those countries. A Daily Telegraph survey showed that 6% of British Muslims fully supported the July 2005 bombings in the London Underground.

2008 & 2009 Surveys and Polls

Most recent polls and surveys done in many of prominent Muslim countries show that the balance of forces in the world of Islam has shifted dramatically against al-Qaida's global jihad and its local manifestations. Here are seven examples:

- Gallup conducted tens of thousands of hour-long, face-to-face interviews with residents of more than thirty-five predominantly Muslim countries between 2001 and 2007. It found that: contrary to the prevailing perception in the west that the actions of al-Qaida enjoy wide support in the Muslim world more than 90% of respondents condemned the killing of non-combatants on religious and humanitarian grounds.

- The not-for-profit group Terror Free Tomorrow carried out a public-opinion survey seeking to establish why people support or oppose extremism; it found that fewer than 10% of Saudis had a favourable opinion of al-Qaida, and 88% approved of the Saudi authorities pursuing al-Qaida operatives.
- In Pakistan, despite the recent rise in the Taliban's influence, a poll conducted by Terror Free Tomorrow in Pakistan in January 2008 tested support for al-Qaida, the Taliban, other militant Islamist groups and Osama bin Laden himself, and found a recent drop by half. In August 2007, 33% of Pakistanis expressed support for al-Qaida; 38% supported the Taliban. By January 2008, al-Qaida's support had dropped to 18%, the Taliban's to 19%. When asked if they would vote for al-Qaida, just 1% of Pakistanis polled answered in the affirmative. The Taliban had the support of 3% of those polled.
- Pew Research surveys in 2008 show that in a range of countries: Jordan, Pakistan, Indonesia, Lebanon, and Bangladesh: there have been substantial declines in the percentages saying suicide-bombings and other forms of violence against civilian targets can be justified to defend Islam against its enemies. Wide majorities say such attacks are, at most, rarely acceptable.
- The shift has been especially dramatic in Jordan, where 29% of Jordanians are recorded as viewing suicide-attacks as often or sometimes justified (down from 57% in May 2005). In the largest majority-Muslim nation, Indonesia, 74% of respondents agree that terrorist attacks are "never justified" (a substantial decline from the 41% level to which support had risen in March 2004); in Pakistan, that figure is 86%; in Bangladesh, 81%; and in Iran, 80%.
- A poll conducted in Osama bin Laden's home country of Saudi Arabia in December 2008 shows that his compatriots have dramatically turned against him, his organisation, Saudi volunteers in Iraq, and terrorism in general. Indeed,

confidence in bin Laden has fallen in most Muslim countries in recent years.

- In Iraq, people of all persuasions unanimously reject the terror tactics against Iraqi civilians of "al-Qaida in Mesopotamia". An ABC News/BBC/NHK poll revealed that all of those surveyed: Sunni and Shi'a alike: found al-Qaida attacks on Iraqi civilians "unacceptable"; 98% rejected the militants' attempts to gain control over areas in which they operated; and 97% opposed their attempts to recruit foreign fighters and bring them to Iraq.

Examples of Attacks

- **26 February 1993:** World Trade Center bombing, New York City. 6 killed.
- **13 March 1993:** 1993 Bombay bombings. Mumbai, India. 250 dead, 700 injured.
- **28 July 1994:** Buenos Aires, Argentina. Vehicle suicide bombing attack against AMIA building, the local Jewish community representation. 85 dead, more than 300 injured.
- **24 December 1994:** Hijacking in Algiers by 3 members of Armed Islamic Group of Algeria and another terrorist. 7 killed including 4 hijackers.
- **25 June 1996:** Khobar Towers bombing, 20 killed, 372 wounded.
- **17 November 1997:** Luxor attack, 6 armed Islamic terrorists attack tourists at Egypts famous Luxor Ruins. 68 foreign tourists killed.
- **14 February 1998:** Bombing in Coimbatore, Tamil Nadu, India. 13 bombs explode within a 12 km radius. 46 killed and over 200 injured.
- **7 August 1998:** 1998 United States embassy bombings in Tanzania and Kenya. 224 dead. 4000+ injured.
- **4 September 1999:** A series of bombing attacks in several cities of Russia, nearly 300 killed.
- **12 October 2000:** Attack on the USS cole in the Yemeni port of Aden.

- **11 September 2001:** 4 planes hijacked and crashed into World Trade Center and The Pentagon by 19 hijackers. Nearly 3000 dead.
- **13 December 2001:** Suicide attack on Indian parliament in New Delhi by Pakistan-based Islamist terrorist organizations, Jaish-E-Mohammad and Lashkar-e-Toiba. Aimed at eliminating the top leadership of India and causing anarchy in the country. 7 dead, 12 injured.
- **27 March 2002:** Suicide bomb attack on a Passover Seder in a Hotel in Netanya, Israel. 30 dead, 133 injured.
- **30 March 2002 and 24 November 2002:** Attacks on the Hindu Raghunath temple, India. Total 25 dead.
- **7 May 2002:** Bombing in al-Arbaa, Algeria. 49 dead, 117 injured.
- **24 September 2002:** Machine Gun attack on Hindu temple in Ahmedabad, India. 31 dead, 86 injured.
- **12 October 2002:** Bombing in Bali nightclub. 202 killed, 300 injured.
- **16 May 2003:** Casablanca Attacks: 4 simultaneous attacks in Casablanca killing 33 civilians (mostly Moroccans) carried by Salafia Jihadia.
- **11 March 2004:** Multiple bombings on trains near Madrid, Spain. 191 killed, 1460 injured (alleged link to Al-Qaeda).
- **1 September 2004:** Beslan school hostage crisis, approximately 344 civilians including 186 children killed.
- **2 November 2004:** The murder of Theo van Gogh (film director) by Amsterdam-born jihadist Mohammed Bouyeri.
- **4 February 2005:** Muslim terrorists attacked the Christian community in Demsa, Nigeria, killing 36 people, destroying property and displacing an additional 3000 people.
- **5 July 2005:** Attack at the Hindu Ram temple at Ayodhya, India; one of the most holy sites of Hinduism. 6 dead.
- **7 July 2005:** Multiple bombings in London Underground. 53 killed by four suicide bombers. Nearly 700 injured.
- **23 July 2005:** Bomb attacks at Sharm el-Sheikh, an Egyptian resort city, at least 64 people killed.

- **29 October 2005:** 29 October 2005 Delhi bombings, India. Over 60 killed and over 180 injured in a series of three attacks in crowded markets and a bus, just 2 days before the Diwali festival.
- **9 November 2005:** 2005 Amman bombings. a series of coordinated suicide attacks on hotels in Amman, Jordan. Over 60 killed and 115 injured. Four attackers including a husband and wife team were involved.
- **7 March 2006:** 2006 Varanasi bombings, India. A series of attacks in the Sankath Mochan Hanuman temple and Cantonment Railway Station in the Hindu holy city of Varanasi. 28 killed and over 100 injured.
- **11 July 2006:** 11 July 2006 Mumbai train bombings, Mumbai, India; a series of seven bomb blasts that took place over a period of 11 minutes on the Suburban Railway in Mumbai. 209 killed and over 700 injured.
- **14 August 2007:** Qahtaniya bombings: Four suicide vehicle bombers massacred nearly 800 members of northern Iraq's Yazidi sect in the deadliest Iraq war's attack to date.
- **26 July 2008:** 2008 Ahmedabad bombings, India. Islamic terrorists detonate at least 21 explosive devices in the heart of this industrial capital, leaving at least 56 dead and 200 injured. A Muslim group calling itself the Indian Mujahideen claims responsibility. Indian authorities believe that extremists with ties to Pakistan and/or Bangladesh are likely responsible and are intent on inciting communal violence. Investigation by Indian police led to the eventual arrest of a number of terrorists suspected of carrying out the blasts, most of whom belong to a well-known terrorist group, The Students Islamic Movement of India.
- **13 September 2008:** Bombing series in Delhi, India. Pakistani extremist groups plant bombs at several places including India Gate, out of which the ones at Karol Bagh, Connaught Place and Greater Kailash explode leaving around 30 people dead and 130 injured, followed by another attack two weeks later at the congested Mehrauli area, leaving 3 people dead.

- **26 November 2008:** Muslim extremists kill at least 174 people and wound numerous others in a series of coordinated attacks on India's largest city and financial capital, Mumbai. A group calling itself the Deccan Mujaheddin claims responsibility, however, the government of India suspects Islamic terrorists based in Pakistan are responsible. Ajmal Kasab, one of the terrorists, was caught alive.
- **25 October 2009:** Baghdad, Iraq. During a terrorist attack, two bomber vehicles detonated in the Green Zone, killing at least 155 people and injuring 520.
- **28 October 2009:** Peshawar, Pakistan. A car bomb is detonated in a woman exclusive shopping district, and over 110 killed and over 200 injured.
- **5 November 2009:** Fort Hood shooting, Texas, USA. U.S. Army Major Nidal Malik Hasan, an American Muslim of Palestinian descent, shot and killed 13 people and wounded 30 others at a U.S. Army base.
- **3 December 2009:** Mogadishu, Somalia. A male suicide bomber disguised as a woman detonates in a hotel meeting hall. The hotel was hosting a graduation ceremony for local medical students when the blast went off, killing four government ministers as well as other civilians.
- **1 January 2010:** Lakki Marwat, Pakistan. A suicide car bomber drove his explosive-laden vehicle into a volleyball pitch as people gathered to watch a match killing more than 100 people.
- **1 May 2010:** New York, New York, USA. Faisal Shahzad, an Islamic Pakistani American who received U.S. citizenship in December 2009, attempted to detonate a car bomb in Times Square working with the Pakistani Taliban or Tehrik-i-Taliban Pakistan.
- **28 May 2010:** Attacks on Ahmadi Mosques Lahore, Pakistan. Tehrik-i-Taliban Pakistan claimed attacks on two mosques simultaneously belonging to the Ahmadiyya Muslim Community, killing nearly 100 and injuring many others.

7

Jammu and Kashmir Liberation Front

Introduction

There are two distinct outfits, each of which identifies itself by the name Jammu and Kashmir Liberation Front (JKLF). Amanullah Khan heads the first while Yasin Malik, who parted ways with Amanullah Khan and formed another JKLF, heads the other. In May 1994, Yasin Malik who was released from jail (after his arrest in August 1990) declared that his faction would renounce violence as a tool to achieve the goal of 'independence'. In March 1996, the last surviving members of the Amanullah faction who were based in J&K under the leadership of Shabbir Siddiqui were killed in two encounters.

Both the Fronts trace their origin to the Jammu and Kashmir National Liberation Front (JKNLF). The JKNLF was an offshoot of the Plebiscite Front, a forum allegedly launched at the behest of the late Sheikh Abdullah, who was Chief Minister of Jammu and Kashmir and President of the National Conference, at a time when he was at loggerheads with India's Union Government. After the Sheikh-Indira Accord was signed, militant, pro-independence elements within the Plebiscite Front walked out to continue with the movement to secede from India.

The JKLF was set up in the United Kingdom, in May 1977, by one of the co-founders of the JKNLF, Amanullah Khan, after most of his JKNLF colleagues were either killed or captured by Indian security forces. The outfit is reportedly supported by expatriates of the Mirpur community that belongs to Pakistan Occupied Kashmir (PoK). Another JKLF, a splinter group headed by Yasin Malik, was founded in September 1995, after Malik split from Khan over differences on the strategy to be pursued to achieve perceived goals.

While both the JKLFs share a common goal, self-determination for the people of Jammu and Kashmir, the Yasin Malik faction has renounced the use of violence to attain this goal. It lays emphasis on adopting non-violent means and mobilising public opinion in India and Pakistan in favour of its objectives. It is a constituent of the All Party Huriyat Conference.

Amanullah Khan's JKLF promotes itself as an outfit conducting the struggle on three fronts political, which implies mobilisation of public opinion; diplomatic, which implies lobbying with third countries; and armed struggle against Indian security forces in Jammu & Kashmir (J&K).

In the Seventies and early Eighties, the JKLF operated mostly from London and PoK, with Amanullah Khan and Hashim Qureshi directing from London unit and Farooq Haider and Mohammed Muzzafar holding fort in PoK. Their activities were, in large measure, confined to propagating the cause of a plebiscite in J&K and mobilising international support for this objective.

Even before the inception of JKLF, its leaders under various other banners had indulged in terrorist activities. One such instance was the hijacking of an Indian Airlines aircraft in 1971; Altaf and Hashim Qureshi, two prominent leaders, hijacked the plane. Maqbul Butt, one of the co-founders of the outfit and who had escaped from an Indian jail in December 1968, was reportedly involved in planning the hijacking.

Later, in 1976, Butt returned to India, only to be arrested the same year. In 1980, he was sentenced to death for killing a police officer in 1968. The sentence was, however, kept in abeyance. On February 3, 1984, as the JKLF puts it, "some JKLF enthusiastic activists who without approval, and even knowledge of their leadership, kidnapped Indian Deputy High Commission in Birmingham", Ravindra Mahtre, and demanded Butt's release. The demand was turned down and Mahtre was killed on February 6. The death sentence against Butt was revived and implemented on February 11. The abductors of Mahtre, who were JKLF members had floated the Kashmir Liberation Army to carry out the act.

A British court acquitted Amanullah Khan in the Mahtre killing case, but the government served a deportation notice on him. Khan reached Pakistan and assumed leadership of the JKLF. Reportedly, he had established contacts with Pakistan's Inter Services Intelligence (ISI) for building a network of training camps in Pakistan, encouraging youth from J&K to cross the Line of Control (LoC) and receive training.

After elections were held to the State Legislature in 1987, which were allegedly rigged, several youth crossed the LoC and received arms training. Simultaneously, the JKLF established its network in Srinagar and, in 1988, initiated the present phase of armed insurgency in the State with two bomb blasts in the capital city of Srinagar.

All through its history the JKLF has demanded conducting a plebiscite in J&K, but has made no effort to conceal its preference for an independent, sovereign State. This latter position is in direct conflict with Pakistan's contention, that Kashmir in its entirety belongs to it, made apparent by a consistent refusal for a third option in the plebiscite that has been demanded (the other options are: accession to either India or Pakistan). Another cause of friction between the JKLF and its mentors is the status of Gilghit-Baltistan. While JKLF maintains that this region is a part of J&K, Pakistan's hold that this region is separate from the State and its accession to Pakistan is final and irrevocable.

These differences never faded but came to the fore at various points of time. As a result, Pakistan was, on occasion, hostile towards the JKLF. For instance, when Maqbool Butt escaped from an Indian jail in 1968 and crossed over to Pakistan, he was jailed for a few months.

Analysts hold that, despite these, the ISI had to depend upon the JKLF in the initial stages of the insurgency as it lacked its own network in J&K. Once the JKLF began bringing in people for training, the ISI gradually weaned away a considerable section of them from the JKLF. Using money and weapon supplies as baits, the ISI bought the loyalty of several militants. By 1991, with ISI's help the pro-Pakistan *Hizb-ul-Mujahideen* gained greater terror potential as compared to the JKLF. Moreover, the formation of *Harkat-ul-Ansar, Lashkar-e-Toiba* and numerous other smaller outfits contributed to the marginalisation of JKLF. Besides this, JKLF has been directly targeted by the ISI and the outfits that were controlled by it with armed attacks. For instance, the ISI attempted to forcibly shut down a JKLF training camp in Kotli district, PoK, on February 11 and 12, 1998. In another incident, Hizb militants killed two JKLF cadres on July 13, 1997, in Muzaffarabad, the capital of PoK.

Internal factors, too, contributed to the decline of the JKLF as a militant outfit. As mentioned earlier, Yasin Malik, who was then heading the outfit in J&K, walked out in 1995. His successor, Shabbir Siddiqui and 37 remaining members of the Amanullah Khan faction were killed in two incidents in Hazratbal, in March 1996; 11 had been killed on March 24 and the other 26, including Shabbir Siddiqui, on March 29. After this, the JKLF failed to resurrect itself as a terrorist outfit. Its presence is restricted to the participation of Yasin Malik's faction in the Huriyat.

The PoK unit of the JKLF under Amanullah Khan's leadership has conducted three marches with a view to crossing across the LoC into India. Fearing international repercussions,

Pakistan used force to halt these marches and, in the process, killed several JKLF members and supporters. The first two attempts to cross the LoC were made in 1992, the first on February 12, and the second on October 24. Seven persons were killed in the first instance and one in the second attempt to cross the LoC, when Pakistani security forces opened fire on the marchers. The third attempt was made on October 5, 199. This time round, there were no casualties when the group was stopped.

All Parties Hurriyat Conference

Formation

The All Parties Hurriyat Conference (APHC), an alliance of secessionist parties and leaders, was formed on March 9, 1993 as a political front to further the cause of Kashmiri separatism. The amalgam has, since then, been consistently promoted by Pakistan in the latter's quest to establish legitimacy over its claim on the Indian State of Jammu and Kashmir.

The origins of the Hurriyat are traced to the 1993 phase of the Kashmir militancy. The initial euphoria of 'armed struggle' had subsided in the light of counter-insurgency operations launched by the Indian security forces. The Jammu and Kashmir Liberation Front (JKLF) with its pro-independence ideology had been marginalised and replaced by a network of Islamist extremist outfits controlled by the Inter-Services Intelligence (ISI), Pakistan's external intelligence agency.

Parallel to this, Pakistan was aggressively pursing an agenda of attempting to portray its proxy war against India as an indigenous uprising against Indian sovereignty and internationalise the Kashmir issue. It was in this context that the Hurriyat was formed as an umbrella body for all over-ground secessionist organisations. Since the international community frowned upon the resort to violence by non-state actors, the Hurriyat was an ideal platform to promote the Kashmiri secessionist cause.

Ideology and Role

According to the Hurriyat Conference, Jammu and Kashmir is a disputed territory and 'India's control' on it is not justified. It supports the Pakistani claim that Kashmir is the 'unfinished agenda of Partition' and needs to be solved 'as per the aspirations of the people of Jammu and Kashmir.'

The APHC perceives itself to be the sole representative of the Kashmiri people, a claim that has so far been endorsed explicitly only by Pakistan.

The outfit's primary role has been to project a negative image of counter-insurgency operations in Jammu and Kashmir and to mobilise public opinion against the Indian security forces. The alliance has consistently followed up local allegations of security force excesses, and in several documented cases, allegedly distorted facts to suit its propaganda. For instance, the Haigam firing incident of February 16, 2001 was portrayed as an assault on a peaceful gathering whereas, as later indicated in news reports and official clarifications, the army contingent fired upon the mob only when they were blocked and prevented from moving.

The APHC enjoys an observer's status in the Organisation of Islamic Conference (OIC). Incidentally, the OIC had dropped hard-line Hurriyat leader, Syed Ali Shah Geelani, from its guest list and instead invited Mirwaiz Umar Farooq for its June 2005 Foreign Ministers Conference in Yemen.

Split

There are currently two factions of the Hurriyat Conference led by Mirwaiz (a hereditary title of one of Kashmir's important religious seats, and also head priest of the Jamia Masjid in Srinagar) Umar Farooq and Syed Ali Shah Geelani. The Mirwaiz-led group, also referred to as the 'moderate faction' along with non-Hurriyat leaders like Yasin Malik undertook, between June 2-16, 2005, the first formal visit of Kashmiri separatists to Pakistan occupied Kashmir (PoK) and subsequently, though unsanctioned by Indian authorities, to Pakistan.

Internal fissures within the Hurriyat Conference had culminated in a formal split on September 7, 2003, with at least 12 of its 26 constituents 'removing' the then Chairman Maulana Mohammad Abbas Ansari and 'replacing' him with Massarat Alam as its interim chief. The dissenters reportedly met at the residence of hardliner and pro-Pakistan Jamaat-e-Islami (JeI) leader S. A. S. Geelani and decided to depose Ansari and 'suspend' the seven-member executive committee, the highest decision-making forum of the APHC. A five-member committee was formed to review the Hurriyat Constitution and suggest amendments to reverse what the dissenters perceive as 'autocratic' decisions taken by the executive committee.

Since then, Geelani has formed his own faction of the Hurriyat called the Tehreek-e-Hurriyat Jammu and Kashmir. On October 12, 2004 he was unanimously elected as its Chairman for a period of three years. A 25-member strong *Majlis-e-Shoora* (advisory council) to assist and advise the Chairman was also announced on the same day. A statement released by the faction said 21 members were elected to the 'shoora' and the Chairman was authorised to nominate four members. It also said all the 14 districts of the State were duly represented in the 'shoora,' the highest decision-making body of the outfit. The Geelani reportedly has 16 constituents.

Organisation

The alliance largely functions as a co-operative body with an Executive Council composing of seven members drawn from the main constituent outfits. The Executive Council is the highest decision-making authority. It currently comprises:

Name	Party
Mirwaiz Umar Farooq (Acting Chairman)	Awami Action Committee
Maulana Abbas Ansari	Ittihad-ul-Muslimeen
Bilal Ghani Lone	People's Conference
Prof. Abdul Ghani Bhat	Muslim Conference

Other important leaders of the APHC faction headed by the Mirwaiz are: Fazal Haq Qureshi of the People's Political Front, who is also a member of the General Council (which has eight members); Javid Ahmad Mir of the Jammu and Kashmir Liberation Forum; Syeda Nuzhat of the Khawateen-e-Kashmir; Chairman of the breakaway faction of the Democratic Freedom Party Syed Saleem Geelani; Mohammad Yousuf Naqash of the Islamic Political Party; Manan Bukhari of the Republican Party; Mohammad Amin Qureshi of the People's Political Conference; Khalil Ahmad Khalil of the People's Conference faction led by Bilal Lone (the other faction is led by his brother Sajad Lone); Tableegul Islam leader Bashir Kant; Allama Iqbal Students Union leader Abdul Manan; Amuatai-e-Islami leader Abdul Hamid Bhawani; Shahid-ul-Islam is the spokesperson.

Both factions are headquartered in Srinagar, capital of Jammu and Kashmir.

The Hurriyat Conference appointed Mirwaiz Umar Farooq as its caretaker chairman on August 8, 2004, saying efforts to unify the factions would continue. The decision was made at the Hurriyat's executive council meeting in Srinagar, attended by five general council members, invited especially for consultations. The executive council met for the first time to discuss the unification of the two factions after Maulana Abbas Ansari resigned on July 7, 2004.

APHC Constitution

(Version as adopted in March 1993)

The Constitution of the APHC says: "The APHC shall be a union of political, social, and religious parties of the state of Jammu and Kashmir with its head office in Srinagar."

It spells the objectives of the conglomerate as:

- To make peaceful struggle to secure for the people of Jammu and Kashmir the exercise of the right of self determination in accordance with the UN Charter and the resolutions adopted by the UN Security Council, however, the exercise of the right of self determination shall also include the right to independence.

- To make endeavour for an alternative negotiated settlement of the Kashmir dispute amongst all the three parties to the dispute India, Pakistan and people of the Jammu and Kashmir under the auspices of UN or any other friendly countries, provided that such settlement reflects the will and aspirations of the people of the state.
- To project ongoing struggle, in the state before the nations and governments of the world in its proper perspective as being a struggle directed against the forcible and fraudulent occupation of the state by India and for the achievement of the right of the self determination of its people.
- To make endeavour, in keeping with the Muslim majority character of the state, for promoting the build up of a society based on Islamic values, while safeguarding the rights and interests of the non-Muslims.
- To make endeavour for the achievements of any objectives which may be ancillary or incidental to the objectives specified above.

Structural Organisation

The Executive Council: The executive council shall consist of seven members from the seven executive parties. They are: Syed Ali Shah Geelani (Jamaat-e-Islami) Umar Farooq (Awami Action Committee), Sheikh Abdul Aziz (People's League), Moulvi Abbas Ansari (Ittihad-ul-Muslimeen), Prof. Abdul Gani Bhat (Muslim Conference), Yasin Malik (JKLF) and Abdul Gani Lone (People's Conference).

The chairman shall hold the office for two years. He shall vacate his office if he ceases to be a member of the executive council. He may at any time resign his office by submitting his resignation to the executive council.

General Council: It had more than 23 parties and organisations as members, including traders and employee unions. While the membership of the executive council as per the constitution can not be increased, the general council can accommodate more members if deemed so or if any party or organisation seeks membership.

Quorum: The quorum for the meetings in the executive council is four members.

Official Spokesman: The executive council may appoint one of its members as the official spokesman of the APHC to explain the view point if the APHC.

Finance: The executive committee shall also act as the finance committee of the APHC.

Constituents

(The original list of 26 parties)

1. Aawami Action Committee	**2.** Jamaat-e-Islami
3. Jammu and Kashmir People's Conference	**4.** Muslim Conference
5. Jammu & Kashmir Liberation Front	**6.** People's League
7. Ittihad-ul Muslimeen	**8.** All Jammu & Kashmir Employees' Confederation
9. Employees and Workers Confederation	**10.** Anjaman-e-Tablig-ul Islam
11. Liberation Council	**12.** Jamiat-e-Ahle Hadith
13. Kashmir Bazme Tawheed	**14.** Jamiat-e-Hamdania
15. Kashmir Bar Association	**16.** Political Conference
17. Tehreek-e-Huriati Kashmiri	**18.** Jamiate Ulama-E-Islam
19. Anjamani Auqafi Jama Masjid	**20.** Muslim Khawateen Markaz
21. Jammu and Kashmir Human Rights Committee	**22.** Jammu and Kashmir People's Basic Rights (Protection) Committee
23. Employees & Workers Confederation (Arsawi Group)	**24.** Students Islamic League
25. Islamic Study Circle	**26.** Auquaf Jama Masjid

Dukhtaran-e-Millat

An all-woman outfit, the Dukhtaraan-e-Millat (DeM) can be categorized as a soft-terrorist outfit in the sense that it uses extra-legal means including threats to impose its doctrines but has not taken to arms so far. The outfit, formed in 1987 has claimed that the Kashmir issue is primarily a religious issue and *jehad* is mandatory. It also supports the accession of the Kashmir valley with Pakistan. The DeM primarily operates in the Kashmir valley and its present strength is reported to be approximately 350.

The outfit has grabbed attention in spurts due to controversial remarks made by its leader, Ayesha Andrabi, particularly in the context of developments since year 2000. Of late, Ayesha Andrabi has been very vocal in supporting a new outfit named Lashkar-e-Jabbar (LeJ). This outfit has come into the news after its activists reportedly threw acid on two women in Srinagar on August 7 on the grounds that they were not dressed in 'Islamic' style. The Lashkar-e-Jabbar had first announced, that it would begin to use violence against Kashmir Muslims who were not dressed in their version of 'Islamic Dress Codes'. While supporting this, Ayesha Andrabi issued a press statement asking for an extension of this deadline to September 10, a request that was promptly acceeded. Later, in an interview published on September 9, she said that the current campaign was the "beginning of a comprehensive social reform movement based on true Islamic thought" and also asked women in Kashmir to stay away from government jobs. These reactions has led to speculation that the Lashkar-e-Jabbar could be a front for the DeM to renew its campaign directed at implementing its version of 'Islamic' social values.

The Dukhtaraan-e-Millat had also opposed recent peace intiatives in the State. It had rejected the cease-fire declared by Prime Minister A B Vajpayee and criticised persons and organisations that accorded a positive response to the cease-fire, going to the extent of calling upon foreign mercenary outfits such as the Lashkar-e-Toiba to take action against senior leader of the All Party Hurriyat Conference (APHC), Abdul Ghani Lone for his reported remarks against Islamic fundamentalist outfits.

Ayesha Andrabi, described as a conservative Muslim and radical feminist, leads this orthodox outfit. The outfit has sought to work in tandem with the insurgency which broke out in 1989. During the 1990's, the outfit was active in organising protests against Kashmiri women who did not adhere to the *burqa* (veil) system. In May 1993, the DeM issued warnings to the women in Srinagar not to venture outside their houses without wearing the veil. It also organises protests against the alleged display of objectionable literature in Jammu and Kashmir. Another issue that the outfit periodically raises is alleged excess of security forces conducting counter-insurgency operations in the State. It has regularly co-operated with the All Party Hurriyat Conference (APHC) in organising protest demonstrations on this issue. In June 2000, the DeM called for a strike against alleged custodial killings by the security forces in Jammu and Kashmir.

Security forces are yet to report any instances of terrorist strikes conducted by the DeM though they suspect that activists of the outfit act as couriers of arms and funds for various terrorist outfits operating in the State. The U.S State Department Report of 1995, held a Dukhtaran-e-Millat activist responsible for a parcel bomb blast at the BBC office in Srinagar in which one person was killed and another two injured.

The DeM has recently been linked to certain cases of money laundering. The Jammu & Kashmir Police in May 2002 while ascertaining an Islamabad-London-Srinagar linked hawala (illegal money transfer) network arrested Imtiaz Ahmed Bazaz of Batmaloo. Bazaz, editor and publisher of a Srinagar magazine Mountain Valley reportedly confessed that he had approached Ayub Thakur, the London-based president of World Kashmir Freedom Movement for funneling Inter Services Intelligence (ISI) funds to the Dukhtaran-e-Millat chief Andrabi.

Furthermore, cases have been registered under the Prevention of Terrorism Act (POTA) against Andrabi on charges of allegedly receiving money from the ISI through hawala channels. A massive search operation was launched on June 9, 2002 to arrest Andrabi, who has reportedly gone underground. This follows the arrest of Syed Ali Shah Geelani, former chairman of the separatist alliance All Party Hurriyat Conference (APHC) on June 9 from Srinagar under the Jammu and Kashmir Public Safety Act, 1978 for allegedly receiving money from the ISI through hawala channels and for later distributing the same to different terrorist groups, including the Hizb-ul-Mujahideen (HM). According to official sources, because Andrabi's husband Qasim Faktu was the financial chief of Jamait-ul-Mujahideen (JuM), she reportedly started getting money from Ayub Thakur through Imtiaz Bazaz to provide finances to JuM as well as the DeM.

J&K 2000

J&K continues to be the prominent hot-spot in the country. Even as Indian security forces have gained an upper hand in the battle against Pakistan-backed militants, a new dimension witnessed in 1999-2000 is suicide attacks by foreign militants on military bases in the state. This was after a downtrend of militant violence witnessed during the first half of 1999. The June-July 1999 clashes in the Kargil sector between the Indian army and infiltrators from Pakistan (mainly Pakistani army personnel and some militants, including mercenaries) mark a major development in the low-key proxy war being conducted by Pakistan against India.

The Kargil episode (which is viewed in Pakistan as a wasted golden opportunity to humble India in J&K) has the potential to encourage a fresh round of the low-intensity conflict in the region. The shadow of Kashmir militancy was evident in the hijacking of the Indian Airlines aircraft IC 814 in the last week of December which was resolved only after three militants were released from Indian jails and flown into Afghanistan, from where they returned to Pakistan. Of them, Maulana Masood Azhar, a Muslim cleric has publicly announced his desire to intensify his involvement in the Kashmir insurgency, strengthening the criticism that India is a soft state that is unable to give a firm response to militant intransigence.

The ground situation indicates that despite government efforts, the casualties of the J&K insurgency has increased in

1999 as compared to that in 1998 (2,538 and 2,261 respectively). This development reverses a declining trend whereby the casualties of this protracted conflict had begun declining after reaching a peak in 1996 (2,903 killed). More than a failure of the government's internal security strategies, this could be an outcome of increased activism by Pakistan's Inter-Services Intelligence (ISI). This activism has manifest itself in ISI-sponsored terrorist activities which have been spreading from their traditional zones of Punjab, J&K and the North-East to other regions of the country, particularly the capital, New Delhi, where several incidents of bomb blasts and arms seizures have been attributed to ISI agents. Similarly, there is a growing nexus between the ISI and other terrorist groups in India. The UP-Nepal border is now a major conduit point aimed at creating violent disruption in India.

The North-East, too, continues to be in turmoil even as more evidence of linkages between insurgent groups and the ISI emerges. While insurgency in Mizoram has largely subsided, security forces continue to battle with terrorism in Assam, Manipur, Nagaland and Tripura. Despite a cease-fire between the security forces and several insurgent groups in Nagaland there have been reports of violence. In a major development the General Secretary of the National Socialist Council of Nagaland—Isak-Muivah (NSCN-IM) Thuengaling Muivah was arrested in Bangkok on January 19, 2000 for travelling from Karachi on a false passport. This may prove to be a setback to the negotiations currently underway between the government and the NSCN-IM as the Karachi visit raises suspicions on the intentions of the NSCN-IM. At a time when Indian troops were battling in Kargil, the United Liberation Front of Assam (ULFA) was involved in providing details of troop movements to Pakistani intelligence. Also, the ULFA assassinated a State Minister.

Several initiatives made by the government in 1998 and the first half of 1999 to herald peace in strife torn areas are yet to fructify. While Assam saw a major decline in civilian and security personnel casualties during 1999 as compared to those in 1998 (291 and 603 respectively) there was an increase in the number of terrorists killed (212 and 180). The same was the case in Nagaland, while there was a marginal rise in civilian and security forces casualties in Tripura.

J&K 2001

Despite visible signs of improvement in certain theatres of conflict in the first three-quarters of 2001, the internal security situation in India continues to be critical. Even as the fall-out of the September 11 terrorist attacks on targets in the United States remains unclear for India, indigenous and cross-border terrorist violence in Jammu & Kashmir (J&K), insurgency and ethnic violence in the North East, left-wing extremist (Naxalite) movement in parts of Andhra Pradesh, Bihar, Jharkhand, Chhattisgarh, Madhya Pradesh, Maharashtra and Orissa, and violence perpetrated by the private armies in Bihar are problems that continue to fester. The proxy war unleashed by Pakistan through its support to various terrorist groups, and the activities of the Inter-Services Intelligence (ISI), Pakistan's external intelligence agency, in various parts of India, particularly in J&K, the Northeast and some Southern States, continues to remain the major factor in India's internal security scenario. Another serious dimension that poses an enormous challenge to the internal security scenario is the large-scale induction of lethal and sophisticated weapons, narcotics, and fake currency from across India's borders with Pakistan, Nepal, Bangladesh and Myanmar.

A negative fall-out that India is likely to face in the near future is the international community's changing perception of Pakistan. Strident diplomatic efforts by India, being conducted since the latter half of the Nineteen Nineties, had begun to pay dividends, when Pakistan was being globally perceived as a consistent supporter of cross-border terrorism. However, the scale and the complexity of September 11 terrorist attacks in US necessitated President George W. Bush to engage Pakistan as an ally in its campaign against international terrorism. Irrespective of the mutating US and the global community's perception of Pakistan as also its emergence as a 'frontline state' in the US efforts to eradicate Osama bin Laden and the Al Qaeda terror network, the ISI continues its policy of aiding terrorist outfits active in Jammu and Kashmir and other Islamist extremist outfits in other parts of India.

India has been countering a foreign sponsored Islamist terrorist network, active in J&K and other parts of the country, since the last decade. As India has consistently maintained that international cooperation is a necessity to deal with the scourge of Islamist terror, there was no hesitation in supporting the US-led international coalition against terrorism, launched after the September 11 attacks. While supporting the US-led military strikes against Osama bin Laden and his Al Qaeda network, the prime suspect in the September 11 terrorist attacks, and their sponsor, the Taliban regime in Afghanistan, India has also emphatically qualified that the war against terrorism should not be restricted to Osama bin Laden and the Taliban. A disquieting development is that in launching the offensive against the Taliban and bin Laden, the US led global alliance has co-opted Pakistan, a country which India identifies as the principal sponsor of terrorists and foreign mercenaries active in J&K.

Any effective strategy to counter the threat posed by the Islamist terrorist network needs to take into account Pakistan's role in creating and nurturing these forces and its relationship with the Taliban in Afghanistan. The Pakistani state and the Taliban have been co-sponsors of a terrorist network that essentially relies on *madrassas* (religious seminaries) and the training camps located in Pakistan and Afghanistan. Pakistan and Taliban have also shared the task of training and transforming these Islamist extremists into global terrorists. There is little evidence to construe that Pakistan has, despite US pressure, chosen to alter the perverted course of its history. Indeed, Pakistan's continuing support and succour to terrorism in J&K was propounded once again in the backdrop of the Jaish-e-Mohammed's (JeM) *fidayeen* (suicide) attack in Srinagar on October 1, 2001, in which 38 persons were killed. The JeM

Chief, Maulana Masood Azhar, who was released in exchange for the hostages aboard aircraft IC 814 in December 1999 in Kandahar, continues to move unhindered in Pakistan. Moreover, even as it redraws its strategy with the Taliban, its erstwhile protégé, the Pervez Musharraf regime has sought to continue providing legitimacy to foreign mercenaries initiating terrorist violence in Jammu and Kashmir as an 'indigenous freedom movement'. In the light of such contradictory policy formulations, the current US reliance on Pakistan would have far reaching critical consequences on South Asia's regional security environment in general and India in particular.

In the context of the global campaign against international terrorist networks, India has emphasised that Islamist terrorist violence being inflicted on Western and Indian targets emanate from the same Islamist extremist sources and are supported by common allies, Pakistan, bin Laden's Al Qaeda and the Taliban in Afghanistan and hence requires a multilateral response. Furthermore, India has consistently pointed out that any fight against international terrorism needs to effectually discern the relationship between Pakistan and international Islamist terrorist networks. Any attempt to ignore this issue in order to facilitate Pakistan as a 'frontline state' and retain its support in the current offensive against the Taliban, Osama bin Laden and his Al Qaeda network, would prove to be counterproductive in the long run.

J&K remains the most serious internal security challenge in the country despite significant peace measures initiated by the government in the year 2000-2001. The unilateral government cease-fire, which came into effect on November 28, 2000, was extended thrice and eventually withdrawn on May 23, 2001, having been in force for approximately six months. This failed to reduce the level of violence as statistics for this period show. All the Pakistan based terrorist outfits had rejected this initiative and stepped up their level of violence in an environment where security forces were ordered by the government to refrain from initiating any offensive operations against terrorists in the State.

While announcing the termination of the cease-fire, the government had also invited Pakistan's then Chief Executive and now President, General Pervez Musharraf, to visit India for a composite dialogue, including the Kashmir issue. Gen. Musharraf, who assumed his country's Presidency on June 20, 2001, arrived in New Delhi on July 14. The Agra Summit, which was held on July 15-16 2001, failed to produce a breakthrough in the context of J&K's terrorist violence. While Pakistan continued to emphasise on the historical background of the Kashmir 'dispute', India responded by focussing on the issue of cross-border terrorism supported and encouraged by Pakistan.

Earlier, the Union government released a statement on April 5, inviting all Kashmiri groups to participate in negotiations to find a solution to the Kashmir problem. K C Pant, Deputy Chairperson of the Planning Commission was appointed as the government's nominee for the proposed talks. This initiative too failed with the main over-ground secessionist outfit, the All Party Hurriyat Conference (APHC) refusing to join the negotiations on the grounds that it was not exclusively invited to the talks.

As a whole, all peace initiatives failed to change the ground situation and there was an escalation of terrorist violence in J&K. In the first ten month of 2001, 3066 people have been killed in terrorist violence which when compared to the 2774 deaths recorded in the first ten months of 2000, indicates that violence in this year may surpass that of 2000. These trends were only a continuation of the scenario in the year 2000. Casualties in terrorist violence increased to 3,288 in 2000, the highest figure for any year since the present phase of militancy began in 1988-89. There were 2,259 terrorism-related deaths in 1999.

J&K 2002

The US has exercised persistent pressure on Pakistan to curb cross-border infiltration of terrorists into J&K. Pakistan has declared that it would put an end to such infiltration 'permanently', but there is no clear evidence or stabilizing trends to suggest that there has been a fundamental shift in Pakistan's strategy in J&K. The Pakistani president, General Pervez Musharraf, in a televised address to the nation on January 12, 2002, had declared his government's commitment not to support or permit the use of its territory for terrorism anywhere in the world, including J&K, and this was a commitment he reiterated in his address to the nation on May 27. Available evidence, however, suggests that the Pakistani government continues its sponsorship of cross-border terrorism, and terrorism remains an instrument of its state policy.

Indian diplomatic pressure on Pakistan intensified after the May 14, 2002, *fidayeen* attack on an Army cantonment in Kaluchak, Jammu, in which 36 persons were killed and 48 others injured. India has been maintaining a major military build up along the borders with Pakistan since five terrorists of the Jaish-e-Mohammed (JeM) attacked India's parliament on December 13, 2001, and killed nine security force (SF) personnel and a parliament staff member. All the five terrorists were killed during the attack. Earlier, on October 1, 2001, JeM mercenaries attacked the J&K State Legislative Assembly complex in Srinagar and killed 36 people, including eight SF personnel and 24 others.

India has been countering a foreign primarily Pakistani sponsored Islamist terrorist network, active in J&K and other parts of the country, for over a decade, and has consistently maintained that international co-operation is necessary to deal with this menace. There was, consequently, no hesitation in supporting the US-led international coalition against terrorism. At the same time, India has been emphasizing that Islamist terrorist violence being inflicted on Western and Indian targets emanate from the same extremist sources and are supported by common allies, including Pakistan, the Al Qaeda network of Osama bin Laden, and a range of ideological affiliates not only across the Islamic world, but also now located in many of the Western nations. India also maintains that any fight against international terrorism will have to recognize the relationship between Pakistan and the networks of international Islamist terror. Though the US led global alliance has co-opted Pakistan as a 'frontline state' in its war on terror, available evidence suggests that Pakistan's Inter Services Intelligence (ISI) continues its policy of aiding terrorist outfits active in J&K and other Islamist terrorist outfits in other parts of India.

This is evident in J&K where, despite several peace initiatives and international pressure on Pakistan to abjure terrorism as a foreign policy instrument, terrorist violence has been sustained at high levels. As a result, between January 1 and August 4, 2002, a total of 1728 persons, including 1011 terrorists, 217 security force personnel and 500 civilians were killed in terrorist related violence in the State. In the year 2001, fatalities totalled 4507 persons, including 2850 terrorists, 1067 civilians and 590 security force personnel. This was only a continuation of the escalating trends in the year 2000, when peace initiatives failed to check the levels of violence. The trends indicate that the cosmetic changes within Pakistan in the post-9/11phase have failed to impress the *jehadi* groups operating in J&K.

In the aftermath of 9/11, links between the Al Qaeda, Taliban and terrorists in J&K are increasingly recognized by the global community. There is now overwhelming evidence that groups such as the Harkat-ul-Mujahideen (HuM), JeM and Lashkar-e-Toiba (LeT) had direct ideological, material and operational links with the Taliban and Al Qaeda.

Meanwhile, several peace initiatives were undertaken in 2001 in an effort to resolve the Kashmir issue 'politically'. Through an official statement on April 5, 2001, the Union government invited all Kashmiri groups to participate in negotiations to end the crisis. Two days prior to this, Union Home Minister L.K. Advani announced the nomination of K.C. Pant, Deputy Chairman of the Planning Commission, as the government's nominee for the proposed talks.

India and Pakistan's conflicting positions on the J&K insurgency had also been emphasised during the Summit meeting between Indian Prime Minister Atal Behari Vajpayee and President Musharraf during the latter's visit to New Delhi and Agra between July 14-16, 2001. While Pakistan, in the run-up to the Summit, continued to emphasise the territorial dispute and the façade of 'an indigenous freedom movement', India responded by fixing the focus on cross-border terrorism. As most analysts had foreseen, the Summit failed to change ground realities. 87 people were killed in J&K during the three days of the Summit meeting itself.

J&K 2006

Jammu and Kashmir: Since 2002, terrorism-related fatalities have demonstrated a secular decline in Jammu and Kashmir (J&K). Although the State continues to suffer from a substantial degree of violence and subversion, the military regime in Pakistan which was forced to scale down its proxy-war under intense international scrutiny momentarily has shown no indication of dismantling the vast terrorist infrastructure on its soil. Amidst the hype on people-to-people contacts and confidence-building measures (CBMs), the fact remains that the reduced levels of violence is primarily tactical. In the India-Pakistan calculus, there always exists a possibility of Islamabad seeking to up the ante in order to extort concessions from India.

There were 1732 terrorism-related deaths in J&K during 2005. Continuing with decline in violence, 873 people have died in year 2006 (till October 1). More than 40,000 people have lost their lives in the conflict since 1989, and even at present, an average of 100 lives is lost each month in J&K.

Even as talks between India and Pakistan continue under the aegis of the Composite Dialogue, terrorist violence in J&K, and sporadically in other parts of the India continue, even as Pakistan complains bitterly about the slow pace of 'progress' towards the goals it seeks to secure on the negotiating table, having failed to achieve these through a vicious campaign of terrorism over 17 years.

Fatalities in Terrorist Violence – 2006

Year	Civilians	Security Force Personnel	Terrorist	Total
2001	1067	590	2850	4507
2002	839	469	1714	3022
2003	658	338	1546	2542
2004	534	325	951	1810
2005	520	216	996	1732
*2006	285	125	463	873

***Data till October 1, 2006**
Source: Institute for Conflict Management database.

In realistic terms, it is clear that the process is headed nowhere and there is every likelihood of an eventual breakdown, transient or permanent. The reasons are not far to seek. First, the peace process remains, in substantial measure, tactical rather than substantive, with Pakistan in particular treating the negotiations as a parallel instrument to terrorism to exert pressure on India. Further, the hiatus between the rival positions on Kashmir is unbridgeable, and it is unsurprising, consequently, that the two sides are yet to commence substantive discussions on this issue. The restoration of communication links, people-to-people exchanges, Track Two diplomacy and a range of confidence building measures have all gone smoothly and have largely been successful. The Indian High Commission in Islamabad, for instance, issued 90,000 visas to Pakistanis in the year 2005 in comparison to 60,000 in 2004, a reflection of rising popular bonhomie. In particular, the bus services (Srinagar-Muzaffarabad and Amritsar-Lahore) and coordinated relief efforts in the aftermath of the October 2005 earthquake have been received well by people of both the countries. The ground situation in J&K, however, remains a cause for concern, with terrorism related killings and a continuous stream of infiltrators across the Line of Control (LoC) and international border, though the secular decline in levels of violence, which commenced after the 9/11 attacks in the US, has been sustained - albeit only marginally between 2004-2005.

Worse, terrorist attacks by Pakistan-backed groups have occurred in places as far as Mumbai, Delhi, Bangalore and Varanasi. Furthermore, arrests and seizures connected with Pakistan-backed terrorist groups across India, outside J&K and the Northeast, numbering at least 76 modules during the 2004-06 period indicate the level of penetration and subversion. These modules have been neutralised in locations that extend from Uttaranchal in the North, to Andhra Pradesh in the South, and from Gujarat in the West to West Bengal in the East. These terrorist modules were tasked to target security and vital installations, communication links, and commercial and industrial centres, as well as to provoke instability and disorder by circulating large quantities of counterfeit currency and by drug trafficking.

Meanwhile, the Prime Minister, Dr. Manmohan Singh, announced on May 25, 2006, the formation of five Working Groups to discuss various issues relating to Jammu and Kashmir. Addressing a press conference at the end of the two-day Roundtable Conference in Srinagar, he said that setting up of the Working Groups was the "best way to move forward and ensure that the views of different segments are incorporated." The Groups will deal with improving the Centre's relations with J&K, furthering the relations across the Line of Control (LoC), giving a boost to the State's economic development, rehabilitating the destitute families of militants and reviewing the cases of detainees and ensuring good governance. The Prime Minister also declared his Government's readiness to talk to terrorist groups if they gave up the path of violence. "Anybody who shuns violence and gives up the path of terror, we are willing to find ways and means to interact with all such groups," he said. On the issue of alleged human right violations by the security forces, he said, "our armed force is not an armed force of occupation. They have a proud record, though there could be some aberrations, but these aberrations cannot be allowed. There should be zero tolerance for human rights violations for all our security forces."

J&K 2007

Jammu and Kashmir: Since 2002, terrorism-related fatalities have demonstrated a secular decline in Jammu and Kashmir (J&K), and this trend continued in 2006, with a total of 1,116 persons killed. More than 40,000 people have lost their lives in the conflict since 1989, and, even at present, an average of nearly 100 lives is lost each month in J&K.

Fatalities in Terrorist Violence in Jammu and Kashmir

Year	Civilians	Security Force Personnel	Terrorist	Total
2001	1067	590	2850	4507
2002	839	469	1714	3022
2003	658	338	1546	2542
2004	534	325	951	1810
2005	520	216	996	1732
2006	349	168	599	1116
Source: Institute for Conflict Management database. (**Note:** Compiled from news reports and is provisional)				

Despite the declines in indices of violence, the State continues to suffer from high levels of violence and subversion. Pakistan's military regime, which was forced to scale down its proxy-war under intense international scrutiny, has nevertheless shown no indication of dismantling the vast infrastructure of terrorism on its soil. According to the Union Home Ministry's (MHA) "Status Paper on Internal Security Situation" (presented in Parliament on November 30, 2006), the terrorist infrastructure in Pakistan and Pakistan occupied Kashmir is yet to be dismantled and is being "used by Pak based and Pak ISI sponsored outfits like JeM [Jaish-e-Mohammed], LeT [Lashkar-e-Toiba], Al-Badr, HM [Hizb-ul-Mujahideen], etc."

Amidst the hype on people-to-people contacts and confidence-building measures (CBMs), it is evident that the reduced levels of violence in J&K primarily reflect a tactical rather than strategic shift in the Pakistani calculus, as a two-pronged strategy of parallel talks and terrorism is pursued by the Musharraf regime to secure its ambitions against India.

Talks between India and Pakistan thus continue under the aegis of the Composite Dialogue, even as terrorism in J&K, and sporadically in other parts of the India, persists. At the same time, Pakistan has been complaining bitterly about the slow pace of 'progress' towards the goals it seeks to secure on the negotiating table, having failed to achieve these through its vicious campaign of terrorism over 17 years. The peace process, consequently, remains, tactical rather than substantive, as the hiatus between the rival positions on Kashmir remains unbridgeable, and much of the 'progress' has been in peripheral areas, such as the restoration of communication links, people-to-people exchanges, Track Two diplomacy and a range of confidence building measures. At the same time, the ground situation in J&K remains a cause for concern, as a stream of infiltrators continues to find its way into the terror wracked State. While the various CBMs currently operational between the two countries may have strengthened processes of 'emotional enlistment', have failed to alter India's and Pakistan's stated positions on the Kashmir issue, or to change the fundamentals of the conflict in and over Kashmir. An end to the bloodshed in the State, consequently, seems as unlikely today as it was at any given point since the dramatic escalation of the militancy in 1989-90.

J&K 2010

The external factor remains critical, though the internal responses have had significant impact on insurgent trajectories in several theatres. On the J&K front, for instance, the comparative calm remains principally a consequence, not of any dramatic Indian initiatives or successes, but of Pakistan's growing internal difficulties and the overwhelming media and international focus on the support regional and international terrorism secures on that country's soil. Nevertheless, while the tap has been turned down, it is evident that the infrastructure of the anti-India *jihad* continues to be held in reserve by the Pakistani state, and the 'flow' of terrorism continues to be calibrated to synchronize with shifting Pakistani policies and perceptions. Significantly, 2009 saw a spurt in infiltration over 2008, the first time since 2002 that there has been a year-on-year increase. According to MHA data, there were 473 infiltration bids in 2009, as against 342 in 2008. Of these, 367 were thwarted, and 93 terrorists were 'neutralized' arrested or killed while 227 terrorists were forced back into Pakistan-held territories. Nevertheless, 110 terrorists are estimated to have managed to get into J&K, with an estimated 70 per cent foreign and 30 per cent local component. There is also mounting evidence of an escalation of tensions along the Line of Control (LoC) and International Border (IB), with Pakistani troops repeatedly firing on Indian Forces, usually to divert attention from or to facilitate terrorist infiltration. At least 28 incidents of ceasefire violation were recorded along the LoC in 2009.

With regard to the Pakistan-backed Islamist terrorism in J&K and across the wider Indian theatre, the most significant and potentially threatening unknown, in the medium and long term, remains the outcome of the US 'AfPak' enterprise. This is a project that has been hobbled by persistent incoherence, with each announcement of a 'surge' accompanied by unrealistic 'exit' deadlines that can only give encouragement to the enemy, and fuel greater violence. A possible failure of the AfPak campaigns threatens not only the descent of the entire target region into anarchy, but would have crucial consequences on India's internal security. A premature Western withdrawal from Afghanistan would restore the open alliance between the Pakistani state and the Islamist extremists to a "pre-9/11 plus" status, with even more virulent capacities and networks being directed outwards and substantially into India.

8

Terrorist Outfits in Jammu & Kashmir

LASHKAR-E-OMAR (THE ARMY OF OMAR)

Formation

Lashkar-e-Omar (LeO) is a new terrorist group reportedly founded in January 2002 and is a conglomerate of Harkat-ul-Jihad-i-Islami (HuJI), Lashkar-e-Jhangvi (LeJ) and Jaish-e-Mohammed (JeM) cadres. It was formed after the arrests of several front-ranking Islamist leaders in Pakistan following President Pervez Musharraf's address to the nation on January 12, 2002, in which he committed himself to dismantling the structures and networks of terrorism based in his country. The etymology of Lashkar-e-Omar is yet not clear. According to some reports, it is named after Mullah Mohammed Omar, chief of the Taliban militia. Other reports have indicated that the name is allegedly a direct homage to Syed Ahmed Omar Sheikh, a front-ranking JeM terrorist who was, on July 15, 2002, sentenced to life by an Anti-Terrorism Court in

Hyderabad, Sindh, for his role in the abduction-cum-murder of US journalist Daniel Pearl.

The LeO first came into prominence in November 2001 when it reportedly claimed responsibility for an attack on a church in Bahawalpur in Punjab. A police personnel and 17 Christians, including five children, were killed and nine others injured when six unidentified gunmen opened indiscriminate fire at a church in Model Town, Bahawalpur, on October 28, 2001.

Ideology

Their version of Islam is akin to that of the Taliban militia of Afghanistan. The LeO's ideological underpinning is a mixture of Islamist fundamentalism and totalitarian thinking.

Leadership and Structure

The LeO, according to media reports, was formed as a loose coalition of terrorists. While the group provides new cover for terrorist actions of LeJ, JeM and HuJI, it also includes several like-minded 'freelancers'. Omar Sheikh, currently in prison, and Amjad Hussain Faruqui of the HuJI, a fugitive accused in the Daniel Pearl case, are both closely linked to the LeO. They and their terrorist colleagues were associated with the various training camps in Afghanistan when the Taliban was in power there. Omar Sheikh was reportedly one of the instructors at one such camp. LeO cadres comprise of various Taliban members, certain Al Qaeda terrorists and terrorists from the HuJI, LeJ and JeM. Reports have indicated that Pakistani cadres of terrorist groups and Islamist parties allied with Osama bin Laden's International Islamic Front (IIF), who managed to survive the US air strikes in Afghanistan and crossed over into Pakistan, are also part of the LeO. According to a May 2002-report, the LeO consists of handpicked cadres of the HuJI, JeM and LeJ and was formed primarily to carry out 'punishment acts' of terrorism against Americans on Pakistani soil.

The Lashkar-e-Omar is reportedly headed by Qari Abdul Hai alias Qari Asadullah alias Talha, chief of the LeJ's Majlisi-Shoora (Supreme Council). Qari Asadullah reportedly formed his faction of the LeJ after parting ways with LeJ founder Riaz Basra in October 2000. Basra and three of his associates were killed in an encounter in Mailsi, Multan on May 14, 2002. According to a June-2002 media report, since the LeJ was proscribed, Qari Asadullah decided on the name Lashkar-e-Omar and also succeeded in incorporating terrorist cadres from other proscribed groups like the JeM and LeT into the new group.

The LeO is stated to be patterned after bin Laden's IIF. Besides, cells of the group comprising 5-15 cadres also exist. Therefore, according to official sources, it has become difficult to infiltrate such a homogenous group of motivated cadres. Most of the key members of the conglomerate are veterans of the 1980s jihad in Afghanistan against the erstwhile Soviet Union.

Operational Strategies and Linkages

Official sources have indicated that what makes Lashkar-e-Omar a serious threat is the fact that most of its cadres are members of the same class and camp trained by Amjad Faruqui. Faruqui, a HuJI terrorist, is wanted for his involvement in the murder of Pearl. LeO also has suicide cadres in its ranks. The LeO is allegedly involved in the suicide bombing outside the Sheraton Hotel in Karachi on May 8. In that incident, 14 persons, including 12 French nationals, were killed. Security agencies suspect that there exist more LeO *fidayeen* (suicide) squads and that these would target foreign nationals, particularly Americans and Britons residing in Pakistan.

The LeO has close linkages with the Al Qaeda and several terrorist groups active in the Indian State of Jammu and Kashmir. Karachi based Al-Rashid Trust (ART) is reportedly funding the Lashkar-e-Omar. The ART is one of the 27 groups and organisations listed by US State Department on September 22, 2001 for involvement in financing and supporting a network of international Islamist terrorist groups,

Activities and Incidents

- The Lashkar-e-Omar is suspected to be involved in the terrorist attack on a church in Model Town, Bahawalpur in Punjab on October 28, 2002, in which a police personnel and 17 Christians, including five children, were killed and nine others injured.
- It is reportedly closely linked to the abduction-cum-murder case of US journalist Daniel Pearl and JeM terrorist Omar Sheikh has been sentenced to life for involvement in this case.
- The group, according to official sources, is allegedly involved in the March 17, 2002 grenade attack on a church in the heavily guarded diplomatic enclave in Islamabad in which five persons, including a US diplomat's wife and daughter, were killed and 41 others injured.
- Besides, the LeO was reportedly involved in the suicide bombing outside the Sheraton Hotel in Karachi on May 8, 2002 and the June 14-attack on the US consulate in Karachi, in which 10 persons, including five women, were killed and 51 others injured.

HIZB-UL-MUJAHIDEEN

Of the terrorist outfits currently operating in Jammu and Kashmir (J&K), the Hizb-ul-Mujahideen (HM) is the one of the largest, with a cadre base drawn from indigenous and foreign sources. It is one of the most important terrorist outfits in terms of its effectiveness in perpetrating violence across the State at regular intervals. The HM is one of the 32 outfits proscribed under the Prevention of Terrorism Act, 2002.

Formation and Objectives

The HM came into being in the Kashmir Valley in September 1989 with Master Ahsan Dar as its chief. Dar was later arrested by security forces in mid-December 1993. It was reportedly formed as the militant wing of the Jamaat-e-

Islami (JeI), an Islamist organisation. The Jamaat-e-Islami is reported to have set up the Hizb at the behest of the Inter Services Intelligence (ISI), Pakistan's external intelligence agency, to counter the Jammu and Kashmir Liberation Front (JKLF), which had advocated complete independence of the State. Many of the early Hizb cadres were former JKLF members.

In June 1990, the HM 'Constitution' was approved and Mohammed Yusuf Shah, popularly known as Syed Salahuddin, was appointed Patron and Hilal Ahmed Mir as Amir (chief). Apparently, differences between JeI elements and the non-JeI faction started developing within the HM which led to a split with one faction being led by Salahuddin whereas the other was led by Hilal Ahmed Mir (killed in 1993).

The Hizb-ul-Mujahideen stands for the integration of J&K with Pakistan. Since its inception, the HM has also campaigned for the Islamisation of Kashmir.

Leadership, Command Structure and Areas of Operation

Headquartered at Muzaffarabad in Pakistan occupied Kashmir (PoK), the Hizb-ul-Mujahideen with an estimated cadre strength of at least 1500, is presently headed by Syed Salahuddin. The patron of HM in PoK is Ghulam Nabi Nausheri.

Ghazi Nasiruddin is the outfit's 'chief commander of operations' in the Kashmir Valley. He succeeded Saif-ul-Islam alias Ghulam Rasool Khan alias 'Engineer' Zaman, who was killed in a major counter-insurgency operation on April 2, 2003, at Nowgam Chowk, on the outskirts of capital Srinagar. Saleem Hashmi is the spokesperson of the outfit.

Currently, the HM is organised into five divisions: central division for Srinagar, northern division for Kupwara-Bandipora-Baramulla, southern division for Anantnag and Pulwama districts, Chenab division for Doda district and Gool in the Udhampur district, and Pir Panjal Division for the Rajouri and Poonch districts.

The HM has its own news agency, Kashmir Press International, and a women's wing, Banat-ul-Islam.

The Hizb reportedly has a substantial support base in the Kashmir Valley and in the Doda, Rajouri, Poonch districts and parts of Udhampur district in the Jammu region.

Internal Dynamics

The HM came into the spotlight when it's Salar-e-Ala or 'chief commander', Abdul Majeed Dar, made a conditional offer of cease-fire to the Indian Government at a press conference in Srinagar on July 24, 2000. The endorsement of this offer by the group's supremo Syed Salahuddin followed in an Islamabad press conference on July 25. On August 3, 2000, a high-level official team of the Government of India visited Srinagar and conducted a meeting with Dar and his associates at the Nehru Guest House. However, on August 8, 2000, Syed Salahuddin 'withdrew' the cease-fire at a press conference in Islamabad, reportedly under pressure from the other terrorist groups and their handlers in Pakistan.

On March 23, 2003, Majeed Dar was shot dead by unidentified gunmen in the Noor Bagh area of Sopore Township in north Kashmir when two gun-wielding youth barged into his ancestral house and fired indiscriminately. Two terrorist groups claimed responsibility for Dar's killing: the hitherto little-known, 'Save Kashmir Movement', believed to be a front of the Al Umar Mujahideen, while claiming responsibility, labeled Dar as "an informant of Indian agencies" and "an enemy of the Kashmiri people." Separately, a person describing himself as the spokesperson of Al Nasireen, another obscure group, in a message to a local news agency, said that activists of his group killed Dar for his 'anti-movement activities'. Meanwhile, another person claiming to be a spokesperson for the HM called up the news agency and condemned Dar's killing. Dar had been a front ranking terrorist in the HM before his 'expulsion' in May 2002. In his capacity as 'deputy supreme commander', 'Military adviser' and 'chief commander of operations', Dar played a significant role in the indoctrination, recruitment, launching and training of Hizb cadres. Reports suggest that, while managing the Hizb training camps in Pakistan, he was the only Kashmiri terrorist who had direct access to Prime Minister Nawaz Sharief as also General Pervez Musharraf.

Dar's killing is the culmination of an almost three-year old battle for supremacy being waged by his followers against the faction led by Syed Salahuddin, the HM 'supreme commander' and chief of the 14-member United Jehad Council (UJC), a conglomerate of Pakistan-based terrorist organisations. The Dar initiated 'peace talks' led to dissent within the Hizb, with the Pakistani ranks fearing that an effective process of negotiations may actually be established, to the detriment of Pakistani interests. Subsequently, a war for supremacy ensued within the HM, and a distinctive 'bimodal' operating structure emerged, with separate factions owing allegiance to Dar and Salahuddin. Since the ill-fated peace talks, followers of Salahuddin - who operates from Pakistan - and Majeed Dar, who remained 'underground' in the Kashmir Valley, had a series of internecine clashes. In November 2002, two Salahuddin loyalists were killed in factional conflict reported at the Mirpur and Tarbela camps in PoK. The Hizb leadership in Pakistan has also issued statements claiming Dar's alleged alignment with Indian intelligence agencies. Reports suggest that Dar had been disillusioned with the Pakistani Inter Services Intelligence (ISI) and its military leadership. Dar was 'suspended' by the Salahuddin faction and replaced by Saiful Islam as the Hizb 'chief commander of operations' in Kashmir, on May 4, 2002. Two of his close associates, Assad Yazdani and Zaffar Abdul Fatah, were also 'removed' from positions of command. Again, on May 9, 2002, the Hizb leadership expelled another two 'divisional commanders' in south Kashmir. Even as Dar and his associates were accused of assisting Indian security forces, many of his loyalists were killed by cadres of the Salahuddin group. Faced with Dar's rising popularity within the HM ranks, Salahuddin and the ISI had, in the recent months before the former's death, initiated several moves to marginalize and target Dar and his associates in the terrorist ensemble.

The Salahuddin faction is also widely believed to have carried out the January 31, 2003, killing of the editor of *News and Feature Alliance* (NAFA), Parvaz Mohammad Sultan, in Srinagar. NAFA had been prominently reporting on the internal feud in the HM for the preceding two weeks prior to Sultan's killing. The NAFA reports had mentioned that the Valley-based faction led by Dar had 'overthrown' the Salahuddin faction. Within hours of Majeed Dar's murder clashes broke out at HM camps in PoK between the slain leader's followers and the faction led by Salahuddin. Violent confrontations are believed to have taken place at camps in Kotli, Mirpur, Oggi, Jungal-Mangal, Haripur and Gadhi-Dupatta. Reports have indicated that Salahuddin was fidgety over the prospect of an imminent test of strength in the camps.

In a major counter-insurgency operation on April 2, 2003, HM 'chief commander of operations', Saif-ul-Islam was killed at Nowgam Chowk, on the outskirts of Srinagar. Within a span of 10 days, two front ranking cadres of the HM had been liquidated. An emergency meeting of the 'command council' of the HM in Muzaffarabad named Ghazi Nasiruddin as the new chief for Kashmir, to succeed Saif-ul-Islam, on April 3. However, sources indicate that a process of churning is underway within the HM and its guardians in Pakistan. The HM has for long been regarded as having a considerable number of Kashmiris in its ranks. However, the relative dominance of foreign cadres within the HM has, in the past, progressively impaired the operational capacity of the group. Strained relations between local and foreign cadres have, at times, culminated in violent clashes in some places. Prior to his elevation as the 'chief commander', next only to chief Syed Salahuddin, Saif-ul-Islam had functioned as a 'divisional commander' in south Kashmir for seven years. When Salahuddin removed Abdul Majeed Dar and some 'divisional commanders' loyal to him in January 2002, Saif-ul-Islam was installed as 'chief commander of operations'. Dar had fallen out of favour with Salahuddin and the ISI ever since he announced an ill-fated cease-fire in July 2000.

Media reports have indicated that, two months prior to his death, Pakistani intelligence officials had been urging Majeed Dar to return to Pakistan. Although the Salahuddin-led faction was hostile to Dar, the ISI was keen on a rapprochement. More important, Dar believed that American pressure on Pakistan to move forward with the dialogue process would ensure his safety. But, subsequent events have proved otherwise and the recent killings have led to a split in the HM, with followers of the slain Dar saying that they were parting ways with 'supreme commander' Salahuddin. "We have launched our own faction of Hizbul Mujahideen," Tufail Ahmed, a former 'operational chief' of the Hizb, and Dar supporter said in a March 27, 2003, report. Ahmed is the younger brother of Zafar Abdul Fateh, who was expelled along with Majeed Dar by Salahuddin in May 2002. He claimed that commanders of the new faction on both sides of the border had 'unanimously' appointed Ahmed Yasin as their 'chief commander'. "Around 40 per cent of the Hizb activists are with us," claimed Ahmed.

The two Hizb factions have often blamed each other for the arrest and deaths of their leaders in J&K. Seven Hizb 'chief operational commanders' have been killed in J&K since 1989, according to the *Daily Times*. They include Ahsan Dar, Ashraf Dar, Maqbool Allai, Commander Baangro, Naseerul Islam, Masood Nantary, and Abdul Majeed Dar. Barring Majeed Dar, all these 'commanders' were killed in encounters with the Indian security forces. Saif-ul-Islam's name now also belongs to this list. At least two of these 'commanders' were reportedly killed after they formed splinter Hizb factions.

Links

The HM is closely linked to the Jamaat-e-Islami, both in the Kashmir Valley and in Pakistan. Overseas, it is allegedly backed by Ghulam Nabi Fai's Kashmir American Council and

Ayub Thakur's World Kashmir Freedom Movement in the USA. Early in its history, the Hizb had established contacts with Afghan Mujahideen groups such as Hizb-e-Islami, under which some of its cadre is alleged to have received arms training.

The HM is reported to have a close association with the Pakistani Inter Services Intelligence and the United Jehad Council, and other terrorist organizations operating out of Pakistan. Hizb chief Syed Salahuddin also heads the UJC.

The proscribed Students Islamic Movement of India (SIMI) is also believed to have links with the Hizb-ul-Mujahideen.

LASHKAR-E-TOIBA
'Army of the Pure'

Formation

Formed in 1990 in the Kunar province of Afghanistan, the Lashkar-e-Toiba (also known as Jama'at-ud-Da'awa) is based in Muridke near Lahore in Pakistan and is headed by Hafiz Muhammad Saeed.

Its first presence in Jammu and Kashmir (J&K) was recorded in 1993 when 12 Pakistani and Afghan mercenaries infiltrated across the Line of Control (LoC) in tandem with the Islami Inquilabi Mahaz, a terrorist outfit then active in the Poonch district of J&K.

1. Proscription: The LeT is outlawed in India under the Unlawful Activities (Prevention) Act.

It was included in the Terrorist Exclusion List by the US Government on December 5, 2001. The US administration designated the Lashkar-e-Toiba as a FTO (Foreign Terrorist Organization) on December 26, 2001. It is also a banned organization in Britain since March 30, 2001.

The group was proscribed by the United Nations in May 2005.

The military regime of Gen. Pervez Musharraf banned the Lashkar-e-Toiba in Pakistan on January 12, 2002.

2. Objectives/Ideology: The LeT's professed ideology goes beyond merely challenging India's sovereignty over the State of Jammu and Kashmir. The Lashkar's 'agenda', as outlined in a pamphlet titled Why are we waging jihad includes the restoration of Islamic rule over all parts of India. Further, the outfit seeks to bring about a union of all Muslim majority regions in countries that surround Pakistan. Towards that end, it is active in J&K, Chechnya and other parts of Central Asia.

Hafiz Saeed, a scholar of Islam, has said that the purpose of Jihad is to carry out a sustained struggle for the dominance of Islam in the entire world and to eliminate the evil forces and the ignorant. He considers India, Israel and US to be his prime enemies and has threatened to launch Fidayeen (suicide squad) attacks on American interests too.

The Lashkar-e-Toiba does not believe in democracy and nationalism. According to its ideology, it is the duty of every 'Momin' to protect and defend the interests of Muslims all over the world where Muslims are under the rule of non-Muslim in the democratic system. It has, thus chosen the path of Jihad as the suited means to achieve its goal. Cadres are drawn from the Wahabi school of thought.

Jihad, Hafiz Saeed said during the All Pakistan Ulema Convention held on July 17, 2003, at Lahore, is the only way Pakistan can move towards dignity and prosperity.

The LeT has consistently advocated the use of force and vowed that it would plant the 'flag of Islam' in Washington, Tel Aviv and New Delhi.

3. Leadership and Command Structure: The outfit's headquarters (200 acres) is located at Muridke, 30 kms from Lahore, which was built with contributions and donations from the Middle East, with Saudi Arabia being the biggest benefactor.

The headquarters houses a Madrassa (seminary), a hospital, a market, a large residential area for 'scholars' and faculty members, a fish farm and agricultural tracts. The LeT also reportedly operates 16 Islamic institutions, 135 secondary schools, an ambulance service, mobile clinics, blood banks and several seminaries across Pakistan.

LeT publishes its views and opinion through its Website (http://www.jamatuddawa.org/), an Urdu monthly journal, Al-Dawa, which has a circulation of 80,000, and an Urdu weekly, Gazwa. It also publishes Voice of Islam, an English monthly, and Al-Rabat - monthly in Arabic, Mujala-e-Tulba - Urdu monthly for students, Jehad Times - Urdu Weekly.

Hafiz Muhammad Saeed is the Amir (chief) of Lashkar-e-Toiba. While Yahiya Mujahid serves as the spokesman of the outfit, Maulana Abdul Wahid is one of the senior leaders. Abdullah Muntazer is the 'Spokesman for International Media' and editor of the outfit's Website. Saeed's son Talha reportedly looks after the LeT activity at its base camp in Muzaffarabad, capital of Pakistan occupied Kashmir. Saeed's son-in-law, Khalid Waleed, is reportedly part of the LeT office in Lahore.

According to a November 2005 report of Rediff, the LeT leadership consisted of: Hafiz Mohammed Saeed (Supreme Commander); Zia-Ur-Rehman Lakhvi alias Chachaji (Supreme Commander, Kashmir); A. B. Rahman-Ur-Dakhil (Deputy Supreme Commander); Abdullah Shehzad alias Abu Anas alias Shamas (Chief Operations Commander, Valley); Abdul Hassan alias MY (Central Division Commander); Kari Saif-Ul-Rahman (North Division Commander); Kari Saif-Ul-Islam (Deputy Commander); Masood alias Mahmood (Area Commander, Sopore); Hyder-e-Krar alias CI (Deputy Commander, Bandipora); Usman Bhai alias Saif-Ul-Islam (Deputy Commander, Lolab); Abdul Nawaz (Deputy Commander, Sogam); Abu Rafi (Deputy Divisional Commander, Baramulla); Abdul Nawaz (Deputy Commander, Handwara); Abu Museb alias Saifulla (Deputy Commander, Budgam);

Its cadres are organised at district levels with 'district commanders' in charge. Within Pakistan, the outfit has a network of training camps and branch offices, which undertake recruitment and collection of finances.

It comprises cadres mostly from Pakistan and Afghanistan and a sprinkling of militants from Sudan, Bahrain, Central Asia, Turkey and Libya. Funded, armed and trained by the Inter-Services Intelligence (ISI, the external intelligence agency of Pakistan), it has presently a little over 750 cadres (this number keeps changing) in Jammu and Kashmir (a vast majority of the foreign mercenaries operating in the Valley).

The policy making apex body consists of Amir (chief), Naib Amir (deputy chief) Finance chief etc. At the field level, it has Chief Commander, Divisional Commander, District Commander, Battalion Commander and down below on army pattern.

4. Area of Operation: While the primary area of operations of the Lashkar-e-Toiba is Jammu and Kashmir, the outfit has carried out attacks in other parts of India, including in New Delhi, Mumbai, Bangalore, Hyderabad, Varanasi, Kolkata, Gujarat, etc. It reportedly has cells in many cities/towns outside Jammu and Kashmir.

The LeT has been able to network with several Islamist extremist organizations across India, especially in J&K, Andhra Pradesh, Tamil Nadu, Karnataka, Maharashtra and Gujarat. LeT is actively engaged in subversive activities in the States of Maharashtra, West Bengal, Bihar, Hyderabad, Delhi, Haryana and Uttar Pradesh at the instance of ISI to expand the frontier of violence outside J&K by subverting fringe elements. Of all the Pakistan-based terrorist groups, the LeT is the only group with support bases across India.

The Lashkar-e-Toiba has training camps spread across Pakistan and Pakistan occupied Kashmir (PoK). Its camps, recruitment centres/offices are spread across the length and breadth of Pakistan and PoK in Muzaffarabad, Lahore, Peshawar, Islamabad, Rawalpindi, Karachi, Multan, Quetta, Gujranwala, Sialkot, Gilgit (in the Northern Area of PoK), etc. LeT reportedly has 2,200 offices across Pakistan.

The LeT allegedly carried out the terrorist attack at the Indian Institute of Science campus in Bangalore on December 28, 2005, in which one person was killed; Earlier, on October

29, 2005, it engineered the serial explosions in New Delhi killing at least 62 persons; It is also suspected to have carried out the Varanasi attack on March 7, 2006 in which 21 civilians died and 62 others were injured; Three suspected LeT terrorists were shot dead during an abortive attempt to storm the headquarters of Rashtriya Swayamsevak Sangh (RSS), a right-wing Hindu organization, at Nagpur in Maharashtra on June 1, 2006; The LeT, according to Mumbai Police, carried out the 7/11 serial bombings in Mumbai in which at least 200 people were killed.

Arrests made during March-April 2004 near Baghdad brought to light links between the LeT and Islamist groups fighting the United States military in Iraq. In March - and possibly even earlier - United States forces detained Pakistani national Dilshad Ahmad and four others in Baghdad. Ahmad, a long-time Lashkar operative from the Bahawalpur area of the province of Punjab in Pakistan, had played a key role in the Lashkar's trans-Line of Control (LoC) operations, serving between 1997 and 2001 as the organisation's commander for the forward camps from where infiltrating groups of terrorists are launched into Jammu and Kashmir with Pakistani military support. Ahmad is believed to have made at least six secret visits to Lashkar groups operating in J&K during this period.

5. Training and Operational Strategies: The outfit provides training to both militant cadres and the Ulema (religious scholars). Its militant cadres are given two months training in the handling of AK series rifles, LMGs, pistols, rocket launchers and hand grenades. It also provides a 21-day training programme called Daura-e-Aam and a three months specialized training programme called Daura-e-Khas.

The Ulema are provided with a 42-days course. At the time of induction, the young recruits are made to go through a fresher course called Bait-ur-Rizwan.

Lashkar-e-Toiba is credited for having initiated the strategy of Fidayeen (suicide squad) attacks in J&K. It has formed two sub-groups called 'Jaan-e-Fidai' and 'Ibn-e-Tayamiah'. While the first group consists of highly motivated terrorists, the second comprises terrorists suffering from incurable diseases.

Compared to other terrorist outfits in J&K, the LeT has commanded significant attention primarily due to two reasons. First, for its well planned and executed attacks on security force (SF) targets and secondly, for the massacres of non-Muslim civilians. After the Kargil war of May-July 1999, (when Pakistani troops and mercenaries, including those of the Lashkar, were forced to withdraw from peaks on the Indian side of the Line of Control - LoC), the outfit launched its Fidayeen strategy whereby small groups (2-5 members) of Lashkar cadres would storm a security force camp or base. In another frequently used strategy, groups of Lashkar cadres, dressed in SF fatigues, would arrive at remote hill villages, round up Hindu or Sikh civilians, and massacre them. These two strategies have been designed to achieve maximum publicity and extract public allegiance, mainly out of fear. On December 8, 2001, two LeT suicide squad cadres managed to penetrate inside a SF convoy and opened fire killing one soldier. They were able to generate adequate confusion to escape from the convoy after the attack but were later killed in an encounter with another SF unit.

6. Links: India's National Security Adviser M. K. Narayanan said on August 11, 2006, that the Pakistan-based Lashkar-e-Toiba is part of the "al Qaeda compact" and is "as big as and omnipotent" as the international terror network. "The Lashkar today has emerged as a very major force. It has connectivity with west Asia, Europe.Actually there was an LeT module broken in Virginia and some people were picked up. It is as big as and omnipotent as al Qaeda in every sense of the term," he told a private news channel. Asked how significant the al Qaeda connection was in India, Narayanan said LeT was the "most visible manifestation" of the al Qaeda in India.

LeT has an extensive network that run across Pakistan and India with branches in Saudi Arabia, United Kingdom, Bangladesh and South East Asia.

The outfit collects donations from the Pakistani community in the Persian Gulf and United Kingdom, Islamic Non-Governmental Organisations, and Pakistani and Kashmiri businessmen. It receives considerable financial, material and other forms of assistance from the Pakistan government, routed primarily through the ISI. The ISI is the main source of LeT's funding. Saudi Arabia also provides funds.

The LeT maintains ties to various religious/military groups around the world, ranging from the Philippines to the Middle East and Chechnya primarily through the al Qaeda fraternal network.

The LeT has also been part of the Bosnian campaign against the Serbs.

It has allegedly set up sleeper cells in the U.S. and Australia, trained terrorists from other countries and has entered new theatres of Jihad like Iraq.

The group has links with many international Islamist terrorist groups like the Ikhwan-ul-Musalmeen of Egypt and other Arab groups.

LeT has a unit in Germany and also receives help from the Al Muhajiraun, supporter of Sharia Group, (Abu Hamza Masari- of Mosque Finsbury Park, North London) and its annual convention is regularly attended by fraternal bodies in Saudi Arabia, Kuwait, Yemen, Bahrain, Oman, Kosovo, Bangladesh, Myanmar, USA, Palestine, Bosnia, Philippines, Jordan, Chechnya, etc.

It also has links with the International Sikh Youth Federation (Lakhbir Singh Rode).

7. Links: The outfit collects donations from the Pakistani community in the Persian Gulf and United Kingdom, Islamic Non-Governmental Organisations, and Pakistani and Kashmiri businessmen. It receives considerable financial, material and other forms of assistance from the Pakistan government, routed primarily through the ISI. The ISI is the main source of LeT's funding. Funds also come from some sources in Saudi Arabia.

Finances are also generated through Hawala transaction and through infiltrating groups and other conduits.

According to Mohammad Omar Rana, the expenditure on its militia alone is around 35 crores of rupees per annum.

8. Weaponry: AK series rifles, LMG/HMG's, Hand Grenades, Rockets, Pistols, Mortars, Anti-tank mines, Anti personnel mines, Anti Aircraft Gun, Remote Control Device, explosive devices and sophisticated communication system.

JAISH-E-MOHAMMED
(Army of the Prophet)

The Jaish-e-Mohammed (JeM) has been held responsible for the December 13, 2001 terrorist attack on the Indian Parliament in New Delhi. The outfit has been banned by the Indian government under provisions of the Prevention of Terrorism Act (POTA) on October 25, 2001. The US Secretary of State, Colin Powell, in a notification on December 26, 2001, designated the outfit as a foreign terrorist organistation.

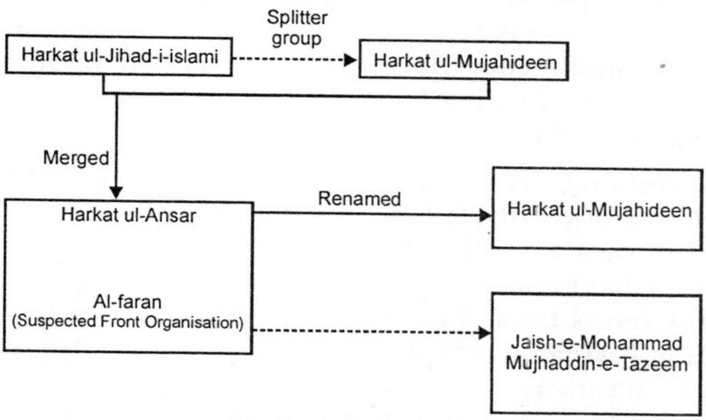

Evolution of Group

1. Formation: The Jaish-e-Mohammed (JeM) is a relatively new terrorist outfit, compared to other major outfits active in Jammu and Kashmir (J&K). Like the Lashkar-e-Toiba (LeT), the JeM too is an outfit formed, controlled and manned by

Pakistan. The outfit was launched on January 31, 2000, by Maulana Masood Azhar in Karachi after he was released from an Indian jail during the terrorists for hostage swap of December 31, 1999, following the hijacking of the Indian Airlines Flight IC 814.

The formation of the outfit was endorsed by three religious school chiefs, Mufti Nizamuddin Shamzai of the Majlis-e-Tawan-e-Islami (MT), Maulana Mufti Rashid Ahmed of the Dar-ul Ifta-e-wal-Irshad and Maulana Sher Ali of the Sheikh-ul-Hadith Dar-ul Haqqania.

The outfit's creation can be linked to the popularity surrounding Masood Azhar after his release from India. Maulana Masood Azhar was the general secretary of the newly established Harkat-ul-Ansar (HuA) in 1994 and was on a 'mission' in J&K when he was arrested on February 11. When he was released, the HuA had been included in the US list of Foreign Terrorist Organisations which had compelled the outfit to rename itself as the Harkat-ul-Mujahideen (HuM). However, Masood Azhar decided to float the new outfit JeM rather than rejoin his old outfit. He was also reported to have received assistance in setting up the JeM from Pakistan's Inter-Services Intelligence (ISI), the then Taliban regime in Afghanistan, Osama bin Laden and several Sunni sectarian outfits of Pakistan.

2. Objectives: The Jaish-e-Mohammed is part of the Islamist terror network with its base in Pakistan and active in the terrorist violence in J&K. The outfit, like other terrorist outfits in J&K, claims to using violence to force a withdrawal of Indian security forces from J&K. The outfit claims that each of its offices in Pakistan would serve as schools of jihad. Delivering speeches at various cities and towns in Pakistan after his release, Masood Azhar threatened that the outfit would eliminate Indian Prime Minister Atal Behari Vajpayee who he termed as 'Abu Jahl' (Father of Ignorance). In its fight against India, he added that the outfit would not only "liberate" Kashmir, but also would take control of the Babri Masjid in Ayodhya, Amritsar and Delhi.

3. Leadership and Command Structure: Masood Azhar, the *Amir* (chief) of the outfit was arrested by Pakistani security forces on December 29, 2001, after pressure from India and other foreign countries following the December 13, 2001 attack on India's parliament. However, a three-member Review Board of Lahore High Court ordered on December 14, 2002, that Azhar be released.

There are no reports of any formal governing bodies or councils within the outfit. Unconfirmed reports indicate that the prominent office bearers of the organisation include

a. Maulana Masood Azhar – Amir
b. Maulana Qari Mansoor Ahmed – Nazim Propaganda Wing (he is a resident of Bhurewala, Punjab)
c. Maulana Abdul Jabbar – Nazim, Military Affairs (Former Nazim military affairs, (HuM)
d. Maulana Sajjad Usman – incharge, Finance (Former HuM Nazim Finance)
e. Shah Nawaz Khan alias Sajjid Jehadi & Gazi Baba – Chief Commander J&K (Former Supreme Commander HuM, J&K)
f. Maulana Mufti Mohd. Asghar – Launching Commander (Former Launching Commander of HuM)

4. Operational Strategies: Most Jaish-e-Mohammed attacks have been described as *fidayeen* (suicide terrorist) attacks. In this mode, terrorists of the outfit storm a high security target, including security forces' bases, camps and convoys. After storming, they either fortify themselves within the target, killing as many security force personnel and civilians as possible before they are killed by retaliatory action. In other cases, they kill and injure as many as possible before attempting to escape.

5. Area of Operation: The Jaish-e-Mohammed has largely confined its operations within J&K. The only recorded instance of its operations outside J&K has been the December 13, 2001, Parliament attack in New Delhi. However, several of its cadre have, on occasions been arrested or killed by security forces in states other than J&K.

6. External Linkages: The outfit is closely linked, through the Binoria Madrassah in Karachi, with the former Taliban regime of Afghanistan and its Portege,Osama bin Laden and his Al-Qaeda. JeM chief, Masood Azhar was released by Indian authorities in Kandahar and has reportedly met Taliban and Al Qaeda leaders in Afghanistan on various occasions.

The JeM is also reported to have links with Sunni terrorist outfits operating in Pakistan such as the Sipah-e-Sahaba Pakistan (SSP) and Lashkar-e-Jhangvi (LeJ).

7. Major Incidents:

2010

- **July 30:** The CID of the Sindh Police arrested two persons allegedly associated with the JeM at Shershah area in Karachi. The arrested persons were identified as Mohammad Rizwan and Mohammad Daud. Two TT pistols and several rounds of ammunitions were recovered from their possessions. CID (Investigations) Superintendent of Police Mazhar Mashwani said that both militants are affiliated with the JeM, and accused of providing shelter and weapons to their other associates.
- **June 16:** A JeM, identified as Owais, cadre was shot dead by unidentified assailants in Karachi in Sindh

2009

- **December 9:** Security Agencies arrested six people, three foreigners among them, for their alleged links with banned religious outfit Jaish-i-Mohammed and for planning a terrorist attack in Sargodha of Punjab. Among the suspects were two Egyptians, one Yemeni, two Pakistani-Americans and a local. Sources said that these five militants were arrested from the house of one of the suspects in Aziz Bhatti Town. Two computers and some jihadi literature were recovered. The Pakistani-Americans were identified as Omer Farooq and Waqar.
- **November 22:** Out of the two infiltrators killed by the Army at Balakote sector on November 21, one of them

has been identified as a youth from Rajouri District, absconding from his house since October 2002. The SFs are reported to have recovered two Pakistani SIM cards from the possession of the slain militants. He was reportedly absconding from his house since October 4, 2002 and was said to have crossed over to Pakistan. He was associated with the Jaish-e-Mohammed (JeM) outfit and underwent training in different camps in PoK and Pakistan.

- **November 21:** An infiltration bid was foiled by the SFs, killing two intruders and forcing their associates to retrieve to Pakistan occupied Kashmir (PoK) in the Balakote sector of Poonch District. However, in the process, one trooper was also killed and two others injured. Intercepts revealed that a group of five to seven militants of JeM outfit were launched from Dandot area of PoK (half of Dandot village falls in PoK) in the night of November 20 by Pakistan Army, which fired on the Indian posts at Tarkundi, adjacent to Dandot, to give covering fire to the militants and engage troops in firing to divert their attention from intrusion. One Pika gun, one AK-47 rifle fitted with an Under Barrel Grenade Launcher, one 12 bore gun, a binocular, one Improvised Explosive Device, one grenade, six AK magazines, two medicine kits and some eatables were recovered from the possession of the slain militants. The slain trooper was identified as Rifleman Suresh Kumar of Rajasthan Rifles (7th Battalion).
- **October 29:** Two Pakistani militants of the Jaish-e-Mohammed (JeM) outfit, including a 'divisional commander' and his body-guard, were killed inside the house where they had been trapped since October 28-night at Sarhuti Top in the Mendhar *tehsil* (revenue unit) of Poonch District in the early hours of October 29. A Government teacher, Mohammad Mushtaq, who had reportedly given shelter to the militants in his house, has been arrested by the Police. The house was completely destroyed in the fire as explosives stored

inside caught fire after being hit by rocket launchers leading to a major blaze. The slain militants were identified as 'divisional commander' Abdul Sattar *alias* Babbar *alias* Omar and his body-guard Shahid Khan *alias* Shahid. Recoveries made from the encounter site include two AK-47 rifles, one Chinese pistol, one wireless set and two AK magazines. According to official sources, Babbar was operating in the twin border districts of Poonch and Rajouri for the last eight years. He was among the militants present in Bhatti Dhar forests encounter in Poonch which had lasted for 11 days from January 1, 2009. Sources also said Babbar was second-in-command after the Jaish chief for Poonch and Rajouri Districts, Dawood, who had been headquartered at Pir Panjal range.

- **September 28:** A young duo of brother and sister shot dead a Jaish-e-Mohammed (JeM) 'commander' Osama, a Pakistani, and injured his two associates and also snatched two AK rifles of the militants while thwarting an attack on their house at Upper Shahdara Sharief in the Kalsian area of Rajouri District in the night of September 27. In the scuffle, two brothers, who were a target of the militants, were also injured. Police sources and eye-witness account revealed that three militants, including Osama, knocked at the house of Gujjar Noor Ahmad at 9pm and also dragged out Vakalat Hussain, Noor's younger brother living adjacent and forced their entry inside Noor''s house. After questioning the two brothers, the militants assaulted 46-year old Noor Ahmed, his wife, Rashida Begum and Vakalat Hussain, describing them as agents of the SFs. In the meantime, Noor's 20-year old son Aijaz Ahmad attacked Osama on his head from the back while 17-year old Ruksana fired from an AK-47 rifle of the militant. Osama was killed on the spot. The brother-sister duo also managed to snatch another AK rifle from the militant and also assaulted the two other militants, who escaped in an injured condition.

- **September 25:** Police arrested a JeM militant from the Bus Stand area of Jammu city and recovered *hawala* (informal money laundering system) money, mobile handsets and SIM cards from his possession. The militant, identified as Zubair Ahmad, a resident of Mendhar town in Poonch District, was arrested soon after he reached the city from Mendhar. Zubair was a close associate of the JeM 'divisional commander' Dawood Ahmed, presently operation from Mendhar.
- **September 13:** The JeM has walled off a 4.5-acre compound outside Bahawalpur in the Punjab province of Pakistan. However, a report added that authorities have ignored the construction despite reports that the compound might be a radical *madrassa* (seminary) or training camp, with senior Police officials claiming there is no militancy problem in southern Punjab.
- **September 6:** The Police shot dead a Pakistani militant of the Jaish-e-Mohammad (JeM), Chota Saad *alias* Umair, and arrested a District commander of the outfit, Ishfaq Ahmad Sofi *alias* Ishfaq, during two related anti-militancy operations in the Sopore area of Baramulla District. Two AK-47 rifles, one hand grenade and some ammunition were recovered from the encounter site. Official sources the two militants were involved in carrying out series of grenade attacks in Sopore town, including one on August 10, 2009 on Central Reserve Police Force camp at Plaza Hotel Sopore in which one shopkeeper was killed. They were also involved in several grenade attacks in Srinagar City, besides killing Reshma Jan *alias* Zahida on June 16, 2009 in model town of Sopore.
- **August 5:** The Government announced that 25 extremist and militant groups and welfare organisations affiliated to them have so far been banned because of their involvement in terrorist activities. In a written reply submitted on August 5 in response to a question in the National Assembly,

Interior Minister Rehman Malik said the banned organisations included Al Qaeda, SMP, Tehrik Nifaz-i-Fiqah Jafaria, SSP, JuD, Al Akhtar Trust, Al Rasheed Trust (ART), Tehrik-i-Islami, JeM, LeJ, TTP, Islamic Students Movement, Khairun Nisa International Trust, Tehrik-i-Islam Pakistan, Tehreek-e-Nafaz-e-Shariat-e-Mohammadi (TNSM), LeT, Lashkar-i-Islam, Balochistan Liberation Army, Jamiat-i-Ansar, Jamiatul Furqan, Hizbut Tehrir, Khuddam-i-Islam and Millat-i-Islamia Pakistan.

- **August 1:** Suspected Jaish-e-Mohammed (JeM) militants opened fired targeting Police and Central Reserve Police Force personnel, killing a Policeman and seriously injuring two CRPF personnel in capital Srinagar.
- **July 6:** The CID of the Sindh Police arrested a militant of the banned outfit JeM from Hyderabad. Abid Hussain was an absconder in the assassination case of a Hindu businessman Gardesh Kumar since 2007. CID Superintendent of Police, Mazhar Mashwani, told after killing Kumar, the militant had managed to escape during an encounter with the Police during a raid in Hyderabad in 2007. Since then, he went into hiding, while the Police arrested his father and brother, who pointed out the location where Kumar's body was buried.
- **June 29:** Police in PoK has revealed that groups like the LeT and JeM are shifting bases to PoK following clampdown on their activities in the wake of the Mumbai terrorist attacks of November 26, 2008. In a confidential report submitted to the Government of Pakistan, PoK Police has said these groups have acquired large pieces of land in and around PoK capital of Muzaffarabad and are pursuing a "jehadi" agenda under the garb of religious activities. "After the ban imposed on the JuD, the front of LeT by the UNSC, Pakistan forces had taken control of their offices... The activities of the outfit had gone underground for some

months, but have again become active," the BBC quoted the report as saying. The report said that the JuD has constructed a mosque, a school and a dispensary on the land acquired by them in Dulasi and further construction is on.

The PoK Police report also mentions the activities of other jihadi groups like the JeM and HuM which have also constructed madrassas (seminaries) near Muzaffarabad. The JeM has also set up an office and seminary near Muzaffarabad. Police has noted that most of the activities of the militant groups have been observed in Neelam Valley, near the Line of Control. Extremist organisations have also reportedly set up offices in Kandil Shahi.

- **June 29:** The Lahore Police claimed arresting seven terrorists linked to the JeM and TTP and recovering explosives and weapons. According to a handout by the Capital City Police office, the Police arrested the terrorists from T-4 Ali Park, Bund Road Lahore after a brief exchange of fire. It said the men planned to launch terrorist attacks in the city. The handout said the suspects were arrested at a check-post near Shera Kot bus station. They were identified as Karim Bukhsh, Abdul Rehman, Muhammad Younas, Shafaqat Farooqi and Hafiz Muhammad Ijaz. The police said two rifles, three pistols, 22 kilograms of explosives and bullets were recovered. It also said the arrested suspects informed Police about their three accomplices residing in the Bund Road area. The Police subsequently raided their hideout and arrested Shehzad and Ijaz Mahmood. However, Muhammad Ramazan, a resident of Rahim Yar Khan, managed to escape. The Police recovered 12 kg of explosives from the suspects' hideout.
- **June 24:** Police arrested Aabid *alias* Assadullah Bhai, a self-styled battalion commander of the JeM, from the Sopore area of Baramulla District, official sources said in capital Srinagar. Aabid, a resident of Peshawar in Pakistan, was active in Sopore and adjoining areas for

the last two years and was involved in many militancy-related activities, they said. One Chinese pistol, a magazine and four rounds were recovered from his possession.

- **April 13:** The 36 hour-long operations in Pulwama District ended with the SFs killing another militant. The SFs later recovered dead bodies of both the Jaish-e-Mohammed (JeM) militants holed up in a residential house of Aglar Kandi area. Inspector General of Police, B. Srinivas, said, "The encounter has ended and both the militants belonging to JeM have been killed. One Army captain sustained injuries in the operation," Both the slain militants were Pakistani citizens and identified as Afaaq and Babar, he added further. Two AK series rifles and some other material were recovered from the site of encounter.
- **April 12:** A militant of the Jaish-e-Mohammed (JeM) was killed and an Army officer injured in an encounter in the Pulwama District. A gun battle broke out in Aglar Kandi area after SFs launched a search operation in the area, official sources said. They said one militant was killed in the firefight so far. One Army officer of the rank of Captain was also injured in the gun battle. According to intelligence inputs, the two militants belong to JeM and are residents of Pakistan. They have been identified as Afaq and Baber. One residential house suffered extensive damage while three other houses were partially damaged in an encounter.
- **March 31:** A soldier, Sepoy Rumpum Gogi, who was injured in the encounter with the Jaish-e-Mohammad (JeM) militants in Kamla forests in the Tral area of Pulwama District, succumbed to injuries at 92 Base hospital of the Army at Badami Bagh Cantonment on March 30, a Police spokesman said. He also said the second militant killed in the encounter has been identified as 'district commander' Azhar alias Usman, a resident of Faisalabad in Pakistan. The other militant killed in the encounter was a local resident.

- **March 29:** Meanwhile, the two militants killed in an encounter in Kamla forests of Tral in Pulwama District a day earlier have been identified as local cadres of the Jaish-e-Mohammed (JeM). One of the slain militants has been identified as Azad Ahmad Bhat, a resident of Dadsara village. Two assault rifles, six magazines, 89 rounds and two grenades were recovered from the possession of the slain militants.
- **March 25:** The Australian Government on March 16 re-listed six groups as terrorist organisations under the Criminal Code, following advice from Australia's security agencies. The re-listing ensures that it remains an offence to associate with, train with, provide training for, receive funds from, make funds available to, direct or recruit for these organisations. The outfits that have been re-listed are: Ansar al Islam (formerly Ansar al-Sunna); Asbat al Ansar; Islamic Army of Aden; Islamic Movement of Uzbekistan; JeM; and LeJ.
- **February 5:** Several banned militant groups met in Muzaffarabad, the Pakistan occupied Kashmir capital, and pledged to continue the *jihad* to "liberate" Kashmir from India. The meeting was organised by a previously unknown group, Tehreek-e-Azadi Jammu and Kashmir, on the eve of "Kashmir Solidarity Day". Groups affiliated to the United Jihad Council (UJC), the umbrella organisation of more than a dozen militant outfits, were in attendance including the Hizb-ul-Mujahideen (HM), the Jaish-e-Mohammed (JeM) and the Harkat-ul-Mujahideen (HuM). The meeting took place at Chattar, a neighbourhood that reportedly houses Government offices, top Government functionaries and political VIPs. The local administration did not prevent the event, held under a tent on a main road. However, there was no comment from the Pakistan Government on the meeting.

- **January 8:** The ten-day long operation by the SFs which targeted about a dozen commanders of the Jaish-e-Mohammed (JeM) outfit in Bhati Dhar forests of Mendhar in Poonch District came to an abrupt end in the evening of January 8 with all militants managing to escape. Army sources confirmed that the operation has been called off and all militants, who were being searched for last 10 days, might have escaped. "The operation, which had started on December 30 afternoon in dense Bhati Dhar forests, is off. All militants were reported to have escaped taking advantage of rugged terrain and prevailing climatic conditions in the area", they said. This was the longest ever anti-militancy operation in Jammu region in two decades.

  Police arrested two more civilians taking the total number of arrests made from Bhati Dhar surroundings for helping JeM militants in converting cave hide-outs into bunkers to four. The two civilians were identified as Mohammed Bashir and Mohammed Iqbal, both residents of village Thera in Bhati Dhar. Earlier, Police had arrested a retired Assistant Sub-Inspector of Police and a woman for assisting the militants.
- **January 5:** While an encounter between the SFs and JeM militants in Bein forests of Bhati Dhar in Poonch District entered the sixth day, two SF personnel sustained splinter injuries in the intermittent firing by the holed up militants. The militants, who are at the position on higher peaks of the densely forested mountainous belt of Bhati Dhar, are reportedly firing intermittently mostly during the night and early hours. Three SF personnel and four militants have been killed so far in the encounter that began on January 1.
- **January 3:** A Special Police Officer (SPO), Naresh Kumar, was killed in the continuing encounter between SFs and two absconding Jaish-e-Mohammed (JeM) militants at Bhati Dhar forests in the Mendhar *tehsil* of Poonch District. With the killing of SPO, the death toll in the three-day long encounter has reached seven.

- **January 2:** Four top militants of the JeM were killed in a fierce three-day long gun-battle at Bhati Dhar forests in the Mendhar *tehsil* (revenue division) of Poonch District. While two Army soldiers and a militant were killed on January 1, three militants were killed on January 2. Official sources said bodies of two soldiers, who were missing in the encounter, were recovered in the morning of January 2. They have been identified as Subedar Rakesh Kumar Singh and Naik K. P. Singh. While one of the militants was killed in the night of January 1 after he came out of the hideout firing on the Army personnel, his three associates were killed on January 2 when their hideout was blasted with a powerful bomb. A large quantity of arms, ammunition, explosives, wireless set, mobile telephones and literature was also destroyed along with the hideout.
- **January 1:** Two Army soldiers and a Jaish-e-Mohammed (JeM) 'area commander' were killed in a gun-battle at Bhati Dhar forests in the Chatral area of Mendhar sub-division in Poonch District while a group of five militants was still trapped in the area. Official sources said troops of Rashtriya Rifles and Special Operations Group personnel had cordoned off Bhati Dhar forests two days back after receiving specific information that a group of six JeM militants had taken shelter there. In the evening of January 1, the militants reportedly opened fire on Army personnel, who retaliated. In the subsequent encounter between the two sides which continued for more than two hours, two soldiers and JeM 'area commander' Abdul Gul were killed.

2008

- **December 18:** The Foreign Ministry has said that the JeM chief Maulana Masood Azhar "is wanted by the law enforcement authorities of Pakistan and is at large." The clarification came after Foreign Minister Shah Mahmood Qureshi told a television channel that Azhar was among the "important people" who had been taken into custody. A few hours earlier, Pakistan High Commissioner to India Shahid Malik told that his Government was still looking for Azhar. "He is not under house arrest. As far as I know, [the report of his house arrest] is wrong. He is not in Pakistan. We don't know where he is," Malik said. Last week, Pakistan Defence Minister Ahmed Mukhtar told that Azhar had been "picked up." These statements came after Pakistani authorities had "confined" Azhar to his home in Bahawalpur in Punjab province.

- **December 17:** Authorities have reportedly claimed neutralizing a clandestine terror network set up by the jailed killer of Daniel Pearl inside the Hyderabad Jail and the Sindh Government has suspended senior Police and jail officials after a large number of cell phones, SIMs and other equipment were recovered. Highly-placed Interior Ministry sources told that the jailed terrorist, JeM cadre Ahmed Omar Sheikh, had also threatened General Pervez Musharraf on his personal cell phone in the second week of November 2008 and planned to get him assassinated by a suicide bomber. The caller reportedly told Musharraf: "I am after you, get ready to die." Subsequent investigations by the authorities revealed the threatening phone call was made by someone from the Hyderabad Central Jail. Being a suspect, Omar Sheikh was placed under observation before it transpired that he was the one who had threatened the former president.
- **December 8:** The Pakistani authorities have placed restrictions on the movement of Maulana Masood Azhar, chief of the outlawed JeM, by confining him to his multi-storeyed concrete compound in the Model Town area of Bahawalpur in Punjab province,. Official sources said Azhar's activities have been restricted in the wake of the India's recent demand to hand him over to New Delhi. Adviser on Interior Rehman Malik said in Islamabad last week that India has given to Pakistan a list of three persons Maulana Masood Azhar,

Dawood Ibrahim and Tiger Memon for their immediate extradition.

India has reportedly sought the arrest and extradition of Masood Azhar while citing a 1989 agreement signed by the director-general of the CBI and the director-general of the FIA which binds both the agencies to collaborate with each other, to trace out the most wanted terrorists and criminals and hand them over to their respective counterpart. Azhar is wanted by the CBI for his alleged involvement in the 2001 attacks on Indian parliament.

- **November 20:** An official spokesman said that two militants of the JeM were killed in a joint operation of the police and army in the Daril-Vilgam village of Kupwara district. The slain militants were identified as Shamsher alias Showkat Bhai and Irfan alias Abu Talib, both residents of Pakistan. Two AK rifles and other arms and ammunition were recovered from the slain militants.
- **October 14:** In Srinagar, Police arrested four persons involved in grenade attacks and recovered arms and ammunition from their possession. They were in close contact with chief operational commander of the JeM, namely Pasha, who had given them instructions to lob grenades in Srinagar City.
- **October 9:** Security forces shot dead the 'chief commander' of the Pakistan-based JeM, identified as Zaheer Ahmad alias Pasha, and his accomplice, Saifullah alias Shoukat Bhai alias Faisal, during a five-hour gun battle in the Sopore area of Baramulla district. The duo were Pakistani nationals. Two AK assault rifles and some ammunition were recovered from the possession of the slain militants of Faisalabad, Pakistan
- **September 27:** The continuing encounter at Kenigam in the Pakharpora-Rajpora belt of south Kashmir ended and the dead bodies of both the holed up JeM militants were recovered. The slain militants were identified as Shaukat Ahmed Dar of Pulwama, and Adnan Bhai of

Balochistan in Pakistan. Three Army personnel and a civilian sustained injuries in the gunbattle. Later an explosion occurred when residents were clearing the rubble injuring 16 persons.

- **September 25:** A JeM militant, identified as Showkat was killed in another ongoing operation at village Kenigam near Pakharpora in the Budgam-Pulwama belt. Another accomplice of the dead militant, identified as Adnan was still fighting the forces.
- **September 7:** Security forces (SFs) killed a 'divisional commander' of the Jaish-e-Mohammed (JeM) outfit, Barkatullah Ansari a.k.a. Hyder of Muzaffarabad in Pakistan occupied Kashmir, during an encounter that ensued after a cordon-and-search operation at Warpora in the Baramulla district. Officials said that three SF personnel sustained injuries in the incident. They added that Ansari was a key co-ordinator between different militant outfits in north Kashmir apart from being involved in a number of attacks on the SFs and civilians in the Sopore-Bandipora region.
- **July 27:** SFs killed two militants - Abdullah, 'Battalion Commander' of the Lashkar-e-Toiba and Abu Baker of Jaish-e-Mohammed in an encounter at village Gujarpati Surigam in the Kupwara district. Abdullah was reportedly involved in killing of two policemen in the Sogam area of Kupwara district in May 2008.
- **July 16:** Two militants of the Jaish-e-Mohammed (JeM) outfit and a Special Police Officer of the Jammu and Kashmir Police were killed and approximately 22 security force personnel sustained injuries in an 18-hour-long gun-battle at Warpora village on the Sopore-Bandipora Road. Officials later said that the slain militants were identified as Hilal Ahmed Sofi of Warpora and a Pakistani militant, namely Ali Mohammad Raza.
- **July 4:** One JeM militant was killed by troops during an encounter between village Barpora and Wagahama

in the Pulwama district. While one Pakistani militant, Shabir Ahmad alias Arsalan, managed to escape in injured condition, an AK 47 rifle and two magazines were recovered from the encounter site.

- **June 16:** During a routine checking, SFs arrested three JeM militants at Shokbaba Bandipora in the Baramula district. The SFs also recovered three hand grenades from their possession.
- **June 9:** The security forces foiled an attempt by some militants of the JeM, HuM and HM to indoctrinate and recruit five youth of Sopore area in the Baramulla District into jehad and other anti-national activities. The youths were likely to be sent to Pakistan Occupied Kashmir for acquiring arms and training in guerrilla warfare.
- **May 23:** The troops launched a search operation in the Panzu area and arrested a militant of the JeM, identified as Bilal Ahmed Chopan. Three Chinese grenades, one AK magazine and six rounds of AK ammunition were recovered from his possession.
- **May 17:** The SFs in an encounter at Laru Jageer in the Tral area of Pulwama district killed six JeM militants while at least four militants, two of them injured, managed to escape. Two of the dead militants were identified as the top wanted JeM 'district commander' Waseem Hassan Ahanger alias Qari Asif and his close associate Mohammad Yousuf Bhat alias Prince. While Qari Asif was active since 2004 and was operating in the Tral area, Prince was reportedly active since 2007 in the Awantipora and Tral areas.
- **April 24:** Superintendent of Police in Handwara, Dr. Haseeb Mughal, said that about 30 militants of the LeT and JeM were still active in the Handwara-Kandi belt of Kupwara district.
- **April 23:** The SFs shot dead a Pakistani militant of the JeM outfit, identified as Abu Umar, at village Nadwal in the Mendhar area of Poonch district. A body-guard

of Abu Umar was reported to have escaped during the exchange of firing, sources said.

- **April 22:** The involvement of Pakistan-based outfits has been observed in most of the terrorist attacks in India as groups from across the border continue to sponsor terrorist and subversive activities in the country, the Union Home Ministry said in its Annual Report for 2007-08. "The hand of Pakistan-based terrorist organisations - LeT and JeM - and, increasingly of the Bangladesh-based HuJI, known to have close links with ISI, has been observed in most of these cases," the 167-page report said. The incidents showed these groups have been using sleeper cells in the country to carry out such activities, and have also been using the territory of other neighbouring countries such as Bangladesh and Nepal, it said.
- **April 19:** The SFs in a day long gun battle killed four heavily armed militants in the Rang forest area, about 6-km ahead of Warnow in the Kupwara district. Three of the slain militants, residents of Pakistan occupied Kashmir, were identified as Amjad Bhai, Abu Saifullah and Irshad Ahmed. While Amjad Bhai was a top wanted 'district commander' of the JeM who had been operating in the Lolab area for the last six years, Abu Saifullah and Arshad were both cadres of the LeT. SSP, Kupwara, Vijay Kumar, confirmed the death of four militants said that four AK rifles and a number of grenades were among the arms and ammunition seized at the site of the encounter.
- **April 11:** JeM and LeT, the Pakistan-based terrorist groups, are among the 44 outfits designated as 'Foreign Terrorist Organisations' (FTO) by the US. Besides these two, other groups active in India - the Bangladesh-based Harkat-ul-Jihad-i-Islami and Pakistan-based HuM - are also in the FTO list issued by the office of the coordinator for counter terrorism of the US Department of State.

- **April 2:** SFs killed two militants of the JeM outfit, identified as Abu Hussain alias Saifullah and Abu Omar, both Pakistani nationals, during an operation at Arin Dardpora in the Bandipora district.
- **March 23:** Pulwama Police arrested an over-ground worker of the JeM outfit, namely Mohammad Ishaq Mir, in the Pulwama town. Officials claimed that a hand grenade was recovered from his possession.
- **March 9:** Troops arrested three suspected JeM militants from Warpora village in the Baramulla district. The arrested were identified as Manzoor Ahmed Dar alias Jana, Ishfaq Ahmed War alias Ishkan and Abdul Rashid War. Two hand grenades were recovered from their possession.
- **February 21:** In a joint operation, the Jammu and Kashmir Police and Army killed three militants of the JeM in Kupwara district. Deputy Inspector General of Police (North Kashmir), B. Srinivas, informed that Police had received specific information regarding the presence of a seven-member group of JeM militants in the dense forest area of Batnar Kooligam in the snowbound Lolab valley. In the encounter that ensued after a cordon-and-search operation, three militants were killed while four others, including two injured militants, managed to escape. Srinivas said that identity of the slain militants was being ascertained with the help of informants and residents of Khurhama area, though some of them insisted that the Jaish 'commander' Pasha was among those killed.
- **January 22:** Maulana Abdul Jabbar, a former commander of the JeM, was arrested during a recent crackdown on extremists, said Interior Ministry sources in Pakistan. They said Jabbar was earlier arrested in 2002 for his alleged involvement in the first three suicide attacks in the country, which targeted Christian centers in Islamabad, Taxila and Murree. He was released in November 2002. He was again arrested in December 2003 in connection with attacks on

President Pervez Musharraf but released in 2006 for lack of evidence, the sources said. Sources added that a security agency had detained Jabbar on suspicion of his involvement in the recent suicide attacks. However, the Interior Ministry spokesperson Javed Iqbal Cheema neither denied nor confirmed Jabbar's arrest, saying it was not in his knowledge.

2007

- **December 29-30:** A 'battalion commander' of the JeM outfit, identified as Abdul Gani Dar alias Jhangvi, was killed in a fierce gun battle at Drubgam village in the Rajpora area of Pulwama district on December 29. A day later, the police recovered the dead body of another Pakistani militant, Abu Shakir, of the JeM from the encounter site.
- **December 6:** Pakistani militants of the JeM and LeT have joined hands with the HuJI of Bangladesh to destabilise India's sovereignty taking the strategic advantage of the eastern border, the Director General of BSF, A. K. Mitra, said. Talking to the media in Agartala, Mitra pointed out that the western frontier of India was relatively tough for Pakistani militants but the eastern border with Bangladesh had become more useful for them and foreign militants were utilising South Bengal border for anti-Indian activities. He disclosed that 14 militants of the LeT and JeM were arrested in South Bengal border, trying to sneak into India from Bangladesh in the past six months. Speaking on the recent terrorist attacks in India, including the recent serial bomb blasts in Uttar Pradesh, Mitra said circumstantial evidence point to a kind of a joint mission by the HUJI, along with LeT and JeM.
- **November 27:** Two JeM militants were killed in an encounter with the SFs near Sangrama in the Sopore-Baramulla belt in north Kashmir. One of them was believed to be a local Kashmiri militant and another Pakistani national. However, both remained unidentified.

- **November 16:** Three suspected Pakistani JeM militants were arrested by the Special Task Force of Uttar Pradesh Police in Lucknow on a tip off that some terrorists were passing through the Tehripulia area.
- **November 15:** Five militants, including four Pakistani cadres of the HuM and a lone Pakistani cadre of the JeM and two soldiers were killed at Dharamwari in an encounter that lasted for over 10 hours.
- **October 30:** Ghulam Sarwar alias Amanullah Bukhari alias Jangi Chacha of Gujranwala, Pakistan, a 'district commander' of the JeM, was killed by the SFs in an encounter in the Bandipora district. Officials said that Bukhari was wanted in over 50 civilian killings in addition to a number of police personnel.
- **October 24:** SFs killed two of the top wanted Pakistani militants of the JeM outfit. SF personnel launched a cordon-and-search operation at Khoshi Mohalla Brar near Chitti Bandi village in the Bandipora district after receiving information that two militants were hiding at the residence of one Ghulam Hassan Paswal. In the ensuing encounter, SFs destroyed the target house, killing both the holed up militants, identified as 'district commander' Saquib and 'battalion commander' Abu Huzaifa alias Ghazi Baba. Two soldiers were wounded in the encounter.
- **October 18:** Two Pakistani militants of the Harkat-ul-Mujahideen (HuM), 'district commander' Dr Zen and his bodyguard, were killed in a gun-battle with the SFs at Lodara village in the Bandipora district However, in the capital Srinagar, a Jamiat-ul-Mujahideen spokesman claimed to news agencies that one of the militants killed was his outfit's "Battalion Commander" Abul Khair alias Mohammad Usman and another was Imran of the JeM. Officials however insisted that one was Zen and another was his bodyguard.

- **October 17:** Security forces foiled an infiltration bid and arrested a JeM militant, Abdul Majid Chowhan, from Dardapora Lolab in the Kupwara district.
- **September 20:** An Army officer, Mukesh Kumar, and one Pakistani 'commander' of the JeM outfit, identified as Jamal alias Bilal Bhai, were killed in an encounter between terrorists and SF personnel at Tral in the Pulwama district.

  One Pakistani 'commander' of the JeM outfit, identified as Amanullah Bukhari, was arrested by SF personnel during a search operation at Bandipora in the Baramulla district.
- **September 17:** Two top Pakistani militants of the JeM were killed in a joint operation by the SFs at Khayyar village in the Bandipore area. Inspector General of Police (Kashmir), Shiv Mohan Sahai, said that SFs launched a search operation in the area following information that three of the top wanted militants of the JeM, led by the most wanted Amanullah Bukhari, were hiding at a house. SFs later neutralized their hideout and gunned down two heavily armed militants, identified as Mohammad Tariq Khan alias Sajid and Mohammad Abu Bakr Ayayee alias Usman. However, Bukhari managed to escape.
- **September 14:** A suspected Pakistani cadre of the JeM was killed by SF personnel at Sodal near Handwara in the Baramulla district. While one SF personnel was wounded, five terrorists managed to escape from the incident site.
- **September 4:** A JeM 'district commander', Abdul Gani alias Abu Mavia alias Mauz, surrendered before the troops in Doda district. Senior Superintendent of Police, Manohar Singh, informed that Abu Mavia had joined militancy in 2002 and received arms training at Balakote training camp in Pakistan occupied Kashmir.
- **August 30:** Security forces killed a Pakistani militant of the JeM outfit, identified as Ali Raja, at Balkul Gali Top in the Kupwara district.

- **August 17:** Police arrested four members of the JeM network, including a woman and her daughter, from Mendhar in the Poonch district. The women, who were arrested from a hide-out at village Bhati Dhara, were identified as Zubaida Begum and her 20-year old daughter Rubeena Begum. Zubaida's husband, Mohammed Razzaq was already under detention since the last two years for his links with the JeM. According to official sources, both the women were instrumental in shifting arms and hawala consignments for the militants.
- **August 11:** Special Operations Group of Jammu Police and Delhi Police, in a joint operation, gunned down JeM 'divisional commander' Saifullah Qari, a Pakistani national and mastermind behind the July 5, 2005-attack on makeshift Ram temple at the disputed Ayodhya complex in Uttar Pradesh and critically injured his associate in a house at Ramzanpura near Janipura Colony in Jammu. The injured militant has been arrested. A Delhi Police Sub Inspector Devinder Singh was also injured in the operation that lasted for half an hour.
- **August 1:** Troops also killed a Pakistani militant of the JeM, identified as Mohammad Talha Reyan, in an encounter at Zaloora in the Sopore area of Baramulla district.
- **July 5:** A militant of the JeM outfit was killed in an encounter with police at Krussan in the Kupwara district.
- **May 22:** Two JeM cadres, identified as 'district commander' Waseem Bhai of Pakistan and Arshid Ahmed Dar alias Umar, were killed by the SF personnel In another encounter at Kesrigam in the Kakapora area of Pulwama district. Official sources said that a soldier, Rajesh Chaudhry of the Rashtriya Rifles, also died in the gun-battle.

- **May 16:** The CRPF personnel arrested one over-ground worker of the JeM outfit, Farooq Ahmad, at Murran road in Pulwama.
- **May 6:** Pakistan-based terrorist groups, particularly the JeM and LeT, are increasingly depending on "surrogate bases" in Bangladesh, Nepal and the Middle East for movement of trained cadres and finances for their operations, indicated the Union Home Ministry. A home ministry document, based on intelligence inputs, said the Bangladesh-based HuJI, linked to the JeM and LeT, is recruiting Indian youths, sending them to Pakistan for training and re-inducting them via Bangladesh to carry out terrorist attacks. "This is evident from the Mumbai local train serial bomb blasts in which 11 Pakistanis infiltrated through the Indo-Nepal border in Bihar, Indo-Bangladesh border in West Bengal and Indo-Pakistan border in Gujarat," the report said.
- **April 26:** Another plot to assassinate the Jammu and Kashmir Chief Minister Ghulam Nabi Azad in a suicide attack during his rally at Bandipora in the Baramulla district was foiled by police with the arrest of three militants, including a Pakistani national. A senior police officer said that a top LeT militant, Showkat Ahmed, was arrested from the capital Srinagar on April 24. During interrogation, he revealed that the LeT, JeM and HM had hatched a joint conspiracy to assassinate the Chief Minister at Bandipora during his rally. Police raided a militant hideout on the outskirts of Srinagar from where two associates of Showkat were also arrested. They included one Pakistani, Abu Sikander.
- **April 21:** The outlawed JeM is reportedly re-organising itself under its new commander Mufti Abdul Rauf, younger brother of the outfit's chief Maulana Masood Azhar. The JeM had established a transit camp in the capital Islamabad for its activists coming from southern Punjab and traveling to Kohat where another

camp had been established. "Mufti Abdul Rauf is spearheading the re-organisation of JeM," the sources said. Rauf appeared on the scene after Maulana Azhar went underground following two suicide attacks on President General Pervez Musharraf. The camp in Islamabad is supposed to serve as the base for the outfit for its propaganda campaign and distribution of pamphlets in the tribal areas.

- **March 17:** A militant of JeM was arrested from village Sangoo-Narbal in Kakapora in the Pulwama district along with three hand grenades, four detonators, 700 grams of explosives and seven AK rounds.
- **March 16:** Rawalpindi Police said that they arrested five cadres of the banned JeM, who were on their way to the Supreme Court building, in Faizabad. The arrested men had been identified as Mohammad Jahangir, Mufti Abdul Rauf, Abdul Haleem, Atiqur Rehman and Kashif. Mohammad Jahangir and Mufti Abdul Rauf were the brothers of Maulana Masood Azhar.
- **February 27:** SFs killed a JeM militant, identified as Mohammad Iqbal alias Bala of Pakistan, during an encounter at Gujjarpatti Chandigam in the Kupwara district. Three of his associates reportedly managed to escape from the incident site.
- **February 21:** The Police control room in New Delhi received a call from a man identifying himself as spokesman of the JeM who threatened to carry out blasts in the national capital if four of its men, lodged in the Tihar jail are not released. The police reportedly has identified the number and a hunt is on to arrest the person responsible for making the call.
- **February 4:** Four suspected JeM militants, including a Pakistani national, are arrested following an encounter with the Delhi Police under the Ranjit Singh flyover near Connaught Place. The police recovered three kilograms of RDX, four detonators, a timer, six hand

grenades, .30 bore firearm, US $ 10,000 and INR 50,000 from them. The encounter followed a tip off available with the Special Cell of the Delhi Police that some JeM members are in the Capital to carry out a major operation and they would meet near the flyover. Joint Commissioner of Police (Special Cell) Karnal Singh said the militants, identified themselves as Shahid Gafur from Sialkot in Pakistan and Bashir Ahmed, Fayaz Lone and Abdul Mazid from Jammu and Kashmir. The three Kashmiris disclosed that they arrived by the Malwa Express earlier in the day.

- **February 2:** Islamabad police arrested 40 students of a Madrassa (seminary) in connection with a protest demonstration by the banned JeM held during the visit of an APHC delegation.
- **January 20:** Police have beefed up security in the Cuttack city amidst intelligence reports indicating that the JeM, Lashkar-e-Toiba LeT and SIMI cadres are planning to orchestrate a terrorist attack during the India-West Indies one-day Cricket Match at the Barabati Stadium on January 24. Official sources told that terrorists are planning to carry out attacks in Cuttack, besides Kochi (Kerala), Bhubaneswar (capital of Orissa), Guwahati (Assam) and Bangalore (capital of Karnataka) prior to the Republic Day on January 26.

  A senior police official in Orissa said, "We have information that Muslim fundamentalists are trying to take advantage of the feeble police presence in certain pockets of the state. We are very watchful and alert." According to the security blueprint, three platoons of police force will guard the hotel where the teams of India and West Indies stay in Bhubaneswar while around 40 platoons would do duty in Cuttack. Plainclothes policemen would also man the nearly 40-km distance from the hotel to the stadium.

- **January 19:** SF personnel foil a terrorist attempt to cause large scale disturbances during Republic Day (January 26) when they arrested five militants of the LeT and JeM from different places at Bandipora in the Baramulla district.
- **January 8:** Security forces (SFs) arrested a Jaish-e-Mohammed (JeM) cadre, Mohammad Maqbool Bhat, at New Colony in the Pulwama district.
- **January 7:** SFs killed two cadres of the JeM outfit, identified as Fayaz Ahmed Sheikh alias Muzzamil Jihadi, a 'Tehsil Commander', and Shabir Ahmed Rather at Dalwan village in the Chrar-e-Sharief area of Budgam district.

2006

- **December 18:** Four of the six terrorists, who were reportedly trapped in three separate operations at Bandipora and Lolab, have been killed by the SFs since December 18-evening. Sources said that SF operation ended with the death of both the holed up terrorists at Kota Satrena in the Bandipora area of Baramulla district. They are identified as Saifullah and Khalid alias Zubair, Pakistani cadres of the JeM.
- **December 4:** The Pakistan-based Lashkar-e-Toiba (LeT) and Jaish-e-Mohammed (JeM) are using territory and elements in Bangladesh and Nepal for movement of terrorists and finances in India, according to a paper prepared by the Union Home Ministry on internal security situation.
- **November 27:** Two suspected Jaish-e-Mohammed militants were arrested by the Delhi Police at the Old Delhi railway station. The arrests followed a tip-off that the duo were aboard the Kalka-Delhi Mail train. Police recovered two kilograms of RDX and INR 5 lakh from them. During interrogation, the arrested persons reportedly disclosed that they were JeM militants.

- **November 21:** Two over-ground workers of the militants, identified as Kamar Din and Mohammad Ashraf, associated with the JeM outfit, are arrested from the Chajroo area of Udhampur district.
- **November 12:** The Union Government has decided to provide maximum security cover for the kin of Prime Minister Manmohan Singh, his predecessor Atal Behari Vajpayee and Congress Party chief Sonia Gandhi, in view of the abduction threat from the Pakistan-based JeM group. Security agencies in Jammu and Kashmir intercepted a wireless message of the JeM, which suggested that militants were planning to kidnap kin of these VVIPs to secure the release of some militants in various jails of India.
- **October 19:** A cadre of the Pakistan-based outfit JeM, identified as Pervez Ahmed Radoo, is arrested by the Special Cell of the Delhi Police on October 14. He was a carrier of arms, explosives and communication equipment for JeM cadres in various parts of the country, including Delhi. The police said JeM chief in Srinagar, identified as Shergill, had entrusted Pervez with triggering explosions in the Capital.
- **October 17:** Head Constable Vikram Singh, driver of Inspector General of Police (Kashmir) S. M. Sahai, is shot dead by terrorists near the General Bus Stand at Batmaloo in the capital Srinagar.

  Terrorists shot dead Constable Dilawar Ahmed at Telbal Morh near the Hazratbal Shrine on the outskirts of Srinagar. The JeM claimed responsibility for both the attacks.
- **October 15:** Police constable Ghulam Mohiuddin is reported to have died and his colleague, Ghulam Hassan, sustained injuries in a terrorist attack in the Lal Chowk area of capital Srinagar. The JeM claimed responsibility for the incident.
- **October 6:** Police arrests two terrorists of the JeM, identified as Liaquat Hussain and Mushtaq Ahmed,

from Pangai in the Thannamandi area of Rajouri district.

- **October 4:** 21 terrorists, belonging to the JeM, Al Barq and Hizb-e-Islami outfits, hailing mostly from the Baramulla and Kupwara districts, surrender before 19 Infantry Division within a day of their infiltration from LoC in the Uri sector.
- **September 28:** A Hawala operator, identified as Naseer Ahmed alias Doctor, is arrested by Nowshera police from the Mendhar area of Poonch district. He is being questioned to ascertain his links with the JeM outfit, including the outfit's 'commander' for Rajouri-Poonch districts, Saifullah Kari.
- **September 24:** Over 1,000 trained Kashmiri militants are "currently stranded" in three camps of the HM in the Hazara region of NWFP, a Press Trust of India report quoted the Pakistan-based Herald magazine. "Of these, the Hisari and Batrasi camps are located in Mansehra district while a third camp is located in Boi in district Abbottabad," Herald reported. It quoted unnamed sources to say that thousands of other terrorists were confined in camps run by half a dozen smaller Kashmiri groups or predominantly Pakistani outfits like the LeT, JeM and Al-Badr Mujahideen in the frontier and Pakistan occupied Kashmir regions. Quoting "knowledgeable sources", the Herald said "until recently", small groups like the Tehrik-ul-Mujahideen, Al-Umar Mujahideen, Jamiat-ul-Mujahideen, Al-Fatah, Al-Jihad, Al-Barq, Tehrik-e-Jihad, and Islamic Front were receiving between 400,000 and 700,000 rupees a month, adding, "Large organisations like HM, LeT, JeM, Al-Badr Mujahideen and others received more money, ranging between two to three million rupees."

  A JeM cadre, identified as Arshad Ahmed alias Tipu, surrenders before SFs in the Doda district.

- **September 20:** Javed Ahmed alias Atish alias Jugnoo, a 'section commander' of the JeM, is killed by the SF personnel at village Rannaie in the Doda district.
- **September 17:** Abu Jandal, a former bodyguard of Osama bin Laden, claims that Al Qaeda operatives were behind the hijacking of the Indian Airlines plane in December 1999, which culminated in the release of JeM chief Maulana Masood Azhar and two other terrorists, Mushtaq Ahmed Zargar and Omar Sheikh, at Kandahar in Afghanistan.
- **September 16:** Three JeM militants are killed during a cordon-and-search operation at Gurwatan Sarpathri in Pir Panjal foothills in Shopian area. One of the killed militants is believed to be a Pakistani national.
- **September 12:** Prime Minister Manmohan Singh said that that Pakistan has not done enough to control terrorist outfits like the LeT and JeM.
- **September 9:** SFs arrest Mohammad Rizwan, a member of the banned JeM, from the outskirts of Karachi in Pakistan. He was involved in several heinous acts of sectarian terrorism and the provincial government had him on their most wanted list.
- **September 4:** A cadre of the JeM, Qadiryar, is killed in an encounter with SF personnel at Midora in the Pulwama district.
- **August 30:** SFs arrest two cadres of the JeM at Lolab valley in the Kupwara district along with five hand grenades.
- **August 29:** Two teachers are arrested as Rajouri district police today raided terrorist hide-outs in the Mendhar, Darhal, Gambhir and Rajouri towns to neutralize the network of Amzad, 'financial chief' of the JeM, who was reportedly arrested earlier.
- **August 24:** The Anti-Terrorist Squad of the Mumbai Police said that the two Pakistani terrorists, one of whom was killed in an encounter on August 21, had plans to attack five places in Mumbai, including the

Bhabha Atomic Research Centre at Anushakti Nagar and Siddhivinayak Temple. During interrogation, Mohammad Riaz Nawabuddin, who was arrested on August 21, has revealed that the duo had obtained training at a JeM camp in Pakistan.

- The Special Operations Group of police in Jammu arrests three activists of the JeM and HM from Tikri on the Jammu-Srinagar national highway when they were shifting a Hawala consignment from Rajouri to Kashmir.
- Two JeM cadres, identified as Gulshan Ahmed and Tariq Ahmed Hazzan, are arrested from the Kupwara district.

❐ August 23: The Union Government said that Pakistan's external intelligence agency ISI continues to provide "directions" and "logistics" support to terrorist groups like the JeM, LeT, HM and Al-Badr for terrorist related activities in Jammu and Kashmir.

❐ August 18: An intelligence agency has handed over six suspects, belonging to the proscribed JeM, to police in connection with the March 2, 2006-suicide attack outside the US consulate in Karachi.

❐ August 17: Terrorists attack personnel of the Jammu and Kashmir Police and CRPF at three places in the capital city of Srinagar on with silencer-fitted pistols, killing two of them and injuring two others. One of the injured succumbs to his injuries later.

Inspector General of Police (Kashmir), S M Sahai, said that a freshly inducted JeM module has carried out the attacks. Ismail Hamza, an aide to the JeM leader Maulana Masood Azhar, denies that a British national arrested in Pakistan in connection with the plot to blow up US-bound airliners had ever been a member of the group.

❐ **August 16:** The father of Maulana Masood Azhar, chief of the JeM, said that Rashid Rauf, identified by Pakistan as a key player in the failed plot to blow up transatlantic airliners in London, left the movement to join rivals more interested in Al Qaeda's anti-Western message. He said that Rauf was a member of the JeM before he joined Al Qaeda.

- August 8: The Jammu Police shot dead two suicide squad (Fidayeen) cadres of the JeM outfit, including one identified as Mohammed Basharat alias Khalid, a Pakistani, in an encounter at Jagti near Nagrota in the early hours and foils their plot to strike in the Jammu City on or before the Independence Day (August 15).

  Hassan Bhai, a front ranking JeM cadre, who was also a close associate of the outfit's chief Maulana Masood Azhar, is killed in an encounter with the police in the Keshwan forests of Doda district.
- **August 1:** A Police Constable and two JeM terrorists, including a Pakistani national, are killed in an overnight encounter at Chidipora in the Pulwama district. Two CRPF personnel, Mohammad Aziz and Kapil Kumar, are killed by cadres of the JeM at Dalgate in the capital Srinagar. A civilian is also injured in the attack, which took place near a crowded bus stop.
- **July 19:** In three separate incidents in capital Srinagar, terrorists open fire on police personnel killing two of them and injuring another. Subsequently, JeM claims responsibility for the attacks, which took place at the Bus Depot near Hazratbal Shrine, Soura Sabzi Mandi and Lal Chowk.
- **June 25:** Two Pakistani terrorists of the JeM outfit are killed in an encounter with the security forces in the Dardsun area of Kupwara district, while three others managed to escape. A JeM spokesperson confirms the death of two cadres of his outfit, but claims that four soldiers are also killed and three others sustained injuries in the gun-battle.
- **May 30:** A police personnel is killed and ten persons sustain injuries in separate grenade attacks in the

capital Srinagar. In the first incident, terrorists hurl a grenade towards an escort vehicle of the Human Rights Commission near Iqbal Park killing police constable Ghulam Nabi Kanjoo on the spot and injuring six persons, including a woman and her two infants. The Jaish-e-Mohammed (JeM) claims responsibility for the attack.

- **May 22:** Thirty-four persons, including 23 civilians, are injured in separate grenade attacks in Srinagar. Subsequently, the JeM claims responsibility for these attacks.
- **May 15:** Two civilians and one CRPF personnel are wounded when terrorists targeted a security bunker with grenades at Kawdara in the capital Srinagar. The JeM claimed responsibility for the attack.
- **May 6:** Two youths, who had forcibly been inducted by a JeM 'commander', are rescued by the troops from the Dachhan area of Doda district.
- **May 3:** A police personnel is wounded when terrorists lobbed a hand grenade targeting the Police Station at Khanyar in the capital Srinagar. A spokesperson for the JeM claimed responsibility for the attack.
- **April 27:** Troops arrested a suspect, Mohammed Sharief Khatana, during a search operation from the Kanthali area of Udhampur district along with some clothing which he had planned to give to Abu Sufian, Abu Muslim and Manzoor Ahmed, cadres of the JeM outfit.
- **April 16:** Four civilians are wounded when unidentified terrorists triggered a grenade blast targeting a picket of the Central Reserve Police Force at Rainawari Chowk in the capital Srinagar. The JeM is reported to have claimed responsibility for the attack.
- **April 16:** Police kills a top ranking cadre of the JeM, identified as Aftab Ansari, at Kokernag in the Anantnag district.

- **April 14:** Terrorists trigger out seven grenade blasts in the capital city of Srinagar, killing five civilians and injuring 44 persons, including 14 SF personnel. A local news agency, Current News Service, reported that four terrorist groups - JeM, Jamiat-ul-Mujahideen (JuM), Al-Mansooran and J&K Islamic Front - claimed responsibility for these blasts.
- **April 11:** A JeM cadre, identified as Haider alias Imtiyaz, is killed during an encounter with the SFs at Lolab in the Kupwara district.
- **April 10:** Two JeM cadres, identified as Mustaqeem and Commando, are killed during an encounter with the security forces at Sukhnai village in the Doda district.
- **April 4:** Cadres of the JeM abduct Ghulam Rasool Jan, a police constable, from his residence and subsequently killed him at Kehlil in the Tral area of Pulwama district.
- **March 17:** The SFs shot dead four foreign mercenaries of the JeM outfit, including 'district commander' Abu Mehtab, in an encounter at village Morian Chatru in the Manjakote area of Rajouri district.
- **March 14:** A 'Divisional Commander' of the JeM, Jaish Zubair Lone alias Irfan, and his associate, Ihtisham Ali alias Abu Saliha, are killed in an encounter with the troops at Chandhara Pampore village in the Pulwama district.
- **March 11:** Authorities in PoK are reported to have arrested eight terrorists in Muzaffarabad, including Mufti Abdul Raouf of the JeM.
- **March 5:** Twenty-three civilians and two CRPF personnel are injured during a JeM triggered grenade attack on a CRPF vehicle near Rajpora Chowk in Pulwama town.
- **March 4:** Six civilians and three police personnel sustain injuries in a JeM triggered grenade attack near Rainawari in the capital Srinagar.

- **February 19:** Two JeM terrorists, Ali Muawia, a 'district commander', and Abu Khalid, a 'battalion commander', are killed by the SFs in a gun-battle at Ganai in the Tral town of Pulwama district. One AK-56 rifle and one pistol are recovered from the incident site.
- **February 2:** Two JeM terrorists, identified as 'district commander' Shah Ali and Abrar Hazarvi, are killed in an encounter with the police at Madhari jungle in the Poonch district. Two AK-47 rifles, eight magazines, 121 rounds, one Kenwood radio set, four grenades, Rs 1860 in Indian currency, Rs 1500 in Pakistan currency, two pouches and one diary are recovered from the incident site.
- **January 1:** A JeM 'divisional commander', Osama Bukhari alias Mohammed Arshad, is shot dead in an encounter with the troops at Dodaj under the jurisdiction of Darhal police station in Rajouri district. Two police personnel, Mohammed Ishfaq and Abdul Qayoom, are wounded in the incident. Bukhari, a resident of Bahawalpur in Pakistan, was instrumental in a number of killings in the Thannamandi and Darhal areas, according to official sources. One AK-47 rifle, three magazines, 100 rounds, one Chinese pistol with two magazines, two Chinese grenades, one wireless set, four diaries, 10 letter pads, one pouch, matrix codes, some documents and photo identity cards are recovered from the incident site.

2005

- **December 29:** Three terrorists, including a top JeM 'commander', are killed in an encounter with the SFs at Khrew Pampore in the Pulwama district. According to defence sources, the slain terrorists include 'deputy divisional commander' of the outfit, Qari Suhail, and two of his accomplices Afaq and Danish.
- **December 21:** Police arrest five JeM cadres from the outskirts of Kishtwar town in Doda district. Two of them hail from Anantnag district in Kashmir valley

and three from Kishtwar. They were identified as Sajjad Ahmed Khanday, Shabir Ahmed Akhoon, Tanveer Ahmed, Shahid Hussain and Sajjad Hussain Bhat. A BSNL mobile telephone, four BSNL SIM cards and Rupees 10,000 in cash are recovered from their possession.

- **December 19:** A top JeM 'commander', identified as Qari Zarar, is killed in an encounter with the SF personnel at Lalpora village in the Kupwara district.
- **November 30:** A group of JeM terrorists shoot at and injure a police constable, Zahoor Ahmed, at Khanyar in the capital Srinagar.
- **November 25:** SFs arrest a JeM cadre from the Pulwama district along with some arms and ammunition.
- **November 24:** A top JeM leader, identified as Zia, is killed by the troops at Dhobiwan village in the Tral area of Pulwama district.
- **November 21:** A Pakistani cadre of the JeM group is killed and two soldiers wounded in a midnight encounter in the Jawahar Nagar area of capital Srinagar. One AK-56 rifle, two magazines and 15 rounds are seized from the incident site. Inspector General of Police (Kashmir Zone), K. Rajendra Kumar, said that Sajid alias Qari Saifullah was hiding in the house of a former official of All India Radio behind DAV School for the last several days. Kumar also informed that Saifullah is a 'divisional commander' of the JeM.
- **November 11:** An alleged conduit of the JeM, who shuttles between India and Bangladesh and has ferried the terrorists involved in the July 5-Ayodhya attack, is arrested by the Special Cell of the Delhi police at Old Delhi railway station.
- **November 7:** Troops kill a Pakistani cadre of the JeM, identified as Mohammad Rustum, during an encounter at Warnow in the Lolab valley of Kupwara district.

- **November 6:** SFs in the Punjab province of Pakistan detain 32 activists of banned religious organisations during Eid celebrations ahead of the cricket Test match between Pakistan and England. Government prepares a list of 190 activists belonging to JeM, SSP and other terrorist outfits and arrest 32 of them from Multan, Bahawalpur, Sargodha and Faisalabad.
- **November 2:** A few hours before the swearing in of Ghulam Nabi Azad as the tenth Chief Minister (CM) of Jammu and Kashmir, a Fidayeen (suicide squad) terrorist detonated a powerful car bomb in the Nowgam area of capital Srinagar near the old residence of outgoing CM, Mufti Mohammad Sayeed, killing at least 10 people and injuring 18 others. A caller, who identified himself as Jaish-e-Mohammed spokesperson, Abu Qadam, telephoned local media organisations in Srinagar and said Mohammad Mubashir, a resident of Abbaspora in Pakistan occupied Kashmir, was the Fidayeen who carried out the attack.
- **September 30:** Security forces raided a terrorist hideout at Wan Diwalgam in the Kokernag area of Anantnag district and killed a JeM terrorist, identified as Mohammad Rafeeq Wagay.
- **September 23:** An 'area commander' of the JeM, Khurshid Ahmed Butt alias Kamran alias Fayaaz, was arrested by the Delhi Police from the Pampore area of Pulwama district.
- **August 1:** A 'sector commander' of the Jaish-e-Mohammed, identified as Adil, is shot dead by the troops in the Phagala area of Poonch district. One AK rifle, 190 rounds, seven magazines, one radio set and Rupees 20,000 were recovered from the incident site.
- **July 27:** A JeM cadre, identified as Sajjad Ahmed Aatish, hailing from Bahawalpur in Pakistan, is killed by the security forces (SFs) at Imbarzalwari in the Sopore area of Baramulla district.

- **July 22:** A Jaish cadre, Arnas, is killed by the security forces during an encounter at Dyalgam in the Kokernag area of Anantnag district.
- **July 13:** In Kupwara district, a JeM cadre is killed by the troops at village Kanthpora and one AK rifle, two magazines and 50 rounds of ammunition were seized from his possession.
- **July 11:** A 'district commander' of the JeM, Momin Khan of Pakistan occupied Kashmir, is killed along with his local associate Mohammad Iqbal Wani in an encounter with the SFs at village Chhatawach-Shopian in the Pulwama district.
- **July 9:** Four Jaish-e-Mohammed cadres, including Jamal Bhai, 'chief operations commander' and Mullah Naseer, 'Deputy chief', are killed during an encounter with the SFs in Pulwama district.
- **July 3:** SFs kill two cadres of the Jaish-e-Mohammed at Killora in the Shopian area of Pulwama district.
- **June 10:** Acting on a tip off about four JeM cadres hiding in the Sofipora Wullarhama village on Sangam-Pahalgam road in Anantnag district, SFs launched a cordon and search operation around the village Imambara (structure for the Muharram celebrations) and killed two terrorists after an exchange of fire injured a solider. Subsequently, the structure caught fire and two other terrorists holed up inside are believed to be killed in the rage.
- **June 8:** A Jaish-e-Mohammed 'commander', identified as Zulfikar, and an Army Major are killed and two soldiers sustain injuries during an encounter at Katari Gala in the Rajouri district.
- **June 6:** Two JeM cadres, including 'district commander' Abu Lareb, are killed by the troops in an encounter at Naika Majari in the Poonch district.

  An unidentified Jaish-e-Mohammed terrorist is killed by troops at village Sokar in Darhal area of Rajouri district.

- **June 5:** Five JeM terrorists, including a 'commander' identified as Shah Ji and his body-guard Manhaz Ali, are killed during an anti-insurgency operation at Kalalkas Jamola in the Rajouri district.
- **May 31:** Abu Hassan alias 88 of the JeM is killed during an encounter at Makhi forest in the Surankote area of Poonch district.
- **May 5:** JeM cadre, Ishaq alias Abu Kasha Asgari, is shot dead by the SFs at Hari Safeda in the Surankote area of Poonch district. One AK rifle, two magazines, two grenades and a wireless set was recovered from the incident site.
- **May 4:** A cadre of the Jaish-e-Mohammed, Sajjad, is shot dead and two others, Omar and Arif, were arrested by the Army subsequent to an encounter at village Tharsa in the Deedah area of Udhampur district.
- **April 26:** The Karachi Police arrest two terrorists of the JeM, Mohammad Anis and Nafees Siddiqui, and seize six locally-made bombs and more than 55 kilograms of explosive material during a raid at a house in the Orangi Town area.
- **April 10:** Two JeM cadres, Rizwan and Farooq Ahmed Kullay, are killed during an encounter that ensued after troops from the Assam Regiment launched a cordon-and-search operation in the Danora forest area of Pulwama district. Official sources in Pulwama said that one pistol and a self-loading rifle, which had been snatched by Jaish cadres during a bank robbery at Imam Sahib, Shopian, last year, were recovered from the incident site.
- **April 9:** According to *Asia Pulse,* Australia has re-listed six groups as terrorist organisations, warning that anyone associated with them faces up to 25 years in jail. Attorney-General, Philip Ruddock, named the six organisations as Lashkar-e Jhangvi, Jaish-e-Mohammad, both Pakistan-based and Asbat al-Ansar,

Egyptian Islamic Jihad, Islamic Movement of Uzbekistan, and the Islamic Army of Aden.

- **April 8:** Two cadres of the Jaish-e-Mohammed, including Zahoor Ahmed Bhat alias Abdul Islam, a 'district commander' and Sarfaraz Ahmed, a 'tehsil commander', are killed during an encounter with the SFs at Karewa Manloo village in the Shopian area of Pulwama district.
- **April 6:** Mohammed Rafiq alias Kamran, a 'tehsil commander', and Mohammed Shaffi alias Khalid, a 'section commander' of the Jaish-e-Mohammed, surrender before the army at Kishtwar in the Doda district. They handed over two AK rifles, four magazines and 120 rounds of ammunition at the time of surrender. Subsequently, based on information given by them, the troops raided a JeM hideout at village Chachchi and shot dead two Jaish cadres. Two AK rifles and some ammunition were recovered from their possession.
- **April 3:** Two suspected JeM cadres are killed during an encounter with the security forces at Zahid Bagh Litter village in the Pulwama district.
- **March 15:** The body of a JeM cadre is recovered by the police at Nargali in the Reasi area of Udhampur district. Official sources said that he was believed to have been killed in an intra-gang rivalry.
- **March 4:** Four terrorists of the JeM are killed during an encounter that ensued after SF personnel launched a cordon-and-search operation in the forest area of Tral in Pulwama district.
- **January 19:** *Dawn* reports that the police have traced a network of 19 people suspected of involvement in the July 30, 2004 suicide attack on Pakistani Prime Minister Shaukat Aziz in Fateh Jhang, and arrested three brothers belonging to the proscribed Jaish-e-Mohammad and Jamaat-ul-Furqan outfits.
- **January 3:** Inspector General of Police (Kashmir Zone), Javaid Makhdoomi, discloses at a press conference that

the Pulwama Police had arrested a JeM 'district commander', Sajjad Ahmed Bhat alias Mulla, from the Dr. Munir Khan Kidney Hospital at Sonwar in Srinagar.

2004

- **December 6:** Saifullah, 'district commander' of the Jaish in Bandipore area of Baramulla district, is killed by the security forces.
- **October 1:** Two Jaish-e-Mohammed terrorists, identified as Mohammed Yusuf and Abu Rehman alias Mohammed Farooq, are killed in an encounter with the troops at Dassal Kariyan in the Rajouri district.
- **September 19:** Two Jaish-e-Mohammed terrorists, identified as Mohammad Islam and Saifur Rehman, are killed by the troops during an encounter in the Dooraswani jungle area of Kupwara district.
- **September 17:** Nazir Afghani alias Hamid, a 'district commander' of the JeM, is shot dead by the police at Bazipora forests in the Baramulla district.
- **August 28:** A Jaish-e-Mohammed terrorist, identified as Riyaz Ahmad Ganie alias Tanveer, is killed in an encounter with the security forces at Sanzwatri in Pulwama district.
- **August 27:** Troops shot dead Mohammed Hassan Askari, a 'commander' of the JeM outfit, during an encounter at Choudhary Narh in the Rajouri district.

  Mohammed Ashfaq, an 'area commander' of the Jaish, is killed during an encounter with the troops at Bigial Mohalla in the Mendhar area of Poonch district.
- **August 23:** Abdul Rehman alias Hamza Askaari, an 'area commander' of the JeM outfit is killed by the troops at Darhal in the Rajouri district during a search operation.
- **August 6:** Three JeM terrorists are shot dead by security forces at Konibal in the Pulwama district
- **July 30:** Three terrorists of the Jaish-e-Mohammed (JeM) were arrested during a raid on a house in Javed

Colony near the General Bus Stand in Bahawalpur, Pakistan. The arrested men were identified as Mehdi Kanwal alias Shakir, Sakhawat Hussain and Asad Hussain.

- **July 29:** Nazakat Hussain, a JeM terrorist, was arrested from village Pir Bhera in Rajouri district.
- **July 28:** A Jaish-e-Mohammed cadres was killed in an encounter at Trich in the Kupwara district.
- **July 22:** A 'district commander' of the JeM, identified as Jan Mohammed alias Peer Baba, was shot dead by the police during an encounter at Khurd Malai Nullah in the Arnas area of Udhampur district.
- **July 15:** A suspected Jaish terrorist, identified as Ghaniur Rahman, was arrested from Hyderabad, Pakistan, for his alleged links to the Al Qaeda and Taliban.
- **June 30:** Two JeM cadres, identified as 'district commander' Osama and Rehman, were shot dead by the troops during an encounter at village Sam Samad in the Thannamandi area of Rajouri district.
- **June 29:** Two terrorists of the JeM were killed in an encounter at Trech in the Kupwara district. Another Jaish cadre was shot dead by the troops during a shootout at Goshbal in the Bandipore area of Baramulla district.
- **June 21:** Two terrorists, affiliated to the Jaish-e-Mohammed outfit, were shot dead during an encounter at Bathnoor village in the Tral area of Pulwama district. Two AK-56 rifles, one wireless set, a tape recorder and five hand grenades were recovered from the incident site.
- **June 18:** A group of terrorists, suspected to be JeM cadres, abducted and later beheaded a civilian and his son in the Tral area of Pulwama district. The two were allegedly killed after the terrorists suspected them to be informers for the security forces'.

- **May 22:** A JeM terrorist was killed at Kandi Chak in the Kupwara district.
- **May 9:** Security forces shot dead two Jaish-e-Mohammed 'commanders', identified as Tariq Hussain and Maqsoom, during an encounter in the Mahore area of Udhampur district. Two AK rifles, nine magazines, 105 AK rounds, one radio set, three hand grenades and Rupees 2110 in Indian currency were recovered from their possession.
- **April 10:** Security forces shot dead the 'district commander' of JeM for Srinagar, Tariq Arshid alias Imran, a resident of Multan, Pakistan, in an encounter at Natipora on the outskirts of Srinagar city.
- **April 8:** Sehrai Baba, the 'chief commander of operations' of Jaish-e-Mohammed, was among five terrorists killed during an encounter with security forces in the Sheikhnaar forest area of Kupwara district. Gazi Asif Zajim alias Sehrai Baba alias Qari Asif, hailing from Karachi in Pakistan, according to official sources, had earlier functioned as the outfit's 'district commander' in Kupwara for two years.
- **April 7:** A Jaish 'district commander' identified as Nayeem Ahmad was shot dead by the Army in Udhampur district.
- **March 28:** Security agencies in Islamabad arrested three terrorists affiliated to the outlawed Jaish-e-Mohammed for their alleged involvement in the December 25, 2003, suicide attack on President Pervez Musharraf.
- **March 26:** Three JeM terrorists and two soldiers were reportedly killed during an encounter at Sonabrari village in the Kokernag area of Anantnag district.
- **March 24:** A self-styled district commander of the JeM, identified as Abu Usman, was killed along with his associate during an encounter with the security forces at Sogam in the Kupwara district. An AK rifle, three magazines, 35 rounds of ammunition, six grenades,

six grenade launchers and a wireless set were recovered from the incident site.

- **March 5:** Senator Lt General (retd.) Javed Ashraf Qazi said in Islamabad that the outlawed Jaish-e-Mohammed was involved in the December 2003 assassination attempts on President Pervez Musharraf.
- **February 20:** The Supreme Court stayed the execution of Jaish-e-Mohammed terrorist Mohammad Afzal, who was awarded the death sentence by the trial court in the December 13-Parliament attack case. The sentence was later confirmed by the Delhi High Court. The Supreme Court suspended the operation of the sentence while issuing notice to the Delhi Government on Afzal's appeal challenging the judgment of the Delhi High Court.
- **February 18:** Three suspected Jaish cadres were killed during an encounter that ensued after a search operation in the hilly terrain of Ahlan Gadole in Anantnag district. Further, two more JeM terrorists were shot dead during an encounter at village Sarhuti in the Mendhar area of Poonch district.
- **February 9:** A Jaish-e-Mohammed terrorist was shot dead by the SF personnel at Chandigam in the Lolab valley of Kupwara district.
- **February 5:** Nine terrorists and a Junior Commissioned Officer of the Army were killed during an encounter at Donil Hill in the Kupwara district. SFs launched an operation after securing information that a group of Lashkar-e-Toiba and JeM cadres had established a hideout in the area.
- **January 19:** Two Jaish terrorists were killed by SFs in an encounter at village Kalla of Mahore tehsil in the Udhampur district. Two AK rifles, eight magazines, four hand grenades, one wireless set, 18 detonators, Rupees 4650 in Indian currency and seven Improvised Explosive Devices were recovered from the slain terrorists.
- **January 13:** During a cordon and search operation launched by the Awantipore Police and a unit of the

Border Security Force (BSF) at Bugmar in Batnoor area of Tral district, two Jaish-e-Mohammed terrorists were killed.

- **January 11:** A JeM terrorist was taken into custody in Bahawalpur, Pakistan, in connection with the assassination attempt on President Musharraf's convoy at Rawalpindi on December 25, 2003.

2003

- **December 29:** One of the two suicide bombers who targeted President Musharraf on December 25 in Rawalpindi belonged to the outlawed Jaish-e-Mohammed and was freed from an Afghan prison during year 2002, unnamed intelligence officials were quoted as saying in the *Daily Times*.
- **December 23:** A JeM cadre and one soldier were killed during an encounter that ensued after the SFs raided a terrorist hideout at Drubgam in the Pulwama district.

  The US Secretary of State redesignates the Jaish-e-Mohammed as a Foreign Terrorist Organization.
- **December 12:** SFs shot dead Abu Babbar, an 'area commander' of Jaish-e-Mohammed, in a gun-fight at Zabbi Toti dhok in the Surankote area of Poonch district.
- **December 9:** In south Kashmir, a terrorist identified as Toofan Khan of the Jaish-e-Mohammad, and a security force personnel were killed during an encounter at Bongam in the Shopian area of Pulwama district.
- **December 7:** Troops shot dead two JeM terrorists during an encounter at Sadiqi Bhata in the Chatroo area of Doda district.
- **December 4:** Authorities in Pakistan occupied Kashmir (PoK) outlawed six terrorist groups including the Khuddam-ul-Islam (formerly known as Jaish-e-Mohammed [JeM]).
- **November 21:** Law enforcement agencies sealed eight offices of proscribed terrorist groups in the Sialkot

district including four offices of the Khuddam-ul-Islam.

- **November 15:** The Pakistan Government proscribes, under the Anti-Terrorist Act 1997, the Khuddam-ul-Islam (KI - formerly known as Jaish-e-Mohammed [JeM]).
- **November 15:** Khudamul Islam (KI - formerly known as Jaish-e-Mohammed [JeM]) is proscribed.
- **September 21:** Four JeM terrorists are killed during an encounter with the security forces in the Gulgam forest area of Kupwara district.
- **September 20:** Two Jaish terrorists and two SF personnel are killed and two SF personnel, including a Major, are injured during an encounter at Tarkundi in the Gambhir area of Rajouri district
- **September 18:** Media report indicates that JeM chief Maulana Masood Azhar met Muttahida Majlis-e-Amal (MMA) leaders recently and promised them his support.
- **September 17:** Nasir Mehmood Awan alias Ansar, a senior 'commander' of the Jaish-e-Mohammed, is killed during an encounter with the security forces at Danmar in the Iddgah locality of capital Srinagar.
- **September 16:** The JeM warns that it would target Indian leaders in suicide attacks that would be "shocking for India". A Jaish spokesperson Wali Hassan Baba reportedly said during a telephonic interview with the Associated Press that the attacks would be retaliation for the killing of Shahnawaz Khan aka Ghazi Baba, 'operational chief' of the outfit, by Indian security forces in Srinagar on August 30.
- **September 10:** Five Pakistan-based terrorist groups, including the Jaish-e-Mohammed, which were proscribed by President Pervez Musharraf on January 12, 2002, are currently functioning openly under changed identities, according to the Herald.
- **September 8:** While acknowledging the killing of its 'operational chief' Gazi Baba alias Shahnawaz Khan

during an encounter on August 30, the JeM appoints Sahrai Baba in his place. Pakistani Urdu daily Jung quoted Jaish 'deputy supreme commander' Wali Hasan as saying that Abu Dajana has been appointed as Sahrai's deputy in Jammu and Kashmir.

- **August 30:** Two terrorists, including Shahnawaz Khan alias Gazi Baba, operational chief of the Jaish-e-Mohammed in Jammu and Kashmir and a key accused in the December 13, 2001 Parliament attack case, are killed in an encounter with the Border Security Force in Noorbagh locality of Srinagar.
- **August 27:** The Buner Police arrest at least ten terrorists affiliated to the Jaish-e-Mohammed (JeM) after a clash between two groups of the outfit over an internal dispute near Ghaurghushti Town in Peshawar.
- **August 19:** Three JeM terrorists are killed during an encounter at Kaninwali in the Pulwama district of south Kashmir.
- **July 27:** Three foreign mercenaries affiliated to the Jaish-e-Mohammed are killed at village Kakora under the jurisdiction of Manjakote police station in Rajouri district.
- **July 14:** Three JeM terrorists are killed and three security force personnel injured during an encounter at Fatlipora village, Budgam district.
- **July 6:** Asadullah Farooqi, reportedly a 'financial advisor' of the JeM, is killed during an encounter at Chota Nar in the Dodaj area of Darhal.
- **July 5:** According to The Friday Times, the JeM, rechristened as the Khuddam-ul-Islam, has split following the expulsion of the outfit's Karachi unit chief Abdullah Shah Mazhar by the Jaish chief Maulana Masood Azhar.
- **July 1:** Abdul Jabbar, former 'supreme commander' of the JeM, is reportedly arrested in Midhranjha, a town near Sargodha, for his alleged involvement in

two terrorist attacks on Christian targets during year 2002.

- **June 30:** Security forces kill four terrorists, including a 'battalion commander' and a 'company commander' of the JeM, at Abhama village in the south Kashmir district of Pulwama.
- **June 26:** Four foreign mercenaries, including Abu Muaviya, a LeT 'district commander', and an Afghani identified as Abu Haamid, 'company commander' of the JeM are killed during an encounter in the Dooraswani forest area of Lolab in Kupwara district.
- **June 12:** A former terrorist of the outlawed JeM is reportedly shot dead by two unidentified assailants in Sector 5-L, New Karachi police jurisdiction, Karachi.
- **June 4:** Three JeM terrorists and one SF personnel are killed while three SF personnel, including a Junior Commissioned Officer (JCO), and a teenaged girl is injured during an encounter in the Surankote area of Poonch district.
- **May 28:** Security forces foil an infiltration attempt near the Line of Control in the Shahpur Karnetian area of Poonch sector killing four JeM terrorists.
- **May 19:** Four women and two children are beheaded by suspected JeM terrorists at village Chowkian in the Kot Dhara area of Rajouri district.
- **May 15:** Maulana Masood Azhar, JeM chief, arrives in Kotli in Pakistan occupied Kashmir (PoK) despite a ban on his entry.
- **May 14:** Pakistan occupied Kashmir (PoK) government announces a ban on the entry of Jaish-e-Mohammed (JeM) chief Maulana Masood Azhar into the region.
- **May 7:** Two Pakistani Jaish cadres, including a 'district commander', are killed during an encounter at Chhampora village in the Vilgam forest area of Kupwara district.

- **April 29:** Two JeM terrorists are killed after an unsuccessful suicide strike on an SF formation at Drugmulla in the Kupwara district.
- **April 25:** SFs foil an infiltration attempt and kill three JeM terrorists at Sagra village in the Mendhar sector of Poonch district. One SF personnel is also killed during the encounter.
- **April 24:** Two JeM terrorists are killed and a SF personnel is injured during an encounter in the Sogam forest area of Kupwara district.
- **April 18:** A Jaish 'district commander' is killed during an encounter at Morha Kalali village, Surankote area of Poonch district.
- **April 2:** Security forces destroy two JeM hideouts at Hari Budha, Mandi area of Poonch district, and kill six foreign mercenaries.
- **March 29:** Security forces kill three JeM terrorists, including a 'deputy district commander', in an encounter in Kishtwar area, Doda district.
- **March 14:** Two JeM terrorists are killed in an encounter in Surankote, Poonch district.
- **March 12:** A JeM terrorist is killed in an encounter in Noida, Uttar Pradesh.
- **March 9:** Special Task Force personnel of Uttar Pradesh Police arrest two Jaish terrorists in Muzaffarnagar.
- **February 20:** Two Jaish terrorists are killed in encounter at Chewa-Safapora, Baramulla district.
- **February 3:** Two Pakistani JeM cadres killed on the Line of Control in Balakote sector of Poonch district.
- **February 1:** A 'district commander' of the JeM and SF personnel killed in Bemina, outskirts of Srinagar.
- **January 31:** Two JeM terrorists killed during encounter at Nayidgam village in the Shopian area of Pulwama district.
- **January 24:** Two foreign mercenaries of JeM killed in encounter in the Mendhar area of Poonch district.

- **January 23:** Lahore High Court's Multan bench refuses to prosecute JeM chief Maulana Masood Azhar on charges of making an anti-India speech. "It is not a crime to make speeches against India," rules Judge Ijaz Ahmed Chaudhry, while dismissing the case.
- **January 22:** JeM 'platoon commander' Habibullah alias Saifullah killed in encounter in Kudara, about 20km from Bandipore.
- **January 14:** An unidentified terrorist kills Ghulam Hassan Chopan, a former spokesperson of the JeM, in Bemina, on the outskirts of the State capital Srinagar.
- **January 13:** JeM terrorists kill a Border Security Force (BSF) personnel and injure another at Batmaloo General Bus Stand in Srinagar.
- **January 8:** In view of the growing resentment against the 'burqa and anti-education drive', JeM withdraws directive through posters issued in the name of its 'Central Jehad Council' and pasted in Khablan, Darhal and Thanna Mandi areas, Rajouri district.
- **January 5:** Three JeM terrorists, including Kamran Khan alias Khijjar, a 'commander', are killed in an encounter in Devla village, Mahore area of Udhampur district.
- **January 4:** Two Jaish terrorists, including a 'commander', are killed in Karmula village, Tral area of Pulwama district.
- **January 3:** Two foreign mercenaries of the JeM are killed and three Border Security Force (BSF) personnel injured in an encounter preceded by an explosion in Laani village, Gool area of Udhampur district.

2002

- **December 18:** A special court in Delhi sentences to death Mohammad Afzal and Shaukat Hussain Guru, JeM terrorists, in the December 13, 2001-Parliament attack case.
- **December 16:** A special court in Delhi convicts Mohammad Afzal and Shaukat Hussain Guru, JeM

terrorists, in the Parliament attack case for various offences under POTA, Indian Penal Code (IPC) and Explosive Substances Act.

- **December 14:** A three-member Review Board of Lahore High Court orders that JeM chief Maulana Masood Azhar be released.
- **November 29:** Canada designates the JeM and Harkat-ul-Mujahideen as terrorist groups.
- **November 21:** Three JeM terrorists and an SF personnel are killed in an encounter in Hafruda forest area, Kupwara-Handwara belt.
- **November 11:** Two front-ranking JeM terrorists, including 'area commander' Imtiyaz Ahmed alias Mohammed Faran, are killed in an encounter in Kurl Chajla, Mankot area, Mendhar.
- **October 21:** A suspected JeM terrorist, one of the 12 accused arrested for plotting to kill Chief Minister Narendra Modi, is killed in Ahmedabad, Gujarat.
- **October 19:** JeM 'commander' A B Usmaan is killed in Dulligam village, Banihal area of Doda district, during a search operation.
- **September 29:** Three JeM terrorists are killed in an encounter in Chunti Pathri and Satarseeran in Kreeri.
- **September 16:** An Additional Sessions Judge in Dera Ghazi Khan grants bail to JeM chief Maulana Masood Azhar. On the other hand, the Home Secretary, on the same day, extends Azhar's detention for a further period of 90 days.
- **September 13:** Detained JeM terrorist Mohammad Afzal, allegedly a key conspirator in the December 2001-Parliament attack case, denies charges that he had a hand in the attack.
- **September 9:** A JeM 'battalion commander' is killed in encounter in Dangarpora, Anantnag district. September 1: Two JeM terrorists, including a foreign mercenary, are killed in encounter near Shopian, Pulwama district.

- **August 28:** A Bahawalpur court extends till September 10, 2002 the judicial remand of JeM chief Maulana Masood Azhar.
- **August 19:** A JeM terrorist is arrested in connection with a bomb blast at a madrassa (seminary) in Sahiwal, Pakistan, on August 16, in which a suspected JeM terrorist was killed.
- **August 18:** Three JeM terrorists, including a 'commander', arrested in Multan, Pakistan.
- **August 16:** Suspected JeM terrorist killed and another injured, reportedly while assembling a bomb at a madrassa (seminary) in Sahiwal district, Pakistan.
- **August 9:** Four JeM terrorists killed in Tangdhar sector of Kupwara district.
- **July 30:** Lahore High Court extends detention of JeM chief Maulana Masood Azhar till August 15, 2002.
- **July 18:** A JeM 'commander', who has taken shelter at a house in Banihal town, from July 17 night, and was holding 15 members of the family hostage, is killed.
- **July 16:** Two JeM cadres killed in an encounter at Chhamb Kailan Dhok, in Loran area, Poonch district.
- **July 15:** Anti-Terrorism Court in Hyderabad, Sindh, awards death sentence to JeM front-ranking terrorist Ahmed Omar Saeed Sheikh in the Daniel Pearl abduction-cum-murder case.
- **July 10:** 'District commander' of JeM, Bilal Ahmed alias Mehmood Bhai of Pakistan occupied Kashmir (PoK), killed in encounter at Krumbhore village in Handwara area.
- **July 2:** JeM 'Area commander' killed in an encounter in the Dranti forests, Rajouri district.
- **May 20:** Three Pakistani cadres of the JeM killed in an encounter at Banota village in the Hill Kaka area of Surankote.
- **May 17:** Three foreign mercenaries of the JeM killed in an encounter at Pathian Wali, in the Lassana area of Surankote, Poonch district.

- **May 14:** Delhi Police files chargesheet against seven persons in the December 13, 2001-attack on India's Parliament. JeM Chief Masood Azhar and two of his Pakistani aides declared proclaimed offenders.
- **May 12:** United States reportedly agrees to let Pakistan try Ahmed Omar Saeed Sheikh, a JeM top-terrorist and prime accused in the abduction-cum-murder of US journalist Daniel Pearl, before initiating any moves seeking his extradition.
- **May 9:** Three front-ranking terrorists of the JeM killed in an encounter at Karnatian dhok in the Shahpur village of Mandi sector.
- **April 28:** Three JeM terrorists killed in an encounter in Pitha Sahib village near Morha Kalar in the Behrot area of Thanna Mandi.
- **April 5:** Notification issued on the regular trial of the four JeM cadres, accused in the abduction cum murder case of US journalist Daniel Pearl. The trial would commence inside the Central Prison in Karachi.
- **March 25:** Maulana Masood Azhar, chief of the proscribed JeM, shifted to his residence in Kausar Colony, Bahawalpur, from the Mianwali Jail.
- **March 24:** Security forces arrest a six-member group of JeM terrorists from the Kunzar area of Tangmarg.
- **March 17:** Foreign Minister Abdus Sattar says in Lahore that JeM terrorist Omar Sheikh will be interrogated in Pakistan.
- **March 14:** US Attorney General John Ashcroft is quoted as announcing the indictment of British-born JeM terrorist Omar Sheikh
- **March 14:** Adnan alias Sunny, a JeM cadre and self-claimed killer of Pearl, is arrested in Lahore,. He appears at a local Urdu daily's office and claims he had slain Pearl.
- **March 10:** Three JeM terrorists, including a hardcore terrorist, Zubair Afghani, killed in an encounter in the Naika Majari forests, Gursai area, Mendhar.

- **March 7:** Reports indicate that US law enforcement officials are seeking the extradition of several other suspects, besides JeM terrorist Ahmed Omar Sheikh, who have been linked to the 1999-hijacking of an Indian air craft, IC-814.
- **March 5:** The constitutional petition filed by Sadia Ahmed Omar Saeed Sheikh, wife of JeM terrorist Omar Sheikh, prime suspect in Pearl case, seeking a restraining order against his extradition, is disposed-of by a division bench of the Sindh High Court.
- **February 22:** Two Pakistani mercenaries of the JeM killed in an encounter at Hardu Bani in the Baramulla district.
- **February 18:** Two foreign mercenaries of the JeM killed in an encounter at Rajara in Poonch district. Separately, two Pakistani JeM mercenaries, including a 'district commander', killed in an encounter at Matti-Gawran in the Anantnag district.
- **February 12:** Sheikh Ahmed Omar Saeed, front ranking terrorist of the JeM and prime suspect in Pearl's abduction case arrested in Lahore.
- **February 5:** Police in Karachi arrest three cadres of the proscribed JeM in the US journalist Daniel Pearl abduction case.
- **February 4:** The JeM, in a statement, says it would confine its activities to J&K and suspend its terrorist attacks in other parts of India. It further says it would also revive suicide attacks to target security force establishments and vital installations in J&K.
- **January 28:** Three JeM terrorists killed in an encounter in Poonch district.
- **January 12:** JeM among five terrorist outfits proscribed, announces President Pervez Musharraf during a televised address to the nation.
- **January 12:** Two JeM terrorists killed in an encounter at Matti-Gawran in Kokernag.

- **January 11:** Maulana Masood Azhar, JeM chief, detained for three months under the provisions of the Maintenance of Public Order (MPO) Ordinance in Pakistan for making provocative speeches against government policies.
- **January 7:** Seven JeM terrorists, including a 'district commander', killed in an encounter at Golad, Poonch district.
- **January 4:** Two Pakistani mercenaries of the JeM killed in an encounter at Kalaban, Poonch.
- **January 2:** JeM says it is shifting its offices to Jammu and Kashmir (J&K) to escape a crackdown by Pakistani authorities. JeM leader Mohammed Abdullah says the outfit's leaders would infiltrate into J&K, despite heavy Indian security.

2001

- **December 29:** Masood Azhar and 29 other outfit members arrested by security forces from Bhawalpur. A day later, he was remanded to police custody for three months and shifted to Mianwali jail in Lahore.
- **December 26:** Masood Azhar briefly detained for four hours at Hyderabad by police while on his way to Bhawalpur. He was leaving Karachi after the outfit was declared a Foreign Terrorist Organisation by US.
- **December 21:** Suspected JeM terrorists kill three women and injure a fourth in Poshkreeri, Anantnag district.
- **December 20:** In a statement, Mohammed Afzal, arrested for involvement in the attack on India's Parliament, said that he had harboured and aided the terrorists responsible for the attack under the guidance of Ghazi Baba, JeM's chief commander for J&K.
- **December 19:** Masood Azhar, speaking in Bhawalpur, Pakistan, denies that his outfit was responsible for the attack on India's Parliament.
- **December 14:** India's External Affairs Minister holds JeM along with LeT responsible for attack on Parliament.

- **December 13:** Five terrorists, later identified as Pakistani JeM mercenaries, attack India's Parliament in New Delhi. Eight security force personnel, a parliament staff member and the five mercenaries are killed.
- **October 1:** Four terrorists, later identified as Pakistani JeM mercenaries, attack the J&K Legislature Complex in Srinagar. 10 SF personnel and the four mercenaries among 32 killed in the attack. While the JeM claimed responsibility for the attack on the same day, it withdrew the claim two days later.
- **August 26:** Qutub Din, an Afghan termed as a top 'commander' of the organisation, killed along with two bodyguards at Khangar Hills, Poonch.
- **June 5:** 11 JeM terrorists, killed in separate operations in Poonch.

2000

- **April 19:** A Jaish terrorist perpetrates the State's first human bomb attack outside the Army headquarters in Srinagar. There were, however, no casualties except for the human bomb.
- **January 31:** The organisation is launched in Karachi by Maulana Masood Azhar

1999

- **December 31:** Maulana Masood Azhar and two other terrorists, are flown to Kandhar, Afghanistan and released in exchange for the hijacked IC 814 and its passengers.

HARKAT-UL-MUJAHIDEEN (Formerly known as Harkat ul-Ansar)

The Harkat-ul-Mujahideen (HuM), a Pakistan-based terrorist outfit, has been in existence twice in the history of that country's involvement in cross-border terrorism. In the interim between the two phases, it continued to exist, but under the name of the Harkat-ul-Ansar (HuA). While the first renaming was an outcome of a reorganisation effected by the Inter-Services Intelligence (ISI), Pakistan's external intelligence agency, among its various sponsored terrorist outfits in Jammu and Kashmir (J&K), the second renaming was necessitated by a US proscription of the outfit.

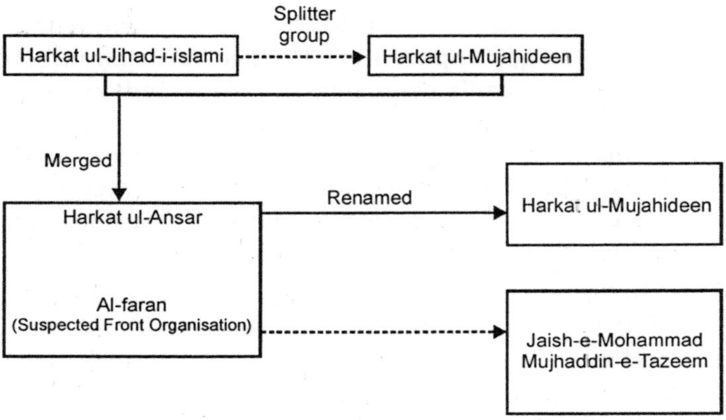

Evolution of the Group

The HuA was categorised as a terrorist outfit by the US in 1997 following reports that it was linked with Osama bin Laden, and his Al Qaeda, a global terrorist network that has struck at several US targets around the world. The outfit immediately adopted the name of Harkat-ul-Mujahideen to escape the ramifications of the proscription. Despite public knowledge that the HuM was a recast version of the HuA, the US had refused to categorise the outfit as a terrorist outfit. However, following the September 11, 2001 terrorist attacks on New York and Washington in the US, the outfit came under scrutiny of the US government for its extensive links with Osama bin Laden, the prime suspect in the terrorist attacks. On September 25, US President George W. Bush signed an order officially banning the outfit.

The HuM was originally formed in 1985, to participate in the *Jehad* against Soviet forces protecting the Communist regime in Afghanistan. It was a formed by a group that walked out of another jehadi group, the Harkat-ul-Jihad-al-Islami

(HuJI). With the Soviet withdrawal from Afghanistan in 1989, the outfit turned its attention to J&K, where terrorist violence had been unleashed by Pakistan supported outfits in 1988.

As the organisation chart shows, the Harkat-ul-Mujahideen merged with another terror outfit, the Harkat-ul-Jehad-al-Islami (HuJI), to form the Harkat-ul-Ansar (HuA) in 1993. This merger apparently failed to form an effective instrument for Pakistan's campaign in J&K as Indian security forces (SFs) arrested three of its top leaders in quick succession. First, Nasrullah Mansur Langrayal, chief of the former Harkat-ul Mujahideen was arrested in November 1993. Three months later, the HuA's General Secretary, Maulana Masood Azhar, and its J&K unit chief Sajjad Afghani were arrested in Srinagar.

The HuA made several attempts to obtain the release of the arrested leaders by abducting SF personnel and foreign tourists and using them as hostages. In the first attempt, made in January 1994, two SF personnel were abducted and subsequently killed when the government refused to release the leaders. A second attempt was made in June 1994 when two foreign tourists were abducted. Following local outcry against these abductions, the hostages were released without any success in their objective. In the third attempt made in October 1994, four foreign tourists were abducted in New Delhi and held in Uttar Pradesh and a demand was again made for the release of the arrested leaders. SFs however, ascertained the terrorist hideout and effected a successful rescue operation and also arrested the leader of the abductors, Umar Saeed Sheikh, a British student of Pakistani origin.

In the fourth attempt, made by a front outfit, Al-Faran in July 1995, six hostages were abducted from various locations. While one managed to escape, the body of the second was recovered in August 1995. The government refused to accept the demands of the abductors and since then there has been no news on the fate of the hostages. It is widely suspected that having failed in their mission, the abductors killed the hostages. These incidents as also reports that the outfit was linked to Osama bin Laden prompted the US government to declare the HuA as a terrorist outfit in 1997. To avoid the repercussions of the ban, the HuA decided to recast itself as the Harkat-ul-Mujahideen.

Meanwhile, Sajjad Afghani was killed during a jailbreak attempt in June 1999. Subsequently, suspected HuM terrorists, hijacked the Indian Airlines Flight IC 814 from Kathmandu, Nepal, forced the pilot to fly to Kandahar, Afghanistan and with the protection and support of the Taliban regime, successfully obtained the release of Maulana Masood Azhar, Umar Saeed Sheikh and Mushtak Ahmed Zargar, commander of the *Al Umar*, a militant group with a predominantly Kashmiri cadre base. The demand for the release of Zargar appeared to be a ploy to convey the impression that the hijacking was conducted for the sake of Kashmiris rather than foreign mercenaries. Certain news reports had speculated that Masood Azhar's brother led the hijackers and his father financed the whole operation.

As mentioned before, the 1993 merger of the Harkat-ul-Mujahideen and the HuJI was not a successful venture. SF sources in India have reported that terrorists claiming allegiance to the three outfits, HuJI, HuM and HuA, have been either arrested or killed throughout the 13-year insurgency in the State.

The HuM's operational capabilities had been severely curtailed by the formation of the Jaish-e-Mohammed (JeM) by Masood Azhar, immediately after his release. News reports from Pakistan suggested that the JeM had weaned away several HuM cadre and other resources. Subsequently, only isolated instances have been reported from J&K where cadre of the HuM have been involved.

Incident

2010 (Data Updated till July 19, 2010)

- **January 31:** A self-styled 'commander' of the HuM outfit, identified as Basharat, who was holed up in an encounter with Security Forces in Baramulla District of Kashmir valley that had started in the evening of

January 30 reportedly managed to escape from the incident site by taking advantage of the darkness.

- **March 12:** The law enforcement agencies warned the authorities concerned that 19 militants were deputed in 12 cities of the province will most likely target NAB offices and ATC. Sources said that a letter had also been forwarded to the authorities concerned, mentioning that some defunct organisations, including Commander Maulana Abdul Jabbar's fraction of JeM, LeJ, HuJI, HuM and HuA, have also joined the TTP.

2009

- **January 2:** Two HuM militants, including a foreigner, were killed in an encounter with the SFs in the Sopore area of Baramulla District. While one of the slain militants was identified as Bashir Ahmad Malla, a local militant, the other militant was believed to be a foreigner whose identity was being ascertained. Two AK rifles were recovered from their possession.
- **March 13:** Police arrested a militant of the HuM outfit, identified as Sarafaraz Ahmad, from the Sopore area of Baramulla District. A Police spokesman said one hand grenade and 12 rounds of AK ammunition were recovered from his possession.
- **May 15:** SFs arrested a 45-year old woman militant of the HuM from Sopore bus stand in Baramulla District and recovered three hand grenades and INR 50,000 in cash from her possession. She has been identified as Naseema, wife of Bashir Ahmad, a resident of New Colony in Sopore town.
- **May 21:** The Karachi Police arrested two suspected Al Qaeda militants and seized explosives and weapons from their possession. The Crime Investigation Department's Superintendent of Police (SP), Fayyaz Khan said suspect Asim hailed from Swat and belonged to the HuM.
- **June 10:** Two militants of the HuM, including the self styled deputy chief of operations of the outfit, were

killed in an encounter with the SFs in the Sopore town of Baramulla District. A Police spokesman said in Srinagar that the SFs launched an operation at Dangerpora in Sopore following receipt of specific information about the presence of two top HuM militants in the area. In the ensuing encounter, both the militants, identified as Kalimullah alias Ali Sher, a resident of Pakistan and the 'deputy chief of operations' and his local aide Mumtaz Ahmad Parray, a resident of Pethseer in Sopore. Two AK-47 rifles, four AK magazines, two pouches and a dairy were recovered from the possession of the slain militants. The spokesman said Kalimullah was involved in the killing of Special Police Officer Fayaz Ahmad on May 31, 2009. He was also involved in a number of grenade attacks on the troops in Sopore in the recent times.

- **October 20:** Police arrested an over-ground worker of the HuM, identified as Jahangir Rasool Reshi, at Watin Chowgal in the Handwara area of Kupwara District. One Chinese pistol with magazine and nine rounds of pistol ammunition were recovered from his possession.

AL BADR

The Al Badr, currently an active terrorist outfit in Jammu and Kashmir, was proscribed by the Government of India on April 1, 2002, under the Prevention of Terrorism Ordinance-2001, which became the Prevention of Terrorism Act on April 28, 2002. It is also designated as a Foreign Terrorist Organization in the United States.

Formation and Objectives

The Al Badr was formed in June 1998 with the professed goal of strengthening the 'Kashmiri freedom struggle' and to 'liberate' the Indian State of Jammu and Kashmir and merge it with Pakistan. The outfit advocates that Kashmiris should be given the right of self-determination in accordance with the United Nations resolutions.

Al Badr reportedly traces its origins to 1971 when a group of the same name carried out attacks on Bengalis in what was then known as East Pakistan. The group also operated as part of the Hizb-e-Islami (HIG) of warlord Gulbuddin Hekmatyar in Afghanistan during the 1980s.

While advocating the idea of a sovereign Kashmir it is also critical of the moderate Kashmiri organisations, such as the Jammu and Kashmir Liberation Front (JKLF). The current Al Badr leadership is also opposed to the United States, Israel and the regime of Saudi Arabia. The outfit has in the past indicated that it perceives Kashmir to be the 'gateway of India' and describes its objective as the 'liberation' of Muslims in the rest of India after 'occupying' Kashmir.

The Al Badr, according to official sources in Jammu and Kashmir, which was earlier operating under the banner of Hizb-ul-Mujahideen (HM), was encouraged by the Inter Services Intelligence (ISI), Pakistan's external intelligence agency, to operate independently in the year 1998. Indian intelligence sources have indicated that a new version of the Al Badr was formed as part of this changed strategy, in 1998, through the induction of foreign mercenaries serving in several other terrorist outfits in Kashmir.

Leadership, Command Structure and Cadre

During the time of its formation, the Al Badr was led by Lukmaan, a resident of Pakistan occupied Kashmir (PoK).

Bakht Zameen, a resident of Punjab province in Pakistan, is the present 'chief commander' of the outfit. Arfeen Bhai alias Lukmaan alias Jannisar is reported to be the 'chief commander' of Al Badr in Jammu and Kashmir. Among the other leaders of Al Badr are: 'launching commander' Irfan; 'deputy supreme commander' Zahid Bhai; 'publicity chief' Jasm Bhat; 'communication in-charge' Abu Mawai.

Al Badr is reported to possess a cadre strength of approximately 200, including 120 foreign mercenaries.

Headquarters and Areas of Operation

The outfit is headquartered at Mansehra in Pakistan. It is also reported to have a camp office in Muzaffarabad, PoK.

Reportage of the past five years has indicated that the Al Badr is active in the Anantnag, Baramulla, Budgam, Srinagar and Kupwara districts of the Kashmir Valley. It also has a presence in the Poonch and Rajouri districts of Jammu region.

Operational Dynamics

The Al Badr is part of the United Jehad Council (UJC), a coalition of Pakistan-based terrorist groups active in Jammu and Kashmir.

It is reported to have training camps in the Manshera area of North West Frontier Province (NWFP) in Pakistan, Kotli and Muzaffarabad in PoK.

It has launched or threatened to launch attacks targeting Indian military installations and prominent government officials in Jammu and Kashmir.

Al Badr cadres are reported to have taken an active part, under the ISI tutelage, in the Kargil intrusion of 1999. The outfit's 'chief commander' Bakht Zameen was reportedly based in Skardu during the intrusion to monitor the movement of his cadres from Pakistan to Skardu and its forward areas.

The outfit, which was defunct for some time towards the end of the 1990s, had, with increasing frequency, begun to claim responsibility for several acts of terrorist violence in J&K during year 2000. Official sources indicated that several terrorists killed in the year 2000 were Al Badr cadres. In one such incident, five terrorists, allegedly part of an Al Badr suicide squad, were killed when troops raided their hideout at Theuru near Ganderbal.

The outfit has opposed the cease-fire on the Line of Control (LoC) declared by India and Pakistan in November 2003. Al Badr has consistently been opposed to any process of dialogue between India and Pakistan. For instance, the outfit's chief Bakht Zameen said in an interview on September 5, 2001, that India was not sincere about holding a dialogue for the amicable settlement of the Kashmir issue. While urging Pakistan to concentrate upon strengthening *Jehad* instead of "wasting further time seeking a negotiated settlement," he also asked the military regime to refrain from initiating any steps that would undermine the 'freedom movement' in Jammu and Kashmir.

The outfit has also sought to enforce Islamist lifestyles in the areas in which it operates. For instance, reports of August 2003 indicated that the Al Badr ordered women in the rural areas of J&K to quit police jobs, wear veils, give up studies after the age of 14 and not to venture out without a male escort. Posters carrying these diktats were seen pasted on street walls and mosques in the Thannamandi and Darhal areas of Rajouri district. The posters, written in Urdu, warned of unspecified consequences if women failed to comply. Earlier on December 20, 2002, in a major terrorist act against women across Jammu region, terrorists killed three young girls, including two college students, at Hasiot village in Rajouri district. The separate incidents were reportedly carried out by a group of three Pakistani terrorists belonging to the Al Badr led by the outfit's 'area commander' Zubair Gul.

The outfit launched a monthly Urdu magazine 'Al Badr' from Karachi and Rawalpindi in January 1999.

Linkages

The Al Badr is reported to have close linkages with the Inter Services Intelligence and Jamaat-e-Islami in Pakistan. During the regime of the Taliban militia in Afghanistan, the outfit's cadres secured weapons and ideological training in many camps across that country.

The Lahore-based *Daily Times* reported on December 27, 2003, that security agencies were investigating the Hizb-ul-Mujahideen and Al Badr's links with the Al Qaeda, Taliban and Gulbuddin Hekmatyar's Hizb-e-Islami. There were reports that the two organisations' former *Mujahideen* were recruiting *Jihadis* for the Taliban and the Hizb-e-Islami from the North-West Frontier Province (NWFP) and Baluchistan.

JAMIAT-UL-MUJAHIDEEN

The Jamiat-ul-Mujahideen (JUM) was the first breakaway faction of the Hizb-ul-Mujahideen (HM) that emerged out of a personality clash between Master Ahsan Dar, the then Chief of the outfit and Hilal Ahmed Mir. Mir, who used the code-name Nasirul Islam opposed the move to transform the Hizb into Jamaat-e-Islami's armed wing. It was formed in 1990 with Sheikh Abdul Basit as its Chief. Its followers are mostly Kashmiris from the Ahle Sunnat (Deoband) school.

The JUM is organised along military lines and a political Amir heads the organisation. It has a 'commander-in-chief' and a 'vice commander-in-chief' who commands four 'divisional commanders' who in turn command the various 'district commanders' and 'area commanders'. According to recent news reports, Engineer Mohammed Salah is said to be the 'Chief Commander' of the outfit while Col. Shamas is one of the important 'District Commanders'. It publishes a monthly magazine *Mahaz-e-Kashmir* in which it enumerates its terrorist operations systematically. Unlike the other terrorist organisations who draw support along sectarian lines, the outfit recruits terrorists from all sects. But, it has not been able to grow into a larger outfit. The Jamiat-ul-Mujahideen played a significant role in the early years of militancy in Jammu and Kashmir. However, it has not been able to maintain its momentum, despite remaining active in several parts of the State over the years. The cadre strength of the outfit is currently reported to be in hundreds. Many of its cadres are still in detention. Several JUM leaders were killed in a series of encounters after 1996, leaving its cadre disorganised and increasingly fragmented. The Jamiat-ul-Mujahideen considers itself as being a 'pure' Kashmiri organization and according to the leadership, all other terrorist outfits have either been suppressed or have accepted Pakistani-recruited cadres in their midst. However, recent reports indicate that as the inflow of Kashmiri youth from Jammu and Kashmir is decreasing, the JUM now needs to recruit Pakistani youth into its ranks. A senior J&K police official said in April 2001 that the top 'commanders' of the Jamiat-ul-Mujahideen had been arrested and the security forces were close to busting the entire outfit.

The Jamiat-ul-Mujahideen is opposed to the All Parties Hurriyat Conference (APHC) whom Abdur Rafeh, a senior leader of the outfit described as a big danger for the terrorist movement in Jammu and Kashmir. According to him, the APHC is an obstacle in the way of the imposition of Islamic laws in the State. The Hurriyat, according to the JUM, has no right to represent the terrorists in Jammu and Kashmir. The outfit has come out strongly against the recent peace initiatives of both India and Pakistan as it considers violence as the only means to settle the Kashmir issue. The JUM also supports the accession of Jammu and Kashmir with Pakistan. The JuI had also termed the surrender of Hashim Qureshi, who had hijacked an Indian Airlines flight to Lahore in 1971, as "an act of treason" and also threatened to "take him to task".

Maulana Ghulam Rasool, alias 'General' Abdullah alias Mohammad Ramzan Sofi, a native of Kupwara, who escaped from a Srinagar jail in February 3, 2000, is running their operation in Pakistan. He had earlier been arrested from Gow Kadal, Srinagar, in 1997 for charges including the triggering of an Improvised Explosive Device (IED) at the Gupkar Road, adjacent to the Jammu and Kashmir Chief Minister Farooq Abdullah's residence, in January 1997. Six persons were killed in the blast. He was reportedly on the list of detained terrorists whom the hijackers of the Indian Airlines flight IC 814 wanted to be set free in exchange for the hostages at Kandahar in December 2000. He had first been arrested in 1993, and during the next seven years, was arrested twice more. But on each occasion, Ghulam Rasool has managed to escape. Along with Nasirul Islam, he had formed a group called the Shabab-ul-Islam with a view to introduce the ideas of 'freedom', 'rights' and *jihad* among the Muslim youth of Jammu and Kashmir. The Shabab-ul-Islam culminated in the formation of the Jamiat-ul-Mujahideen.

In 1991, the outfit was allegedly involved in the killing of Mohammed Sayeed, Joint Director in the Information Department. It is also suspected to have been involved in the killing of H N Wanchoo, a human rights activist in December 1992. The JuI was also reportedly responsible for the Badami Bagh cantonment blast in March 1993 in which 29 persons were killed. The expertise of the outfit is reported to be in carrying out grenade attacks and explosions. A cadre of the Jamait-ul-Mujahideen, who was part of the *fidayeen* (suicide) squad that infiltrated into the Army battalion headquarters at Beerwah in Budgam district and launched an attack on forces inside the camp on September 12, 2000, was consequently killed in an encounter. With the arrests of a JUM terrorist Muzzafar Mirza and his associates in Srinagar and of Nissar Ahmad Gandroo in Kolkata on January 10, 2001, the police foiled their plans to launch terrorist attacks on the eve of Republic Day. Nine people, including four security force personnel, were killed in an explosion outside the local Army Headquarters at Batwara in Srinagar, on December 25. Although the Jamiat-ul-Mujahideen reportedly claimed responsibility for the attack, security forces suspected that the explosion was a joint effort of the Jaish-e-Mohammed (JeM) and another terrorist outfit, the Al-Umar.

LASHKAR-E-JABBAR

The existence of Lashkar-e-Jabbar (LJ) was first reported by the local media in Jammu and Kashmir in August 2001 following two incidents. In the first incident, two unidentified youth poured diluted acid on two school teachers in the Khanyar area of Srinagar on August 7. The next day, an armed terrorist threatened all students and teachers of a girls school in Srinagar of violence unless they adopt 'Islamic' dress codes. Following these, an unidentified person is reported to have informed the local media in Srinagar that his outfit, the Lashkar-e-Jabbar was responsible for these attacks. He added that the outfit meant "business in implementing the Islamic dress code in Kashmir". According to their interpretations, Muslim women must always wear the burqa in public. News reports in the aftermath of this information have also claimed that these attacks were preceded by isolated incidents of firing by unidentified terrorists on unveiled women in south Kashmir in the past two months which left three women injured.

Following this, the outfit was also reported as having fixed September 1, as the deadline for acceptance of its dress codes. The abrupt resurgence of this issue prompted an older outfit, Dukhtaran-e-Millat (DeM), which too projects identical goals, to join the 'movement'. Supporting the LJ's demands, the DeM appealed to the former for a postponement in the deadline. The LJ responded promptly by postponing the deadline to September 10. Meanwhile, the outfit also released a statement on September 8, asking non-Muslim women to wear identifying marks such as '*bindis*' on their foreheads or saffron *duppatas* or to dress in yellow clothes.

Though these developments found little attention in the mainstream press, the impact of the LJ's orders were effective with newspapers reporting a major scramble among Muslim women to get burqas stitched as also brisk sales of black fabric. A news report on September 9 also claimed that about 30 per cent of working women in the State's major towns were seen using burqas as compared to an estimated five per cent who used these before the LJ's announcement. In the light of such a response, the outfit also added a new order that all public transport vehicles must have half a section reserved for women to ensure that there is complete segregation between male and female passengers.

For an outfit that has cornered publicity on a large scale, little is known of its origin or character. There has only been speculation. Some news reports speculate that it is a creation of the DeM, which had failed in the early Nineties when it attempted to force women to accept Islamic dress codes. Another news report claiming to cite intelligence reports submitted to the Prime Minister said that the outfit was promoted by other terrorist outfits to make the use of burqas widespread and consequently to use these for launching attacks on security forces. These intelligence reports have reportedly added that Lashkar-e-Jabbar was also receiving overt and covert support from the Pakistan-based Haqqania Madrassa, which in turn was funded by wealthy Pakistanis and other Muslims living in West Asian countries. The Haqqania Madrassa is also reported to have secured support from the Saudi terrorist, Osama bin Laden, currently based in Afghanistan. Laden is also suspected to be aiding the Lashkar-e-Jabbar.

Most terrorists outfits active in the State, including the Hizb-ul-Mujahideen (HM) and the Lashkar-e-Toiba (LeT) have reportedly condemned the outfit. While the LeT, on August 12, claimed that the aim of those involved in such activities is to malign the outfit (LeT), the Hizb, on the same day, claimed that there was no terrorist outfit existing in the name of Lashkar-e-Jabbar and the activities being carried out in their name signified a deep conspiracy against the 'Kashmiri freedom movement'. Softening this stance, the Hizb, on September 10 released a statement saying that the LJ will be seen as a 'suspect group' until it is proven that it is part of the 'Jihadi movement' in Jammu and Kashmir. Another terrorist outfit, the Jamiat-ul-Mujahideen (JuM), which first criticized the LJ, later changed its stance on September 10, and welcomed the outfit's activities.

The All Party Hurriyat Conference (APHC) too has condemned the use of coercive measures to implement 'Islamic values'. Several other Islamic organisations in the State are also reported to have denounced the "coercive tactics" to make women wear veil, by saying that Islam does not permit any use of force to implement dress codes. These organisations include Jamiat-Ulema Hind, Jamiat-e-Islami Hind and the All India Muslim Majlis-e-Mushawarat.

Security force sources, meanwhile, were cited by news reports on September 10 as saying that patrol and deployment of plainclothesmen were being increased in view of the Lashkar-e-Jabbar's threat. The State Chief Minister Farooq Abdullah was also reported to have taken a serious note of the Lashkar-e-Jabbar threats and has warned police officials that they would be liable to action in case any incident of acid-throwing occurred in their jurisdiction. State security officials were also reported as considering the option of a massive crackdown on the DeM, in view of the suspected links between the two outfits.

HARKAT-UL-JIHAD-AL-ISLAMI (HUJI)
(Movement of Islamic Holy War)

Formation

The Harkat-ul-Jihad-al-Islami (HuJI) is a Pakistan-based terrorist group with an affiliate in Bangladesh. While the exact formation date of the group is not known, its origin is traced to the Soviet-Afghan war. Qari Saifullah Akhtar along with two of his associates, Maulana Irshad Ahmed and Maulana Abdus Samad Sial, all seminary students from Karachi in Pakistan, were instrumental in laying the foundation of a group, Jamiat Ansarul Afghaneen (JAA, the Party of the Friends of the Afghan People), sometime in 1980. Towards the end of its Afghanistan engagement, the JAA rechristened itself as HuJI and reoriented its strategy to fight for the cause of fellow Muslims in the Indian State of Jammu and Kashmir (J&K).

The HuJI continued to exist after the Soviet withdrawal from Afghanistan in 1989 by merging with another Pakistani militant group known as the Harkat-ul-Mujahideen, to form the Harkat-ul-Ansar which subsequently began terrorist operations in J&K. In order to avoid the ramifications of the U.S designation of Harkat-ul-Ansar as a Foreign Terrorist Organization in 1997, it renamed itself as Harkat-ul-Mujahideen in certain areas while its Bangladesh-based unit (formed in 1992) is known as the HuJI Bangladesh (HuJI-B). The HuJI-B functioned, in the initial years, under the Jihad Movement in Bangladesh led by Fazlur Rahman, one of the signatories of the February 23, 1998 declaration of 'holy war' under the banner of Osama bin Laden's World Islamic Front for Jihad against the Jews and Crusaders.

Objectives and Ideology

The HuJI belongs to the Deobandi school of thought and its recruits are indoctrinated in the mould of radical Islam. By describing itself as the "second line of defence for every Muslim", it aims to establish Islamic rule by waging war. The group operating in Bangladesh, HuJI-B, aims to establish Islamic rule in the country by waging war and killing progressive intellectuals. It draws inspiration from Osama bin Laden and the Taliban. At one point of time, it had issued a slogan, *Amra Sobai Hobo Taliban, Bangla Hobe Afghanistan.*

The HuJI supports, like the other Pakistan-based terrorist groups, the secession of J&K from India and its eventual accession to Pakistan, essentially through violence. It also propagates the idea of Islamic rule over all parts of India.

Among the other objectives of the HuJI is the Islamisation of Pakistani society.

Leadership

Bashir Ahmed Mir, the HuJI 'commander-in-chief' for operations across India, was shot dead by police in the Doda district in J&K on January 25, 2008. Operating under the code-name "Hijazi," "Pakistan-trained Mir is believed to have ordered a string of strikes across north and south-east India last year, including the court complex bombings in Uttar Pradesh, the bombing of the Ajmer Sharif shrine in Rajasthan, and the multiple bombings which took place in Hyderabad, Andhra Pradesh, in May and August [2007]." A resident of Chatroo village in J&K, Mir joined the "Harkat-ul-Ansar, which later transformed itself into the Jaish-e-Mohammad, in 1992. He trained in Pakistan-administered Jammu and Kashmir from 1994 to 1995, and was then assigned the charge of instructing new recruits at a HuJI-run camp near Mansehra [Pakistan]. He is believed to have returned to Jammu and Kashmir in 1999, and served with a HuJI unit operating out of the Pir Panjal mountains in the Doda-Anantnag mountain belt." He was appointed commander-in-chief of the HuJI in India in 2004.

After the HuJI lost its base in Afghanistan following the US military operations in 2001, most of its leaders, including Qari Saifullah Akhtar, took shelter in South Waziristan in Pakistan's Federally Administered Tribal Areas (FATA). While an unspecified number of its cadres also made their way into Central Asia and Chechnya to escape capture at the hands of the Americans, many went into Pakistan to establish themselves in the FATA and Buner in Pakistan's North West Frontier Province (NWFP).

The Pakistan-based Shahid Bilal, who is alleged to have masterminded several bomb blasts across the Indian hinterland, is believed to be the operations chief of the HuJI. However, there are conflicting reports on his existence. While some reports have indicated that he was shot dead by unidentified assailants in Karachi on August 30, 2007, some others have reported that Bilal is alive and shuttling from Bangladesh to Karachi. Bilal, a resident of Hyderabad had fled from India to Bangladesh sometime in 2002 and subsequently joined the HuJI. He recruited several persons from Hyderabad to carry out attacks on India and Hyderabad in particular.

According to an August 27, 2007 report in *Indian Express*, "Shahid Bilal, who is also named in the Mecca Masjid blasts, went to Saudi Arabia for training in 2002-2003 and was an understudy of his maternal uncle Farhatullah Ghori, a Jaish-e-Mohammed operative. A resident of Misram Bagh in Hyderabad, Bilal returned to the city in 2005 before the attack on the STF headquarters. Currently based in Karachi, Bilal has operated with Abdul Kalim Pasha in Bidar in the past and has links with fellow-Hyderabadi Rasool Party who used local youths in the assassination of Gujarat Home Minister Haren Pandya. Rasool is also in Karachi."

There have been reports that the HuJI operations are now being handled by Mohammed Amjad after the death of Shahid Bilal.

In August 2004, Qari Saifullah Akhtar was arrested by Dubai authorities and deported to Pakistan. He was in Dubai after he moved out of Saudi Arabia where he was in hiding earlier. Qari fled Afghanistan after the "American invasion in late 2001, taking shelter in South Waziristan before he was spirited out of Pakistan." After deportation, he was detained on the charge of anti-state activities. But he was released by the security agencies on May 21, 2007. An editorial in *Daily Times* on August 9, 2004 stated: "Like Maulana Masood Azhar of Jaish-e-Muhammad, Qari Saifullah Akhtar born in 1958 in South Waziristan was a graduate of the Banuri Masjid in Karachi. He was a crucial figure in Mufti Shamzai's efforts to get Osama bin Laden and Mullah Umar together as partners-in-jihad. Qari Saifullah Akhtar first came to public view when he was caught as one of the would-be army coup-makers of 1995 led by Major-General Zaheerul Islam Abbasi, but saved his skin by turning 'state witness'. (Some say he was defiant but was still let off.) After that, he surfaced in Kandahar and from 1996 was an adviser to Mullah Umar in the Taliban government. His fighters were called 'Punjabi' Taliban and were offered employment, something that other outfits could not get out of Mullah Umar. His outfit had membership among the Taliban too. Three Taliban ministers and 22 judges belonged to his Harkat."

Qari Saifullah Akhtar was also arrested along with his three sons on February 25, 2008 for his alleged links with the October 18, 2007-suicide bombing in Karachi that narrowly missed former Prime Minister Benazir Bhutto but killed about 150 others. However, Akhtar was freed from custody on March 26, 2008 due to lack of evidence.

The HuJI-B's 'operations commander', Mufti Abdul Hannan, who was trained in Peshawar, capital of NWFP, and fought in the *jihad* in Afghanistan, was arrested in Dhaka on October 1, 2005. The HuJI-B is led by Shawkat Osman alias Sheikh Farid and Imtiaz Quddus is the general secretary of the outfit.

Cadre

Although there is no authoritative information on the actual cadre strength, some reports mention it to be around 500-750.

Area of Activity and Influence

While the present global influence of the HuJI is not known, its presence has been reported from more than 20 countries in the past. The HuJI, according to one report, had spread its wings by 2005 to 24 countries, including India, Chechnya, Uzbekistan, Myanmar, Bangladesh, Tajikistan, Iran, Malaysia, Fiji, UK, US, Ireland, the Philippines, and parts of Africa and the West Asia. The outfit, according to a report in *The Friday Times,* maintained branches in 40 districts and *tehsils* (revenue divisions) in Pakistan, including Sargodha, Dera Ghazi Khan, Multan, Khanpur, Gujranwala, Gujrat, Mianwali, Bannu, Kohat, Waziristan, Dera Ismail Khan, Swabi and Peshawar. It also had an office in Islamabad.

Daily Times reported on August 9, 2004 that "In difficult times, the Harkat fighters stood together with Mullah Umar. Approximately 300 of them were killed fighting the Northern Alliance, after which Mullah Umar was pleased to give Harkat the permission to build six more 'maskars' (training camps) in Kandahar, Kabul and Khost, where the Taliban army and police also received military training. From its base in Afghanistan, the Harkat launched its campaigns inside Uzbekistan, Tajikistan and Chechnya. It finally became the biggest *jihadi* militia based in Kandahar located in the middle of the Taliban-Al Qaeda strategic merger."

The HuJI's operations in J&K began in 1991 and it was reportedly managed by a semi-autonomous unit led by 'chief commander' Muhammad Ilyas Kashmiri. According to an estimate in 2002, 650 HuJI cadres were killed in its battle against the Indian army: 190 belonging to both sides of Kashmir, nearly 200 belonging to Punjab, 49 to Sindh, 29 to Balochistan, 70 to Afghanistan, 5 to Turkey, and 49 collectively to Uzbekistan, Bangladesh and the Arab world. However, the HuJI activities in Jammu and Kashmir have progressively declined since 9/11.

The post 9/11 decline in HuJI operations in J&K, however, coincided with the increasing involvement of its Bangladesh based affiliate in several terrorist attacks in the Indian hinterland. The outfit was involved in the attack on American Center in Kolkata on January 22, 2002. The Asif Reza Commando Force (ARCF), which claimed responsibility for the attack, was affiliated to the HuJI, formed and manned largely by Bangladeshi migrants in India and some HuJI militants in India who were trained at ISI-backed training camps in Pakistan. Further, the October 12, 2005 suicide attack on the Special Task Force (STF) office of the Hyderabad Police brought it under the scanner of intelligence agencies. Since that attack in Hyderabad, footprints of the HuJI have been witnessed in most of the terrorist attacks that have taken place in India's urban centres, either directly or indirectly.

The HuJI is believed to have played an important role in the February 2007 bomb blasts in the Samjhauta Express that left 68 persons dead. The May 25, 2007 twin blasts at the Lumbini open air auditorium and a popular restaurant Gokul Chat Bhandar in Hyderabad is also suspected to be the handiwork of HuJI and sleeper cells of the JeM and LeT.

The HuJI has also been linked to the serial bomb blasts in Jaipur on May 13, 2008. "While the SIMI [Students Islamic Movement of India] module might have comprised locals, HuJI could have sent some of its men from outside the state, even from Bangladesh," said Additional Director General of Police (Crime) A. K. Jain, who is supervising the probe.

Available evidence indicates that the HuJI has a strong network in western Uttar Pradesh. The HuJI modules active in Uttar Pradesh are reportedly being monitored from Bangladesh and coordination among the units is allegedly being done by Bilal, the suspected mastermind behind the May 18, 2007 blast at the Mecca mosque in Hyderabad, capital of Andhra Pradesh in southern India, in which 11 persons died. The serial bomb blasts of November 23, 2007 in court premises at Varanasi, Faizabad and Lucknow in which 15 persons died were orchestrated by the HuJI. One of the militants arrested in that case, Sajjad (a resident of Kishtwar in Jammu and Kashmir), is a relative of Mohammed Amin Wani, a HuJI militant arrested in January 2007 by the Delhi Police. According to police, Wani was trained in a camp at Muzaffarabad in Pakistan occupied Kashmir and subsequently in a HuJI camp at Reeshkhore in Afghanistan. He had disclosed to the police about Sajjad who was then HuJI in-charge in Uttar Pradesh. Wani was also instrumental in initiating several young men from western Uttar Pradesh into terrorism, the police said.

The December 22, 2007 arrest of Mohammad Tariq Qasmi and Khalid Mujahid, two HuJI militants involved in the November 23 serial bomb blasts, and the May 22 Gorakhpur blasts, brought to light the deep tentacles of the group in Uttar Pradesh. Qasmi, a qualified *Unani* doctor, is the area commander of HuJI in Uttar Pradesh and was the *intizamiya* (arrangement) in charge of the group. Khalid Mujahid was the head of the action group of the HuJI. Qasmi was reportedly in regular contact with the Pakistan-based HuJI leader, Tauqeer. Brij Lal, the Additional Director-General of Police, stated that money was delivered to Qasmi through local contacts and the bombs were made and supplied by Mukhtar alias Raju, who has made several trips to Bangladesh through the Malda district in West Bengal.

Since 2005, militant groups like the HuJI, Lashkar-e-Toiba and Jaish-e-Mohammed have, with considerable assistance from local groups like the SIMI, established an extensive network in Uttar Pradesh. While the HuJI has a strong network in western Uttar Pradesh, its cadre have reportedly infiltrated into all regions of the State. Recent trends have demonstrated the involvement of technically qualified youth within the HuJI fold and the ability of its cadre "to operate autonomously in small cells, deadly use of explosive devices, careful selection of soft and hard targets and willingness to inflict mass casualties."

The HuJI is reported to have also established several sleeper cells across Uttar Pradesh, Maharashtra, Andhra Pradesh and Rajasthan.

Links

The HuJI is closely linked to the Inter-Services Intelligence, the Taliban and al Qaeda. The group receives patronage and support from Pakistan's Inter-Services Intelligence (ISI), and is also linked with several Islamist groups operating in India, including the Lashkar-e-Toiba (LeT) and Jaish-e-Mohammed (JeM). According to intelligence sources, the group's anti-India operations are planned by the ISI, mostly from the Bangladeshi capital Dhaka. The HUJI-B has coordinated its attacks along with the SIMI, the LeT and JeM. SIMI cadres have provided to the HUJI-B cadres shelter and logistical help prior to the attack. A number of SIMI cadres have also joined the HUJI-B. For example, On April 5, 2006, the Uttar Pradesh STF arrested six persons, including Waliullah, the 32-year old Pesh Imam of a mosque in Phulpur near Allahabad. Waliullah, a former SIMI cadre, was HuJI-B's area commander for eastern UP. On the other hand, the LeT and JeM cadres have taken part in the actual orchestration of the attack. For example, HuJI-B had executed the March 7, 2006 attack in collaboration with the JeM and SIMI at the Sankatmochan Temple and the Railway

Station at Varanasi. The December 28, 2005 attack at the Indian Institute of Science (IISc) Bangalore, in which a Delhi University mathematics professor was killed, was attributed to the HuJI-JeM combine.

Within Uttar Pradesh, the SIMI have provided the HuJI militants shelter and logistical assistance. A number of SIMI cadres have also reportedly joined the HuJI. For instance, On April 5, 2006, the Uttar Pradesh Police arrested six persons, including Waliullah, the 32-year old prayer leader of a mosque in Phulpur near Allahabad. Waliullah, a former SIMI cadre, was the HuJI 'area commander' for eastern Uttar Pradesh. SIMI, with a strong base in some universities of Uttar Pradesh, reportedly enjoys the support of a segment of the Muslim populace in cities such as Kanpur, Rampur, Moradabad, Saharanpur, Lucknow and Azamgarh in Uttar Pradesh.

Further, the HuJI maintains links with militant groups operating in India's Northeast, including the Assam-based United Liberation Front of Asom (ULFA) and the Manipur-based People's United Liberation Front (PULF). The HuJI is reportedly running some of ULFA's camps situated in the Chittagong Hill Tracts in Bangladesh along the border of Tripura.

Proscription

The HuJI is a banned terrorist organisation in India under The Unlawful Activities (Prevention) Act, 2004.

The US State Department designated the HuJI as a Foreign Terrorist Organisation in March 2008 and accordingly all the US financial institutions were required to freeze assets held by the militant group. Earlier, the US administration had classified the HuJI in the 'Other Terrorist Organisations' list in 2003.

Incidents

2009

- **October 18:** The SFs killed a 'district commander' of the Harkat-ul-Jehad-al-Islami (HuJI) outfit, identified as Mohammad Amin *alias* Rahi, at village Sigdi in the Chatroo area of Kishtwar District. Rahi's movement was being observed by the SFs since last week in Sigdi Bhata when he had torched machinery of a contractor, engaged in construction of road and abducted a driver, Satpal Singh of Noorpur, Kangra. The driver was released allegedly after the payment of INR 300000 ransom. One of his associates was reported to have escaped with the AK rifle of Bhat. From the possession of the slain militant, Police have recovered a Chinese pistol with one magazine and six rounds and four Chinese grenades.

- **September 5:** An over-ground worker (OGW) of the Harkat-ul-Jehad-al-Islami (HuJI) and Lashkar-e-Toiba was arrested from the Bus Stand area of Kishtwar town in the afternoon of September 4. A Police spokesman said that a joint team of Army and Police apprehended the OGW when he was carrying some items for the militants to their destination. He was identified as Akhtar Hussain (19), a resident of Patti Mahal. Three I-cards, a mobile phone and some other items were recovered from his possession. The Police said he was a surrendered militant of the LeT outfit. He had surrendered before Rashtriya Rifles (11th battalion) in 2007.
- **April 23:** Police arrested Abdul Razaq Ganie *alias* Abu Vakas, a Pakistan-trained militant belonging to the banned Harkat-ul-Jehad-al-Islami (HuJI) outfit, from Guloora Kultoora in the Kupwara District. On his disclosure, one AK-47 rifle, three AK-47 magazines, 87 rounds of AK-47, two hand grenades and one pouch were recovered.
- **February 2:** Police arrested a 'district commander' of the Harkat-ul-Jehad-al-Islami (HuJI) outfit and recovered arms and ammunition from his possession in the Chatroo area of Kishtwar District. Reports said a Police party intercepted HuJI 'district commander' Mohammed Abdullah *alias* Dulla Bakerwal alias Jameel

at Watsar Chatroo. After a brief encounter, the militant is reported to have surrendered. From his possession, Police recovered one AK-47 rifle, two magazines, seven rounds, one wireless set, one grenade, two magazines and 30 pistol rounds. Dulla Bakerwal was the last surviving HuJI 'commander' in Kishtwar.

2008

- **December 21:** The Jammu and Kashmir Police arrested a senior Harkat-ul-Jihad-al-Islami (HuJI) militant linked to the Faizabad and Varanasi blasts in Uttar Pradesh. Sohail Ahmed, a resident of Chatroo in Kishtwar, is said to be involved in the Faizabad and Varanasi blasts along with his predecessor Sabba, who was killed by Police in Kishtwar few months back.
- **November 9:** A self-styled 'divisional commander' of the HuJI, identified as Mohammad Rafiq alias Irfan, was among two militants killed by the SFs at Kokernag in the Anantnag district. The HuJI 'commander' was active since 2001 in Doda and south Kashmir and was involved in the killing of five personnel of Beacon Project, including Lt Col Ajay Verma, in June 2008. Two AK rifles and other arms and ammunition were recovered from the slain militants.
- **July 15:** *Daily News and Analysis* quoting Intelligence Bureau (IB) sources reported that the Harkat-ul-Jihad-al-Islami Bangladesh (HuJI-B) is recruiting children for its sleeper and information cells in West Bengal. This development has reportedly as a concern area for the State Police as the outfit is known to have a substantially bigger network in the state, especially in Indo-Bangladesh border districts of in Murshidabad, Nadia, North 24 Parganas and South 24 Parganas. An unidentified IB official said, "Huji is mainly targeting school -outs with extremely poor financial background and wooing them with money." The child recruits' assignments include passing on information on police deployment in their respective areas of operation.

"These children are also being used as messengers between HuJI-B linkmen," he added.

- **July 10:** In a case relating to the killing of five General Reserve Engineer Force officers, including Lt Col Ajay Verma, at Watsar in the Kishtwar district of Jammu and Kashmir on June 13, 2008, police arrested seven HuJI militants and was searching for four others. The seven militants were identified as Ghulam Hassan Dangar, Abdul Wahid, Mohammed Hussain, Ghulam Hassan, Noor Din, Irshad Ahmed and Mohammed Qasim.
- **June 24:** A 'commander' of the HuJI, identified as Akhter Hussian Lone alias Hamza, was arrested from the Sumbal area of Bandipora district.
- **May 21:** A suspected militant of the Harkat-ul-Jihad-al-Islami (HuJI), identified as Abdul Rehman, was arrested by the Special Cell of the Delhi Police outside the New Delhi railway station. Police sources said that 3.1 kilograms of RDX, five detonators and a sophisticated timer device were recovered from the Janakpuri locality in west Delhi following his interrogation. No ammunition or weapons were recovered from the suspected militant''s possession.
- **April 23:** The involvement of Pakistan-based outfits has been observed in most of the terrorist attacks in India as groups from across the border continue to sponsor terrorist and subversive activities in the country, the Union Home Ministry said in its Annual Report for 2007-08. "The hand of Pakistan-based terrorist organisations - LeT and JeM - and, increasingly of the Bangladesh-based HuJI, known to have close links with ISI, has been observed in most of these cases," the 167-page report said. The incidents showed these groups have been using sleeper cells in the country to carry out such activities, and have also been using the territory of other neighbouring countries such as Bangladesh and Nepal, it said.

- **April 22:** The Union Minister of State for Home Affairs Radhika Selvi informed the Lok Sabha (Lower House of India's Parliament) that there are reports that some militant groups from the northeast have links with the ISI and some other terrorist organizations of neighbouring countries such as the Bangladesh-based HuJI-B.
- **March 4:** *Press Trust of India* quoting the Bangladeshi newspaper *Pratham Alo* reported that the HuJI-B used to supply grenades to the Pakistan-based Lashkar-e-Toiba (LeT) to carry out attacks in India. An arrested HuJI-B leader, Abu Zandal, has told the police during his interrogation in Dhaka that the outfit had sent several consignments of grenades to the LeT operating in India until 2004. The last such consignment however, could not be delivered as the LeT representative who was supposed to receive it was killed in an encounter with Border Security Force (BSF) near Bangladesh's Kaliganj frontier. Zandal reportedly told the interrogators that the LeT leader Yazdani, who was killed in 2006 by the Delhi Police, used to maintain links with the detained HuJI-B 'operations commander' Mufti Abdul Hannan.
- **January 25:** Bashir Ahmed Mir, the HuJI 'commander-in-chief' for operations across India, was shot dead by police in the Doda district in J&K.
- **January 23:** A fast track court in Lucknow, capital of Uttar Pradesh, sentenced five HuJI militants to life imprisonment for waging war against the State, sedition, conspiracy and other charges. The convicts, Mehboob Ali, Sayeed Shoaib, Mohammad Rizwan, Farhan and Mohammad Saad, were arrested by the Special Task Force from Lucknow on April 5, 2006, along with Waliullah, the prime accused in the Varanasi twin blasts which occurred in the Sankat Mochan temple and near the railway station in March 2006. The court also awarded them 32 years of additional imprisonment under various sections of the Indian

Penal Code, besides imposing a fine of INR 40,000 each. All punishments will run concurrently.

- **January 9:** The Hyderabad city police claimed that the HuJI was responsible for the twin explosions in the city on August 25, 2007, that killed 43 persons. A top police officer said that "Narco-analysis tests conducted on Rafi alias Sheik Abdul Kaleem of Hyderabad gave us names of the key persons involved. Now, we are in the process of gathering evidence against them."

2007

- **December 28:** In a joint operation, the West Bengal Criminal Investigation Department and the Uttar Pradesh Special Task Force arrested Aftab Alam Ansari, a top HuJI militant, from the Cossipore area in the northern part of Kolkata, capital of West Bengal. Ansari is suspected to be one of the masterminds behind the serial blasts in the court premises at Lucknow, Faizabad and Varanasi in Uttar Pradesh on November 23, 2007.
- **December 22:** The Uttar Pradesh Police and central security agencies during a joint operation arrested two militants of the HuJI from Barabanki railway station. The duo, identified as Khalid Mohammed and Tariq, allegedly involved in the serial blasts in the State on November 23, were arrested along with 1.25-kg of RDX and some gelatin sticks. Khalid, who hails from the Jaunpur area of Uttar Pradesh, received training from HuJI militants in Kashmir, while Tariq is a resident of Azamgarh district of the State.
- **December 6:** Pakistani militants of the LeT and JeM have joined hands with the HuJI-B to destabilise India's sovereignty taking the strategic advantage of the eastern border, the Director General of BSF, A. K. Mitra, said. Talking to the media in Agartala, capital of Tripura, Mitra pointed out that the western frontier of India was relatively tough for Pakistani militants but the eastern border with Bangladesh had become

more useful for them and foreign militants were utilising South Bengal border for anti-Indian activities.

- **November 24:** A HuJI 'district commander', Abdul Rashid alias Sarwar, was killed by his colleagues in the Tatwan forests of Kishtwar district in J&K.
- **November 23:** 15 persons were killed and 80 others injured in the near-simultaneous blasts targeting lawyers in court premises in the three cities of Varanasi, Faizabad and Lucknow in Uttar Pradesh. In Varanasi, three blasts killed 11 persons and injured 45 people. Four persons were killed and 14 injured in two explosions at Faizabad. In Lucknow, there was only one blast and no casualty was reported. Police sources said the banned HuJI was behind the blasts. Ammonium Nitrate and timer devices were used in triggering the blasts in Lucknow and Varanasi.
- **November 22:** Five HuJI militants surrendered along with their arms before Lieutenant General A. S. Sekhon, the GoC 15 Corps, in J & K.
- **November 12:** The Hyderabad city police in Andhra Pradesh arrested Sadiq-ur-Rahman, a HuJI-B militant, from Kisanbagh in the old city area in the course of routine checking for illegal immigrants. Rahman claimed to have breached the security of Prime Minister Manmohan Singh, United Progressive Alliance (UPA) Chairperson Sonia Gandhi and Home Minister Shivraj Patil in April 2007. Police sources said that the 26-year-old Bangladeshi national had attended a meeting at Delhi's Vigyan Bhavan during April 21 to 23 in which all the three dignitaries participated. Police recovered bank passbooks, a telephone directory and other important documents from his possession.
- **September 28:** The Hyderabad Police claimed that they have arrested the younger brother of Shahid Bilal, a suspect in the August 25 twin bomb blasts in the city, and his associate on terrorism charges and causing communal disturbances in the city. The duo was

identified as Mohammed Abdul Majeed and Mohammed Shakeel alias Moulana. A police press release said that Shakeel is a close associate and childhood friend of Bilal and is wanted in at least three criminal cases.

- **September 21:** One Bangladeshi national Ridwan Gazi, who the police claimed was an activist of the HuJI-B, was arrested in Hyderabad in connection with the August 25 twin blasts in the city. Gazi had provided shelter to his accomplice, another Bangladeshi national Musliuddin. In his confessional statement, Gazi said that he had tried to garner support for and spread *Jihadi* activities. Musliuddin had funded his purchase of a motorcycle. He reportedly used to visit madrassas and colleges run by minority groups to lure Muslim youth into *Jihadi* activities.
- **September 6:** Hyderabad Police arrested 10 persons on the charge of plotting terrorist activity in the city. While three persons hailing from the Moosarambagh and Saidabad areas were arrested on the charge of attempting to recruit youngsters for terrorist training, seven more were arrested for aiding and abetting an ISI agent, Abdul Sattar.
- **September 2:** The Hyderabad Police filed a new first information report (FIR) charging 15 persons for their involvement in the August 25 twin blasts in the city. All of them were booked under the Explosives Act and for conspiring to carry out bomb attacks. Police Commissioner Balwinder Singh said that only four of the 15 suspects are in police custody. HuJI-B 'commander' Shahid Bilal is among the 11 who are out of the police custody. The new FIR is largely based on the revelations of Sameer Sheikh alias Nayeem, an alleged LeT operative arrested on the Bangladesh border in West Bengal on April 1, 2007. He is also an accused in the Mumbai train blasts case.
- **August 30:** The Hyderabad city police arrested a Bangladeshi national, Mohammed Gazi, who

resembled the suspected bomber in the August 25 blasts in the city, and his female associate.

- **July 17:** A 28-year-old man, Sheikh Jalil, was arrested from Biramnagar in Basirhat for suspected links with Jalaluddin, the area commander of HuJI who was recently arrested from Lucknow.
- **July 14:** Police arrested a HuJI activist, identified as Nur Islam, who allegedly functioned as a 'carrier' of the outfit from the North 24-Parganas district of West Bengal. Nur Islam was an associate of HuJI militant Jalaluddin arrested in Uttar Pradesh on June 23.
- **July 13:** Security force personnel launched a search operation at Nich Mawar forest in the Anantnag district of J&K, following information regarding the presence of militants there, and in the ensuing encounter a HuJI 'company commander', Yousuf Bimla alias Rizean, was killed.
- **June 23:** The Uttar Pradesh Police arrested an 'area commander' of the HuJI operations in India, Jalaluddin alias Amanullah Mandal alias Babu, a resident of Bhilparha in the South 24 Pargana district of West Bengal and his associate, Naushad alias Haafiz, in Lucknow. Nine kilograms of high explosives, an AK-47 rifle, two magazines and 60 cartridges of AK-47, 20 hand-grenades and 10 detonators were seized from their possession.
- **June 21:** The Uttar Pradesh Police arrested two terrorists belonging to the HuJI along with seven kilograms of RDX, six detonators, five watches including three improvised watches equipped with timer wire, two batteries and a switch remote. They were identified as Mohammed Yaqub, a resident of Tarapur under Badhapur police station of Bijnore district and Nasir, a resident of Naumi village under Badhapur police station of Bijnore district.
- **May 7:** A Home ministry document reportedly said that the Pakistan-based terrorist groups, particularly the LeT and JeM, are increasingly depending on

"surrogate bases" in Bangladesh, Nepal and the Middle East for movement of trained cadres and finances for their operations. The document, based on intelligence inputs, said the Bangladesh-based HuJI, linked to the JeM and LeT, is recruiting Indian youths, sending them to Pakistan for training and re-inducting them via Bangladesh to carry out terrorist attacks.

- **March 1:** Unidentified militants killed a released HuJI militant, Mohammed Amin, and his father Ahmedoo Baksh, in a rented house on outskirts of Kishtwar town in the Doda district of J &K.
- **January 4:** Two suspected HuJI militants, Lutful Rahman and Mohammed Amin Wani, were arrested by the Delhi Police. Rahman, a Bangladeshi national, was arrested in Adarsh Nagar locality of North-West Delhi, while Mohammed Amin, who hails from Jammu and Kashmir, was arrested in South Delhi's Nizamuddin area. Deputy Commissioner of Police (Special Cell), Alok Kumar, disclosed: "We have recovered 1.6 kg of RDX, a detonator and a timer from Mohd Amin and INR 4. 5 lakh from Lutuful Rahman."
- **January 4:** Security force personnel killed Abu Salem, a 'divisional commander' of the HuJI, during an encounter at Barf Wali Gali in the Gool area of Udhampur district in Jammu and Kashmir.

TEHREEK-UL-MUJAHIDEEN

Formation

The Tehreek-ul-Mujahideen (TuM) was formed in June 1990 by Yunus Khan, a close associate of Mohammed Abdullah Tairi, chief of the Jammu and Kashmir Jamaat-e-Ahle-Hadith.

Objectives

The TuM aims to merge the Indian State of Jammu and Kashmir (J&K) with Pakistan and also promote a pan-Islamist identity. The protection of Asidih community, a small faction of Sunni Muslims, was a prime motivating factor for the outfit in its early days.

Leadership, Command Structure and Cadre

Sheikh Jamil-ur-Rehman is the *Amir* (chief) of the organization. Maulana Fazlur Rahman, chief of his own faction of the Jamiat-Ulema-e-Islam and currently Member of the National Assembly (MNA), is the patron of the Tehreek-ul-Mujahideen.

Abdul Gani Dar alias Gazalli, 'supreme commander' of the outfit, was arrested by the Border Security Force on March 1, 2002, from the Lal Chowk area in Srinagar, capital city of J&K. A front ranking TuM cadre, he was active in the Kashmir Valley since year 1998.

The group suffered major setbacks in its early years when its founder Yunus Khan, then 'commander-in-chief', was killed in an encounter in 1991. Mohammed Salim Miron who returned from Pakistan occupied Kashmir (PoK) in July 1991 succeeded him. Later, in 1999 security forces in J&K killed its 'commander' Abu Waseem Salafi.

The outfit has a two-tier structure with the apex level consisting of *Amir*, *Naib Amir* (deputy chief), 'operations chief', military adviser', 'intelligence chief' and 'district commanders' and the field level consisting 'divisional commanders' and 'regiment commanders'.

The TuM is dominated by foreign mercenaries recruited from Pakistan and PoK although a certain percentage of its cadres are also drawn from J&K.

Headquarters and Areas of Operation

TuM operates primarily in the Kashmir Valley, especially in the Beeru belt of Budgam district, Ganderbal and downtown localities of Srinagar, Pulwama and Anantnag districts. In year 1990, it opened an office at Muzaffarabad in PoK and sent its cadres for arms training. Ghulam Mohammed

Ghani and Mohammed Shah Wani maintained that office for a considerable period of time.

Linkages

It has received funds from Pakistan, Bangladesh, Saudi Arabia, UK, USA and Gulf Countries primarily through organisations subscribing to the Ahle Hadith tradition. The Saudi Arabia-based Haramain Islamic Foundation has provided extensive funds to the TuM. In 1996, TuM established linkages with the Bangladesh Ahle Hadis Youth Association, which helped the outfit in certain cross border operations. TuM bases in Nepal were utilised to ferry Pakistan-made explosives and movement of cadres from India to Pakistan and vice versa. The Kathmandu network was used extensively by the TuM to distribute funds received through *Hawala* transactions for a number of terrorist groups in J&K.

The outfit has a close association with Lashkar-e-Toiba (LeT), another *Jehadi* group of the Ahle Hadith tradition.

It receives considerable assistance from Pakistan's Inter Services Intelligence (ISI) and the PoK government.

It is one of the members of the Muzaffarabad-based United Jehad Council (UJC), a 15-member conglomerate of Pakistan-based terrorist groups.

The outfit is reported to have carried out joint operations in the Kashmir Valley in the recent years along with the LeT. From 1995 onwards, the ISI started to route funds to the LeT through the TuM.

In Bangladesh, TuM operatives have been supported by local Islamist groups like the Islamic Chhatra Shibir (ICS), Harkat-ul-Jehadi-e-Islami (HuJI), Islamic Okiya Jote, Imam Parishad and Islamic Shashantantra Andolan.

Ever since its formation, the TuM has maintained close links with the Amanullah Khan faction of the Jammu and Kashmir Liberation Front (JKLF) in PoK.

Current Status

The outfit has a limited presence in the Kashmir Valley and its activities have declined in comparison to the Hizb-ul-Mujahideen (HM), LeT and the Jaish-e-Mohammed (JeM). However, due to continuing international pressure on Pakistan since 9/11, major terrorist groups have refrained from claiming responsibilities for their actions and instead outfits like the TuM and the Jamiat-ul-Mujahideen have been encouraged to claim responsibility as part of the ISI's new operational strategy in J&K.

AL UMAR MUJAHIDEEN (AUM)

Formation

Mushtaq Ahmad Zargar formed the Al Umar Mujahideen in December 1989, with a membership primarily drawn from recruits in downtown Srinagar, capital city of the Indian State of Jammu and Kashmir (J&K). The formation of Al Umar Mujahideen is traced to the differences that had emerged within the Jammu and Kashmir Liberation Front (JKLF). Zargar floated the AuM with the tacit endorsement of Srinagar-based cleric Maulvi Umar Farooq, after whom the outfit was named.

Mushtaq Ahmed Zargar alias Latram was one of the three terrorists released on December 31, 1999, by the Indian Government in exchange for the passengers of the hijacked aircraft IC 814 at Kandahar in Afghanistan. Zargar has since then been based in Pakistan.

The Al Umar Mujahideen is a proscribed organisation under the Prevention of Terrorism Act, 2002.

Objectives

The AuM aims to liberate the Indian State of Jammu and Kashmir through an armed struggle and merge it with Pakistan.

Leadership, Command Structure and Cadre

Mushtaq Ahmad Zargar is the 'chief commander' of Al Umar Mujahideen. With the help of Zahoor Sheikh, an Anantnag-based activist of the secessionist People's League, Zargar crossed over to Pakistan through Trehgam and received training at a camp organised by the JKLF in August 1988. Subsequently, he went to Pakistan for a second round of training during May 1989 and returned through Uri. Later, Zargar is reported to have executed several attacks on security force personnel and a series of murders of the Kashmiri Pandits (descendants of Brahman priests). Zargar, who is responsible for over 40 murders and was a key figure in the terrorist ascendancy in downtown Srinagar, was arrested on May 15, 1992.

Manzoor Ahmad Ganai is reportedly the 'chief commander and organiser of training'. Latif-ul-Haq who is the 'acting chief commander' and Jamshed Khan, the 'deputy chief commander' are among the other important leaders of the outfit.

Shabir Ahmad Zargar, who was reportedly chief of the Al Umar Commando Force, a striking wing of the AuM and a close confidant of Mushtaq Ahmad Zargar, was arrested by the Border Security Force in Srinagar on October 2, 2002.

The AuM has a two-tier structure: The supreme command and field formations. The former consists of a 'chief commander', two 'deputy chief commanders', 'military adviser', 'publicity chief', and 'intelligence chief' and the latter consists of 'district commanders' and 'regimental commanders'.

Apart from the Syed Salahuddin-led Hizb-ul-Mujahideen (HM), Al Umar Mujahideen is the only other terrorist group, which is led by a Kashmir Valley-based terrorist.

The outfit reportedly has a strength of 700 cadres.

Operational Strategies

In the early phase of terrorist violence in J&K during the 1980s, the Pakistani external intelligence agency, Inter Services

Intelligence (ISI) perceived the AuM as an instrument through which the ascendancy of the JKLF, which had favoured independence for Kashmir could be challenged.

Apart from attacks on civilians and security forces, Zargar also indulged in extortion and used his 'influence' to intervene in local business and property disputes in Srinagar. At least seven abductions for ransom are reportedly attributed to him. In one instance, Zargar reportedly ordered a ban on the use of Maruti vehicles in Srinagar in order to help a Srinagar businessman who held the dealership for a rival motor company.

On the eve of Legislative Assembly elections in Jammu and Kashmir during September-October 2002, the ISI reportedly appointed Mushtaq Zargar, AuM chief, as the 'chief coordinator' to carry out attacks on candidates and political parties. It has been reportedly working in tandem with the Jaish-e-Mohammed (JeM) and guides the organisation in J&K.

Headquarters and Areas of Operation

The AuM headquarters is located at the Narul locality in Muzaffarabad, Pakistan occupied Kashmir (PoK).

It is primarily active in the Srinagar, Baramulla, Kupwara and Pulwama districts of the Indian State of Jammu and Kashmir and at Muzaffarabad in Pakistan occupied Kashmir.

Linkages

The outfit has, since inception, been funded and supported by the ISI. It also secures substantial assistance from the PoK government based in Muzaffarabad.

It is one of the members of the Muzaffarabad-based United Jehad Council (UJC), a 15-member conglomerate of Pakistan-based terrorist groups.

The AuM had also forged links with the Khalistan Liberation Force (KLF) and supplied arms to them during the phase of terrorism in the Indian State of Punjab.

During year 2002, some of the AuM cadres reportedly joined the Lashkar-e-Omar, which is a conglomerate of Harkat-ul-Jehadi-e-Islami (HuJI), Lashkar-e-Jhangvi (LeJ) and Jaish-e-Mohammed (JeM) cadres.

OTHER EXTREMIST AND SECESSIONIST GROUPS

Muttahida Jehad Council (Also known as the United Jehad Council)

The Muttahida Jehad Council (MJC), a conglomerate of Pakistan-based *Jehadi* outfits, was formed in November 1990 to bring under a single platform all the outfits involved in the terrorist violence in Jammu and Kashmir (J&K).

The MJC, for long an alliance of 13 *Jehadi* organizations led by Syed Salahuddin of the Hizb-ul-Mujahideen (HM), has reportedly been restructured and three Pakistan-based groups, the Lashkar-e-Toiba (LeT), Jaish-e-Mohammed (JeM) and Al-Badr Mujahideen have been brought into the MJC. This new adjustment is called *Muwakhaat* ('agreement on the basis of brotherhood') that is aimed at putting an end to the internal differences among the groups waging the Kashmir *Jehad*.

According to reports, reorganizing the command and control structure of the HM-led MJC was part of a strategy change to enable the Pakistani intelligence to have tighter control over its running. With the restructuring, no component member of the UJC would now be allowed to launch an attack in J&K, unless approved by the Council. To this end, most of the smaller groups, which had reportedly become irritants for the Inter-Services Intelligence (ISI), have been merged to reduce the number of their representation in the Jehad Council from thirteen to five. Al Barq, Tehreek-e-Jehad, Islamic Front, Brigade 313 and the Kashmiri component of Harkat-ul-Mujahideen (HuM) have been merged to form the Kashmir Freedom Force, which would be led by Farooq Qureshi of the Al Barq. The Muslim Janbaz Force, Al Jehad Force, Al Fateh Force, Hizbullah and Jamiat-ul-Mujahideen (JuM) have also been merged to form the Kashmir Resistance Force which would be led by Ghulam Rasool Shah.

The headquarters of the MJC is at Muzaffarabad in Pakistan occupied Kashmir (PoK). At the time of inception, all the terrorist outfits operating in J&K were required to register with the MJC. The council aims at joining forces and resources to augment the terrorist operations in J&K. The Muttahida Jehad Council also acts as the primary public voice of the terrorist outfits currently active in the State of Jammu and Kashmir.

Azam Inquilabi was initially appointed the Chairman of MJC. Subsequently, since he was found to be ineffective in increasing the lethality of the terrorist operations, Tanvir ul Islam replaced him as the chief. With a view to expanding the terrorist canvas in J&K, the Pakistani establishment is reported to have organized a meeting of the various MJC constituents in December 1995. Consequent to the meeting, Syed Salahuddin, 'Supreme Commander' of the Hizb-ul-Mujahideen was appointed the Chief of the conglomerate. The HM chief was 'elected' as the MJC chairman for the fourth time at a meeting in Muzaffarabad on November 6, 1999.

Consequent to the unilateral cease-fire announced by the HM on July 24, 2000, the MJC expelled the outfit from the conglomerate and removed Syed Salahuddin as its chief. Mohammad Usman, a representative of the Muslim Janbaz Force who was appointed as the acting Chairman, replaced him. While criticizing the Hizb cease-fire, the MJC said that it was "wastage of sacrifices and passage to servitude". MJC rejected the cease-fire with the argument that India had a "history of breaking promises and pacts and that atrocities and excesses by security forces were unabated in Kashmir." Following the withdrawal of the cease-fire by the outfit on August 8, efforts began within the conglomerate to re-induct HM. The outfit was re-inducted and Salahuddin re-appointed as Chairman on October 22, 2000 through 'voting' wherein the HM is alleged to have secured a majority vote of eight votes. The Tehreek-ul-Mujahideen, Al Umar, Al Barq and the Hizb-ul-Momineen are reported to have opposed the re-induction while indicating that the HM should formally admit to its cease-fire being a 'mistake' and request for pardon.

The following terrorist outfits are currently members of the Muttahida Jehad Council:

1. Hizb-ul-Mujahideen
2. Jammu Kashmir Liberation Front
3. Harkat-ul-Ansar
4. Tehrik-e-Jehad
5. Tehreek-ul-Mujahideen
6. Jamiat-ul-Mujahideen
7. Al Jehad
8. Al Umar Mujahideen
9. Jammu Kashmir Islamic Front
10. Muslim Janbaz Force
11. Hizbullah
12. Al Fatah
13. Hizb-ul-Momineen
14. Lashkar-e-Toiba
15. Jaish-e-Mohammed
16. Al-Badr Mujahideen

Bibliography

Aijaz (G H). Roots of Kashmir freedom Movement. KTV. 3 No. 2-3; 1978.

Akbar Khan (Maj. Gen.) Raiders in Kashmir. Srinagar, Rebus Pub. House, 210.

Anand (Adrah Sain). Development of the Constitution of Jammu and Kashmir. New Delhi, Light and Life Publishers, 1980. P 377, 2nd ED. 1994. P 517.

Atal (Hira Lal). Nehru's Emissary to Kashmir Oct. 1947. New Delhi, Army Educational Stores, 1972. P 183.

Azad (Jagen Nath). Iqbal aur Kashmir. Srinagar, Ali Mohammad & Sons, 1977. Chap 12-13 (Urdu).

Bakshi (Gulam Mohammad). Kashmir Today Through Many Eyes. Bombay, P.C.C. P 135.

Balraj Madhok. Jammu, Kashmir and Ladakh : Problem and Solution. New Delhi, Reliance Pub. House, 1987. P 83.

Bamzai (PNK). Kashmir and Central Asia. New Delhi, Light and Life Publishers, 1980. P 251.

Bamzai (PNK). Cultural and Political History of Kashmir. New Delhi, M.D. Publications, 1994, 3 Volumes.

Bazaz (P. N). The History of Struggle for Freedom in Kashmir. New Delhi, Pamposh Publisher, 1995. P 744.

Bazaz (P. N). Democracy Through Intimidation and Terror: The Untold Story of Kashmir Politics. New Delhi, Heritage Pub; 1978. P 222.

Bazaz (P. N). Inside Kashmir. Srinagar, Kashmir Publishing Co; 1941. P 412.

Bhat (Bihari Lal). Socio- Religious Reform Movements in Kashmir 1900- 1047. Department of History, University of Kashmir, Srinagar. 1990, P 298.

Bhat (R. K. K Kaul). Political and Constitutional development of J & K State from 1846.

Bidya Bhushan. Evolution of Democratic Institution in Indian Polity: A Study of Jammu and Kashmir. New Delhi, ESS ESS Publications, 1989. P 172.

Burke (S M). The Kashmir Dispute. In Pakistan's Foreign Policy; a historical analysis London. Oxford Uni. Press 1973. Chap.2. P 16-46.

Chohan (Amar Singh). Historical Study of Society and Culture in Dardistan and Ladakh. New Delhi, Atlantic Publishers, 1983. P 264.

Chopra (Surrendra). UN Mediation in Kashmir; a study in power politics. Kurukshetra, Vishal Publishers, 1971. P 290.

Choudhar (G W). Kashmir. In Pakistan's Relations with India. Merut, Meenakashi Prakashan, 197, Chap.3, P 54- 104.

Cohen (Maurice). Thunder over Kashmir. Bombay, Orient Longman, 1955. P. 118.

Collins (Larry) and Lapierre, Dominique. Mountbaten and Independent India. New Delhi, Vikas Pub. House. (Reprint 1994) P 50-62.

Dabla (Bashir A). Working of Women in Kashmir. Jaipur, Rawat Publications, 1991, P 124.

Dhar (P. N). Kashmir problem; Political and Economic Background. India Quarterly V 7. 2; Apr-June, 1951, P 142-162.

Dogra (Ramesh Chander). Jammu and Kashmir: A select annotated Bibliography, Delhi, Ajanta Publications, 1986, P247.

Encyclopedia of India. General Editor P.N Chopra. New Delhi, Rima Publishing House, 1992, 36 Vols.

Farhat Jaben. Position of Women in Kashmir (1900- 1947). Department of History, University of Kashmir, Srinagar, 1984, P 136 (M Phil Thesis).

Gajendragadkar (P B). Kashmir Retrospect and Prospect. Bombay, University of Bombay, 1967. P 147.

Ganai (Abdul Jabbar). Kashmir and National Conference and Politics 1975-1980. Gulsahan Publishers, 1984. P 168.

Gani (Mohammad Yosuf). Emergence and Role of Muslim Conference in Kashmir. 1932-1939. Dept. Of History, University of Kashmir, Srinagar, P209.

Gopal (Sarwapalli) Ed. Kashmir and Indo-Pak Relations and Question f Kashmir. In Jawaharlal Lal Nehru; an anthology, Delhi, Oxford Univ. Pres, 1983. P 216 & 223-225.

Grover (Virendra) ed. The Story of Kashmir: Yesterday and Today. New Delhi, Deep & Deep Pub. 1995, 3V.

Gulam Shah. State Subjectship in Jammu and Kashmir Srinagar, Jupiter Publishers, 1988. P 112.

Gururaj Rao (H.S). Legal Aspects of Kashmir Problem. Bombay, Asia Publishing House, 1967. P 379.

Hari Om. Debacle in Kashmir. New Delhi, Anmol Pub; 1992. P 274.

Hari Ram. Special Status in Indian Federalism; Jammu and Kashmir. Delhi, Deema Publishing House, 1983. P 230.

Ikbal Kaul. Kashmiri Pundits Through the Ages, KSRV. 16 No. 4-5; P 53-57.

Jammu and Kashmir. Srinagar Riot Enquiry Committee report. Chairman, Barjor Dalal, Srinagar, Govt, Press 1931. P 54.

Juneja (V P). Indo-Pak War 197, New Delhi, New Light Publisher, 1972. P 214.

Kak (B L). Kashmir: The Untold Story of Men and Matters. Jammu, Jay Kay Book House, Jammu, 1987. P 144.

Karan Sing. Her apparent; and autobiography. V.1 Sadar-i-Reyasat V. 2. Delhi, Oxford Univ. Press, 1982.

Kashmir On Trial; State versus Sheikh Abdullah. Lahore, The Lion Press. 1947. P 224.

Kashmir V.K Krishna Menon's Speech in Security Council Jan-Feb.195, New Delhi, Publication Division. 1958. P 223.

Kaul (B. M.). Confrontation with Pakistan. Delhi, Vikas Pub. House, 1971. pt I. P 30117.

Khan (Bashir Ahmad). Ahl-i-Hadith Movement in Kashmir 1901- 1981. Department of History, University of Kashmir, Srinagar, 1984, P 152,

Khan (Mohammad Ayub). Foreign Policy. In Friends not Master; a political autobiography. London. Oxford Univ. Press, 1967. Chap. 9, P 121- 153.

Khan (Mohammad Ishaq). Islam in Kashmir: Historical Analysis of its Distinctive Features In Islam in India; Studies and Commentaries edited by Christian W. Troll. Delhi, Vikas Publishing House, 1985, V. 2, P 86- 97.

Korbel (Joesf). Danger in Kashmir. Princeton, Princeton Uni. Press, P 351.

Krishna Mehta. This Happened in Kashmir. Delhi, Publication Division, Govt. of India, 1954. P 171.

Lakhanpal (P L) . Essential documents and Notes on Kashmir Dispute. Delhi, international Pub; 1958. P 272.

Lamb (Alistair). Kashmir a Disputed Legacy 1846-1990. Karachi, Oxford Univ. Press, 1993. P 368.

Lamb (Alistair). Crisis in Kashmir; 1947-1966. London. Rutledge, 1966. P 163.

Lawrence (Walter). The Valley of Kashmir, London, Henry Frowde, 1895, Reprinted in India by Chinar Pub. House, 1992, Srinagar, P 478.

Manzoor Fazli. Socialist Ideas and Movements in Kashmir1919-1947. New Delhi, Eureka Pub: 1980. P 218.

Mattoo (Abdul Majid) Nurbakshis of Kashmir. In Islam in India: Studies and Commentaries edited by Christian W. Troll Delhi, Vikas Pub. House, 1985, V2, P 98- 113.

Menon (V P). Integration of Jammu and Kashmir. in his The Story of the integration of Indian States. Bombay, Orient Longman's, 1956. P 390- 415.

Misra (K. K.). Kashmir and India's Foreign Policy Allahabad, Chaugh Pub; P 605.

Mrani (M R). Paradise Under the Shadow of Hell; India's war on Kashmir as seen by Non- Muslims and Neutral observers. Lahore. Imperial Printing Works. 1948. 5 Parts.

Mullik (B. N). My Years with Nehru; Kashmir. Bombay, Allied Pub; 1971. P 320.

Noorani (A G). The Kashmir Question. Bombay, Manaktalas, 1964. P 125.

Pankkar (K.M). Gulab Singh; 1792-1858 Founder of Kashmir. London, Hopkinson, 1930. P 172.

Pathik (Jyoteeshwar). Cultural Heritage of the Dogras. New Delhi, Light and Life Publishers, 1980. P 177.

Rahamatullah Khan. Kashmir and United Nations. Delhi, Vikas Pub. House, 199.

Rai (Mridula) Hindu Rulers, Muslim Subjects: Islam, Rights and the History of Kashmir, Permanent Black, New Delhi. 2004, P 335.

Raina (N. N). Kashmir Politics and Imperialist Manoeuvres 1846-1980. New Delhi, Patriot Publishers, 1988. P 276.

Ruksana Jabeen. Role of Ulema in Modern Kashmir 1846 to 1947 A.D. Dept. of History, Uni. of Kashmir Srinagar, 1990, P 178.

Sanaullah Bhutt. Kashmir in Flames; an Untold Story of Kashmir's Political Affairs. Srinagar. Ali Mohammad & Sons, 1981. P 244.

Saraf (Mohammad Yusuf) Kashmir's Fight for Freedom Vol. 1 and 2, Ferozsons, Lahore, 1977.

Sen (L.P.) Slender was the Thread; Kashmir Confrontation 1947-48. Bombay, Orient Longman, 1969. P 308.

Sharma (B.L). The Kashmir Story. Bombay, Asia Publishing House, 1967. P 271.

Sharma (D C). Documentation on Kashmir. Jay Kay Book House, Jammu. P 384.

Singh (L.P.) Confrontation with Pakistan, the Second Kashmir War 1965. In his India's Foreign Policy, the Shastri Period. New Delhi, Uppal Publishers, 1980 P. 69-81.

Siser Gupta. Kashmir; a Study in India- Pakistan Relations Bombay, Asia Pub, House, 1966. P 511.

Sufi (G.M.D). Islamic Culture in Kashmir. Simla, The Army Press, 1925. P 393.

Telan (G M). Options on Kashmir: The Debate in Pakistan, Indian Express, Dec. 5, 1994.

Telang (G M). Kashmir in Retrospect: Dead End for Pakistan, Indian Express. Dec. 17. 1994.

Teng (M K) & Kaul (Santosh) Ideological Foundations of National Movement in Kashmir; 1901-1930 JPS V. 4, No. 11; P 25-33.

Teng (Mhohan Krishen). Kashmir Constitutional History and Documents. New Delhi, Light an life Pub; 1977.P 639.

Veena Zutushi. Role of Kashmir Pundits in the Freedom Struggle of J & K State 1931-1947. Department. of History. Uni. of Kashmir, Srinagar, 1981. P 162.

Vidya Bhushan. Permanent Residents of Jammu and Kashmir and Their Fundamental Rights. Indian Journal of Political Studies,Vol. 9. Dec. 1985 P86-94.

Wani (G.A.) Kashmir History and Politics, 1846 –1994 A Select and Annotated Bibliography, Second Edition, Srinagar, Tariq Enterprise, 1995 P-230.

Zutshi (Chitralekha) Languages of Belonging, New Delhi, Permanent Black. 2003 P 359.

Zutushi (U K). Emergence of Political Awakening in Kashmir. New Delhi, Monahar Publication, 1986. P 252.

Index

J

K